T0290476

Financial Success for Young Adults and Recent Graduates

MANAGING MONEY, CREDIT, AND YOUR FUTURE

Janet C. Arrowood

Published in partnership with the
National Society of Collegiate Scholars

Rowman & Littlefield Education
Lanham, Maryland • Toronto • Plymouth, UK
2006

Published in partnership with the
National Society of Collegiate Scholars

Published in the United States of America
by Rowman & Littlefield Education
A Division of Rowman & Littlefield Publishers, Inc.
A wholly owned subsidary of The Rowman & Littlefield Publishing Group, Inc.
4501 Forbes Boulevard, Suite 200, Lanham, Maryland 20706
www.rowmaneducation.com

Estover Road
Plymouth PL6 7PY
United Kingdom

British Library Cataloguing in Publication Information Available

Library of Congress Cataloging-in-Publication Data
Arrowood, Janet C.
  Financial success for young adults and recent graduates : managing money, credit, and your future / Janet C. Arrowood.
    p. cm.
  "Published in partnership with the National Society of Collegiate Scholars"—
  ISBN-13: 978-1-57886-409-6 (hardcover : alk. paper)
  ISBN-13: 978-1-57886-410-2 (pbk.: alk. paper)
  ISBN-10: 1-57886-409-7 (hardcover : alk. paper)
  ISBN-10: 1-57886-410-0 (pbk.: alk. paper)
  1. Young adults–Finance, Personal. 2. College graduates–Finance, Personal. I. Title.
HG179.A77 2006
332.0240084'2–dc22   2005037437

∞™The paper used in this publication meets the minimum requirements of
American National Standard for Information Sciences—Permanence of
Paper for Printed Library Materials, ANSI/NISO Z39.48-1992.
Manufactured in the United States of America.

This book is dedicated to my parents, William and Nina Arrowood, who wittingly and unwittingly gave me the foundation to be a planner, saver, and investor.

It is also dedicated to the fine staff of the Young Americans Center for Financial Education/Young Americans Bank in Denver, Colorado. They do a fabulous job of educating young adults about managing and handling money by teaching them how to save, invest, plan, and run a business, and by making sure they understand the role of financial planning in present and future successes.

Contents

Acknowledgments

Special thanks to Debbie Pierce, Vice President of Communications at Young Americans Bank, for arranging the client focus group. That group of young adults and their parents provided invaluable guidance in the structuring and contents of this book. They also gave a lot of their time to write responses to questions and agreed to let me use their responses in this book. And as always, a big thank you to Tom Koerner, who believed in this book and supported me all the way.

Introduction

Young adults today are living in truly interesting times. You are on the verge of making an incredible number of life and career choices. You're probably between the ages of 16 and 25, and you are faced with an almost overwhelming number of decisions—some of which will last your entire life—like it or not.

It seems like everyone—your parents, your teachers and professors, your friends, and the talking heads on television—go on about "financial planning" and "money management." But do you really know what these terms mean? Why should you even care? After all, you're young, you have years ahead of you to plan for the future, and you'll earn lots of money over your lifetime. Right.

There is an incredible amount of information available to help you manage your money and your life. The Web, TV, books, and magazines are filled with ideas, rules, and suggestions. This book goes much further, with checklists, case studies, examples, and real-life planning information. You'll find information about many things:

- Getting and managing loans and credit cards
- Finding the money for college
- Realistic savings programs
- Handling debt
- Getting insurance
- Understanding taxes
- Understanding benefits
- Banking options
- Making major purchases
- Avoiding bankruptcy and other financial problems
- How money and investments work (or don't work!)

There are questions and exercises at the end of each chapter, and charts and worksheets throughout the book. I hope you'll find the time to work on them, maybe with several of your friends.

You'll meet some real people and see the mistakes they made, the changes they have made, what they would have done differently, and what they feel they are doing "right." You'll also hear from some of your peers—they and their parents have answered a number of questions about money, and their opinions may surprise and interest you. Finally, many of the points made in this book are illustrated using the case of the fictional—but all too real—twins, Alex and Phoenix.

1

The Basics

Money and finances are funny, complicated things, so we'll start out simple, and move on from there.

How do you define financial success? How do you define personal success? A parent of two teenagers describes success this way:

> Having financial success is being able to meet your needs and your wants, having funds for emergencies and fun, and having enough to plan your future, and to share with others. Personal success means having a spiritual peace with who you are and where you're at no matter what the circumstances.—Devyn N.

What do you consider to be the three biggest mistakes people your age make with their money? Why are these mistakes? How might these mistakes be avoided? A teenager, Kris, responded:

> Big mistakes that teenagers make with money generally tend to be spending it too quickly and not investing it wisely. I know entirely too many people who spend their work checks immediately instead of taking the time to invest some of them. Kids generally do not look to their future financial needs. I think that further economic education would help kids and teenagers better understand investments.—Kris Z., a teenager in Colorado

Another teenager put it this way:

> 1. Not saving. 2. Overspending. 3. Bad credit. These are mistakes because they give you a slow start. These mistakes are avoided by being educated.—Kai Ge Y

Two more teenagers (a brother, 15, and a sister, 17) put it this way:

> 1. Peer pressure. 2. Modern day fads. 3. Spending every penny. They drain you of income. Having a parent to help guide you through your financial journey [helps avoid these mistakes]."Derek N., 15

> 1. Spending it all in one place. 2. Spending based on peer pressure. 3. Fads and fashion. Leaves nothing for emergency in the future. Take financial classes at school [to avoid these mistakes]."—Vanessa N., 17

How do you think teenagers and young adults define personal and financial success. Do you think they equate having "things" with being personally and/or financially successful? A parent of two teenagers has this view:

> I think most teens, young adults, twenty-somethings, thirty-somethings, etc., etc. think that personal and financial success are synonymous. Just spend a day watching MTV "Cribs." It is a battle for our kids' mind-set. We actively teach them how leveraged people are. We show them the price tags and calculate the monthly payments for those "wanna-be" lifestyles. We show them that we could live equally as leveraged lifestyles but *choose* not to."—Devyn N.

CHAPTER 1

Money Management and Financial Planning

In life, it all comes down to these two functions—managing money and planning how to make it grow and get more of it. Many people have opinions about what "financial planning" and "money management" mean. By the time you've finished this book, I hope you will have your own workable approach to building and managing your financial resources.

Think of these functions as the way to manage your life, rather than allowing your life to manage you. With a bit of foresight and planning, you can put the "money" part of your life on semi-autopilot, and live the way you want to. Without planning, it's going to be hard to get all the things you need and many of the things you want—and the things you do get aren't always going to be the things you had in mind. You won't have much control over events in your life.

> **Remember, people rarely plan to fail—they simply fail to plan.**

Right now you probably get lots of advice about managing your money and your life from many sources. Most of this advice is from people or places you either don't want to listen to or should take with a grain of salt. If you're reading this, you are in the right place—this book distills inputs from many sources so *you* can make your own plans and decisions.

Advice and information about managing money and credit are available almost anywhere you turn. Some of the most common sources are:

> **Only you can decide what your dreams will be, but fulfilling your dreams and goals is a daunting task, and it never hurts to seek outside information. No matter whom you talk to, you are the one who manages and controls your life.**

- The Internet
- Your parents
- Your friends
- Your school
- Your employer
- Television
- Seminars and investment events
- Books, magazines, and newspapers

How can you objectively evaluate all this information and make your own educated choices? Where can you turn and what can you do to set and meet your own financial goals and fulfill your dreams?

What do you consider the three biggest mistakes teenagers and young adults make with their money? Why are these mistakes? How might these mistakes be avoided?

Mistakes:

1. Not saving money in the less traditional ways (other than passbook accounts): CDs, stocks, [mutual] funds
2. Not having a vision for the future

3. Not having a healthy respect for debt
4. Living/spending in the moment
5. Living from check to check

These mistakes create an unstable financial foundation. They leverage their income and financial moves predicated on the assumption that this financial house of cards could never be rattled. Then it only takes one small tip to bring the whole thing down. "When I taught elementary school children, I always did a finance unit on my own to 4th graders. Money savvy should be introduced *very* early."—Devyn N., parent of 17-year-old Vanessa and 15-year-old Derek.

Practical Exercises

1. Go to your favorite Internet search engine and search for "financial planning" and "money management" (in quotes). You'll get thousands of hits. Go through at least ten pages of the hits for each topic and pick three that sound interesting.

   Print the files and evaluate the information based on what you believe about financial planning and money management right now. Consider things such as applicability to your situation, the value of setting goals, the quality of information delivered, and so forth.

   If you are at your parents' house, ask them what they think about the accuracy and validity of the information you collected. Do they think the approaches and date are useful in the "real world"?

2. Watch a cable, satellite, or Public Broadcasting Service (PBS) financial show or two and write down five useful things you learned. Ask a friend to watch the same show and do the same thing, then compare notes. Then do an Internet search to see if you can validate the accuracy of the statements you heard from the "talking heads."

3. Read the *Wall Street Journal*, the *Financial Times*, or similar paper or a financial magazine. Pick two or three writers and do a Web search to see what their credentials are—are they stockbrokers? Freelance writers? CEOs? What gives them the "right" to give out the information they do? Should you listen to them? Why or why not?

If you do these exercises, you'll quickly see why it's so important to take information provided by any media with a tablespoon or two of salt.

CHAPTER 2

The Importance of Planning

Why is planning so important? It's *your* life and your money, right? So why would you want someone or something else to decide how you manage either your life or your money?

It's easy and tempting to give control of your life and finances to someone else, but you aren't likely to enjoy the results. Even easier is to simply drift or float along, letting whatever will happen, happen. That's a great approach if you want to spend your so-called golden years supplementing your retirement income by working in a hardware store or a fast food restaurant. It's one thing to work somewhere because you need to have contact with other people; it's another thing altogether to work in a menial job because you can't make ends meet.

FINANCIAL PLANNING

When you are thinking of taking a trip, you probably make a few plans. Even if you're only going across town a small bit of forethought makes the trip faster and smoother. You check the bus schedules to find the best times and routes to meet your schedule. If you're driving somewhere in town, you probably make sure you have the right address, maybe call for directions, and listen to the traffic reports so you are less likely to get stuck in traffic. Maybe you even use your trusty GPS wristwatch system to find the directions.

If you're taking a longer trip, you probably get out maps, maybe call a travel specialist, talk to the airlines, or do an online search. No matter what your style, you do at least a little bit of planning to make sure you get what you want.

Shouldn't that apply to your work and financial lives, too? One way or another, even if you don't think of it as planning, the important activities in your life often involve some sort of coordination, research, or "planning." Handling your money and credit shouldn't be any different, should it?

Let's start off by doing a short exercise that will show you how much you already know about planning. By the time you finish this book, you'll see how much this exercise relates to the planning you'll be doing throughout your working life.

Practical Exercise

What are the steps you would take to plan your first ever cross-country trip? Maybe you're headed to college, moving to a new town to work, going on your honeymoon, or off to your five-year high school reunion. What should/would you plan? Where would you go to get information? List those steps here (you may need more or fewer steps):

Step 1:_____

Step 2:_____

Step 3:_____

Step 4:_____

Step 5:_____

Step 6:_____

Step 7:_____

Step 8:_____

Step 9:_____

Step 10:_____

Step 11:_____

Step 12:_____

Step 13:_____

Step 14:_____

Step 15:_____

CHAPTER 3

Taking (or Giving Up) Control: The Choice Is Yours

I asked a group of young adults (ages 16 to 24) about managing money and planning, and the mistakes they or their friends had made. Here are the 12 most frequent responses they gave. Of course, it's your choice—you can choose to cruise through life without a plan. But before you make that choice, take a few minutes to read what I call . . .

The Top 12 Ways to Give Control of Your Life to Someone Else

1. *Assume someone else will always bail you out.*
   Sure, that's a possibility, but your "personal" costs are awfully high. If someone else is going to pay your way, cover your mistakes, build your investments, or rescue you when your bills are higher than your income, that person is going to demand major or total control over how his or her money is used. There aren't many handouts in life, and the ones you get always seem to come with strings—or maybe ropes and chains— attached.

2. *Declare bankruptcy if you can't pay your bills and credit cards. Why should going into debt be a big deal?*
   It's frighteningly easy to declare bankruptcy in our country, even with the recent law changes. You read about multimillionaires declaring bankruptcy and continuing to drive their Mercedes and live in their $10 million houses, with all their furs, jewels, and expensive toys intact. Maybe so, but they had the means and knowledge to get high-priced legal advice—you don't. If you declare bankruptcy, it is going to follow you for at least seven very long years. You may well lose your car, have to move in with your parents or friends, and find you have no access to any form of credit—cards or loans. You may have a hard time getting a job or getting into the school you want or getting professional licenses.

   Debt is very hard to crawl out from under. The $15,000 home entertainment system or computer system you charge today is going to cost you at least double that and take decades to pay off making minimum monthly payments. Even worse, the stuff will be obsolete after just three or five years, and you won't have the means to replace it.

HAS THIS EVER HAPPENED TO YOU OR YOUR FRIENDS?

Imagine buying a top-of-the-line VCR (what's that?!) for $1,000 ten years ago, and charging it. You've been paying $60–$80 or so each month in order to meet the minimum on your credit card. Now you want a top-of-line DVD-R, and you still have ten years to go to pay off the VCR. Plus, your credit card is "maxed out" so you can't buy that DVD-R anyway.

You're going to end up paying twice as much for something that you no longer need or want, and you could have been saving that money to buy something you do want. Go figure!

You aren't the one in control any more; you have to keep paying for something that is obsolete, broken, or no longer of use. Bankruptcy is a drag on your life for a very long time. The courts and the people and places to which you owe money control your life now.

3. *The future is a long way off—live for today and enjoy yourself right now.*

   It's rough to be a student or newly employed. You are dependent on your parents or low-wage jobs to get the money to buy the things you want and need. When you get that first job with decent pay, the temptation to buy-buy-buy is incredibly strong. Suddenly you can't imagine how you functioned all those years without all that stuff. The credit card companies are wondering the same thing—so they stuff your mailbox with "great" offers.

   Unfortunately, most of the things people buy on credit are "consumable"—they are used and gone in a very short time. Airfare, gasoline, meals out, clothes, electronics, and similar items—all are long gone before the bills are paid off. In the case of trips and food, they are often consumed before the bill shows up. You end up paying for memories long after the memories are gone.

   The tendency when you first have a regular source of income and credit to expand your buying power is to take on fixed expenses that you really can't afford. Credit is a dangerous thing—loans and cards and leases—because a "small" payment each month lets you buy some really major stuff. The same applies to expensive trips, electronics, home entertainment centers, designer clothes, and so forth.

   That Lexus or BMW is something you can't possibly pay cash for. But you could get a new car loan and pay $600–$700 a month. Even better, you could lease your dream car for three or four years and drop the payments to $400–$500 per month. Of course, when the lease ends, you have nothing. You may even have to pay for every extra mile you drove, and replace the windshield, replace the tires, and fix every scratch and ding. Suddenly a leased car isn't so cheap. If you want to keep the car to avoid paying these costs, you probably have to get a high-interest-rate used car loan and pay for the car for another four or five years. This becomes a very expensive way to buy a car—but more on that later.

   You are no longer in control—your credit cards and purchases are running your life.

4. *Investing and saving are too complicated. Think about them "tomorrow."*

   That approach may have worked for Scarlett O'Hara in *Gone with the Wind*, but in real life that attitude is a recipe for disaster. Learning about investing is the first step toward doing it, and there are dozens of ways to educate yourself:

   • Investment clubs
   • Books and magazines
   • Materials from mutual fund companies
   • Information from financial advisors and experts
   • Conversations with your parents
   • Courses at school, and on and on

   Banks are a great place to get started, especially if you may need the money soon and don't want to tie it up for months or years. You can start small—$50 or $100 a month with many mutual funds and less into a savings account. Your money earns interest or grows as the stock market goes up. Learning about investments is both empowering and great fun.

   Of course, you don't have to do this, either. When you have accumulated financial resources, you have financial freedom. When you have to rely on credit and other people for your money, you have financial burdens. Which do you prefer? Remember: tomorrow is a day that never comes—it's *always* today—and yesterday is something that can't be undone.

> **Remember, tomorrow never comes. Today is also the tomorrow you worried about yesterday.**

5. *When you max out your current credit cards, you can always get new ones.*

   Of course you can! As long as you make minimum payments, credit card companies will love you, and places you've never heard of will want your money too. Of course, getting rid of those old cards isn't really an option—you can close the cards and transfer the debt to new cards, but you can't just get new cards and disregard your debt on the old ones.

   Getting new cards when the old ones are "full" is not quite the same thing as buying new clothes when the old ones don't fit or go out of style. You can give old clothes to a charity or a friend, but you can't do that with debt. The only way to "give" debt away is to declare bankruptcy, and the costs of doing that are terribly high.

   More credit cards mean giving away even more control over your life—to the card companies, the bankruptcy courts, and the people who may or may not bail you out when you can no longer pay your bills.

6. *Taking charge of your finances is easy—there are experts all over the place who are never wrong, and you have great intuition about picking stocks.*

   It's easy to pick stocks when you're not investing "real" money. The media have contests all the time where listeners manage an imaginary stock portfolio and make pots of money—in theory. Reality is a bit different.

   There are "stock mavens"—so-called experts—on almost every TV channel and in all the magazines. Of course, by the time you get to hear or read their picks, the news is old and you are catching the wrong train!

AN OLD STOCKBROKER TRICK

In the days before everything was electronic and cable/satellite TV news ruled, stockbrokers got much of their information from magazines. If *Money Magazine* recommended "The Top 10 Stocks to Buy Now," the recommendations were already weeks old by the time the magazine came out. Still, people followed that advice, and stockbrokers knew it.

The stockbrokers would rush to their local airports (since the magazines were often flown in) and get the first copies. Then they would call their clients from pay phones at the airport (few cell phones back then!) and get them to buy the recommended stocks. Even though the information was weeks old, by buying just before the people who got the magazine the next day, the stockbrokers' clients were almost certain to make some money.

Even though the stock picks were essentially useless, the lack of investing savvy on the part of the general public combined with a bit of initiative on the part of the stockbrokers almost guaranteed clients would make money. So the "experts" were "successful" with their stock picks. Right.

   Following the advice of experts without understanding their rationale for recommendations and without having clear goals and an investment plan leaves you wide open. You are open to being taken advantage of, following inappropriate or wrong advice, and never reaching your goals because someone else has taken control of your life and money.

7. *Social Security and company retirement plans will take care of me—why waste hard-earned money on investments? Spending is much more fun!*

   Social Security was never designed to be a full-fledged retirement plan. Rather, its purpose was to provide a supplement to other savings and pension plan income.

   Company retirement plans have taken quite a hit as stocks were hammered in the first three years of this decade. In addition (as the on-again, off-again pension woes at United Airlines, Enron, and many other big companies show), even traditional pensions can get into big trouble.

   Being able to take care of yourself is a valuable life skill and essential pension-building survival skill.

8. *As long as you can work, you will always be able to invest when it's convenient. It will be much easier to take control of your financial life when you're in your 30s or 40s.*

How long were you planning on working anyway? To age 70 or so? That's when Social Security will probably start paying you—and only about 20% (or less) of what you were earning.

Ever had a friend or parent who was laid off? Unfortunately, the bad or unpredictable things seem to be the more reliable events in your working and financial lives.

9. *Working hard is for the birds, or at least for someone else.*

You can always go into business for yourself or count on your inheritance. After all, if you are your own boss you can work when you want, charge what you want for your services, and life will be good. Not!

Counting on money from someone else is rarely a good idea. That big commission falls through, or you lose your job, or you don't get that raise, or your parents need to spend the money you thought you would inherit.

In the long (and short) run, working hard and accumulating the fruits of your labors is going to be the best and hardest choice.

10. *Don't bother buying a house—there are too many other things that are more fun.*

Home ownership is one of the best financial decisions most of you will ever make. It really does cost less to own than to rent, provided you have enough money to make the down payment, a good work history, and an excellent credit history.

Why is home ownership such a good deal? You get to deduct most of the payment from your income, avoiding a lot of income taxes. Your home usually increases in value each year. You can paint it, alter it, or expand it, and the landlord can't say no. The increase in value is virtually tax-free when you sell the house.

A home lasts and increases in value. The things you might buy instead are usually disposable—electronics, sports equipment, trips, fancy cars, meals out, and so on. Homes have staying power.

Peer pressure to spend, spend, spend is all around you. New fads are appearing every day. It's easy to give in, but that pair of low-slung pants won't be around in a year or two—the house will.

11. *Don't even think about diversifying your investments. Everyone knows stocks are the only way to go.*

I've never met "everyone," so he or she must not be very successful.

When it comes to building your assets, slow and steady works better than fast and erratic. Ask your parents how they and the people they work with felt when the stock market started falling in March of 2000 and kept moving south for the next few years. People couldn't buy stocks fast enough, looking for the quick buck. Instead, many so-called investors lost 50–70% of the value of their investments in a few short years.

12. *You can always move in with Mom and Dad.*

Hah!

Independence is hard to earn and harder to keep. Money, savings, and a good job are the keys to maintaining your financial independence. Sure, you can always move back home, but do you really want to? The people who pay the bills assume they have a right to make decisions. If you pay the bills, you make your decisions—but if your parents pay your bills, you may lose that freedom. After all, you loved being there so much you never even wanted your own place, right? The rules, the structure, the nosiness? Made your day, didn't it? You loved asking for money and permission to do things and go places. Think you'll like doing it better in your 20s than you did in your teens?

Money Management and Financial Responsibility—What's in It for You?

This book is a guide to help you form your own money management and financial strategies, plans, and goals. To that end I've incorporated much of the information you need so you don't fall into the pitfalls of the preceding list, and it goes several steps farther and gives you the tools and skills you need to construct your own financial plan and money management approach.

You'll find a number of worksheets, lots of information sources, a number of examples, and real advice and experiences from real people:

- Young adults and recent graduates
- Parents of young adults
- Financial professionals
- Other professional advisors such as lawyers and tax advisors
- Employers

Money is something everyone wants, and few people ever seem to have enough of it. You are at a wonderful point in your life because you:

- Are just starting out
- Don't have lots of habits and ideas to change
- Are at a point when saving small amounts goes a very long way
- Are used to *not* having a lot, and managing to get by
- Can develop plans, goals, and habits, and make them your own

This book will help you do these and many other things that will enable you to develop your personal lifetime money management approach. You'll learn to understand and manage money and credit, build a budget, and so much more. By making these financial management strategies your own, they will become an integral part of your life. Then you are free to move on to the rest of your life: education, career, travel, and anything else that makes you happy, knowing you have the means to live today *and* enjoy the future.

How do you plan to make sure you have the money you need to meet your wants, goals, dreams, and needs? Do you have a budget or financial plan? What is in this plan? How often do you review this plan?

By saving consistently over a long period of time.—Vanessa N., 17

I will invest my money wisely.—Derek N., 15

Invest [in] IRAs, mutual funds, a job. I have a vague budget. Don't spend more than you earn. I don't review it [my plan or budget] too much.—Kai Ge Y.

I attempt to invest and save all of the money I receive from both working and gifts. These investments and savings hopefully will benefit me in the future, and most specifically through college. I do not have an outline financial plan of my own.—Kris Z.

I do not have a "written goal" although I've had an IRA for years that I put money in for my retirement. I chose to go to a less expensive college so that I would have the rest of the money as a nest egg for a home that I plan to purchase in a few years. Lastly, I save money for my near future as opposed to [just] my retirement.—Libby M., a former YAB client working in Denver, Colorado.

Meet the Twins—Alex and Phoenix

I want to introduce you to my favorite twins—Alex and Phoenix. They can be male, female, or one of each—you decide. These two young adults are very similar:

- Same age (of course!)
- Same family background (no surprise here)
- Identical grades and subjects in school
- Same part-time job at the same pay during high school
- Same college, same major
- Same employer at graduation, same career, adjacent cubicles
- Same interests and friends

Of course, all this sameness would get very boring very quickly, so I made sure the twins had a few important differences—very different approaches to managing money, saving money, investing money, and planning for the future. Of course, these aren't real people—but they could be.

We're going to follow the twins throughout this book—they make such perfect examples of what to do and not do with money, credit cards, loans, budgets, and just about anything else you can think of. We'll meet them at various ages and decision points over the next eight years.

Let's start watching Alex and Phoenix, seeing what sort of financial decisions they made, starting with their 16th birthday party.

But first, here's a bit more about them. They grew up in a middle-class family in Anytown, USA. Both their parents work full-time. There are two other children in the family—Mary, who is four years older than the twins, and Mike, who is two years younger than the twins. They lived in the same house all through junior high and high school.

When they turned 16, they got a shared car—a hand-me-down from Mary. They had to pay the insurance and gas, but their parents agreed to handle the maintenance and car registration. No car payments—lucky them!

They attended the same public high school and took the exact same courses. When they turned 16, they found part-time jobs for a catering company near their school. They each worked 15 hours a week during the school year and 28 hours a week during the week before Christmas and over the summers after their junior and senior years.

Both graduated tied for 32nd in their class of 700, and they were accepted to the most prestigious branch of their state university. They majored in computer systems and business management, and got terrific jobs as software system marketing specialists at a top technical company in Denver, Colorado. Two years later, at the age of 24, Alex got a big promotion and Phoenix got fired. Why?

Because along the way they made lots of financial decisions with intended and unintended consequences.

What do you consider the three biggest mistakes people your age make with their money? What are these mistakes? How might these mistakes be avoided?

People my age aren't saving their money for their future which will just hurt them. When we get to the stage of purchasing homes they are unable to do so. Also, people my age are spending too much in credit and are then unable to pay their cards back fully. Hence, most of my friends are dealing with credit card debt . . . which again hurts their chances for buying a home. These mistakes can be avoided by living below their means, thus allowing them to save and pay off their [credit] cards.—Libby M., a young working adult.

Practical Exercises

1. Choose three or four of the "Ways to Give Up Control of Your Life" and explain how you make sure they don't happen to you, or if they reflect your current situation, how you will make changes to take back control.

_____

_____

_____

_____

_____

_____

_____

_____

_____

_____

_____.

2. Come up with two more ways to give up control of your life—they don't have to be purely financial—and explain why these things could be a problem and how you make sure they are not problems for you.

_____

_____

_____

_____

_____

_____

_____

_____

_____

_____

_____

_____

_____.

3. Look at your checkbook for the past year. Make notes about its condition. Can you tell from the entries what you actually bought? Can you tell when and where and how much your ATM withdrawals and fees were? Do you detect frivolous spending you might be able to reduce or manage better? How can you make your checkbook your friend rather that your adversary or enemy?

_____

_____

_____

_____

_____

_____

_____

_____

_____

_____

_____

_____

_____.

4. Think about the people you deal with regularly in your peer (age) group. Are people who always seem to have money and nice things but still save money and control their lives? Are there others who never have money because they spent it all as fast as they earned or got it? What does each group do differently, in your opinion? Here's a chart to help you organize your thoughts:

Chart 3.1. The Spender and the Saver

The Spender/Live for Today	The Saver/Plan for Tomorrow

_____

_____

_____

_____

_____

_____

_____

_____

_____

_____

_____

_____.

5. What are the three most important things the Spender might want to do differently?

_____

_____

_____

6. Is it possible to be too "thrifty"? Do you know someone who saves every nickel he or she gets and never goes anywhere, does anything, or seems to have any fun? What are three things these people do you find alarming or of concern?

   _____

   _____

   _____

CHAPTER 4

More Money Management and Financial Planning

In the introduction, I mentioned "money management" and "financial planning" a number of times. One of the practical exercises even gave you some ideas to explore these concepts on your own. Why is this book hammering these concepts so hard and so often? Because they are essential, key concepts if you want to achieve financial success, be financially responsible, and gain financial freedom.

Let's take some time to look at what these concepts are. What is money management? What is financial planning? Why are they so important? Can you gain your financial freedom without understanding these concepts?

Money Management

Money management is one aspect of financial planning. It is what you do in the "here and now," the steps you take on a daily, weekly, and monthly basis to make sure the money you have stretches to meet your day-to-day needs. Part of money management is dedicating some of what you have to meet future goals.

Money management's foundation is the dreaded "B" word—budget. It's easy to say, "I know what my expenses are—I don't need to write them down and plan how I'll spend my money," but in practice that approach doesn't work. Think about it.

Have you ever gone to the ATM to get money or cashed a paycheck or received your allowance, and two days later a week's worth of money was gone? I'll bet you scratched your head, and said, "I can't possibly have spent all that money already. It's only Monday and I don't get any more money until Friday. How am I going to pay for . . . ?"

We'll look at the ins and outs of building a budget that works for you, not one that works for your parents or friends. Everyone's money management needs and styles are different—as different as their income sources and expenses.

> If you did the Web search in the practical exercises, it would be very interesting to look at the information you collected and compare it with what you are going to read next.
>
> If you got input from your parents, it might also be worthwhile to see what they said compared to what you'll be reading here.

ALWAYS "PAY YOURSELF FIRST"

That means put money into your emergency fund, your retirement savings, your personal savings, your education savings, and so on. To do this requires a budget.

Planning to "put whatever is left at the end of the month" into your savings simply doesn't work—there's almost never anything left—there is always a CD or DVD or gadget or pizza calling your name.

It's tempting to say, "I'm young, so I don't need to think about *that* until tomorrow (or next year, or five years from now)." But tomorrow comes awfully quickly. Just think back over how fast the summers raced by, or high school graduation came, or a party ended. It seemed like the longed-for events would never happen, and then they flew by, almost like a dream.

It's your choice, and I hope you will make the kind of money management choices you can put in place, forget about (90% of the time), and live with.

What are the three most important things you learned about saving and investing money? Where or from whom did you learn these things? Do you follow what you know? Do you spend like there's no tomorrow or save some each month?

> **Your budget is as individual as you are—even if you are a twin. Just ask Alex and Phoenix.**

The most important things I've learned are about rates and fees, managing the [checking/savings] account, and different types of accounts. Young Americans [Bank] has taught me a lot about investing, saving, and looking to the future. I generally save my money unless I have some urgent necessity for it.—Kris Z., a YAB client in Denver.

1. Start when you're young. 2. Pay off debt before investing. 3. Pay yourself first. I learned these from books and people. I also follow what I know. I used to spend like no tomorrow but now I save some each month.—Kai Ge Y., YAB client.

Financial Planning

Financial planning is much broader than day-to-day money management. It includes setting goals for the next month, next year, and five years from now. Financial planning includes "lifestyle" planning—how you'll get a job, decide where to go to school and how to pay for it, how you'll afford an apartment, whether to buy a new or used car, and much more.

Successful financial planning is your ticket to financial independence and freedom.

It's next to impossible to begin financial planning without a budget, income sources, goals, and flexibility. By reading this book, you'll learn ways to build a financial plan that works for *you*.

Without planning, financial responsibility, freedom, and long-term success are simply unattainable.

Why Money Management and Financial Planning Matter

You really can't be a successful money manager without being a savvy financial planner, and vice versa. If you build a budget and stick to it, but don't have plans for the money you aren't spending—in accordance with your budget—you'll either end up with a lot of money in a checking account or you'll be tempted to "blow" the money on something you don't need (and maybe don't really want!).

If you have a great financial plan and well-defined goals, but can't manage your money through a budget, you'll never be able to use your plan and you'll get frustrated.

Why Now? Why Not Wait a Few Years?

There are probably scores of things you want or "need." Your friends and peers have things, and you want these things, too. This version of "keeping up with the Joneses" is a tempting precedent to set for yourself, but one that can cost far more than you ever imagined. Believe it or not, there are ways to have most of the things you want and all of the things you need, and still manage your money, meet your financial goals, and ensure your financial independence.

Let's go back in time to visit with our friends Alex and Phoenix during their high school years. Both have jobs at the same catering service. Both earn $10.00 an hour, plus tips. The tips work out to about $5.00 per hour. They both work about 15 hours a week, and they both pay about 20% of their income in taxes. But that's where the similarities end.

Why? Here's a comparison of what they did with their after-tax income.

Table 4.1. The Saver and The Spender

	The Saver—Alex	*The Spender—Phoenix*
Total (Gross) Income	$225/week	$225/week
Taxes	$45/week	$45/week
Net (Take-home) pay	$180/week	$180/week
Savings %	50% of *gross*	25% of *net*
Savings amount	$112.50/week	$45/week
Investment option	Mutual Funds	Savings Account
Assumed annual interest	8%	2%
Value after one year (estimate)	$6,070	$2,425

What Does This Illustration Mean for You?

Over the course of your working lifetime, saving a mere $67.50 more each week—that's one pizza, one movie, and a few CDs or DVDs—makes a huge difference in your future pot of cash. If you're in your teens or early 20s now, you'd have $125,000 or so in your early 30s (assuming you saved for 12.5 years), $466,000 or so in your 40s, and an amazing $1,388,000 when you retire at age 59. And if you put part of that money in a Roth IRA (more on that later), you'd never owe *any* taxes on a large chunk of your investment!

The Saver and the Spender over the Years

Here's a chart comparing what "The Saver" might have, compared to "The Spender."

Table 4.2. Long-term Accumulation Comparison

Age	*The Saver*	*The Spender*
33	$125,000	$50,000
46	$466,000	$185,000
59	$1,388,000	$552,000

Of course, once you're working in a full-time career, you'll have the chance to save even more. You'll have more money, and your employer will probably offer a 401(k) or other retirement plans (and give you "free" money just for saving!).

Nothing is guaranteed, especially the earnings and growth of a mutual fund or other investments, but you'll see lots of these illustrations in this book, and they show you how you can set and reach financial goals.

Practical Exercises

1. Explain money management in your own words. What is it? What is it *not*? How can you be a more effective money manager? When do you think someone should consult a professional money manager?

_____

_____

_____

_____

_____

_____

_____

_____

_____

_____

_____

_____

_____.

2. Explain financial planning in your own words. What is it? What is it *not*? How can you be a more effective financial planner? When do you think someone should consult a professional financial planner?

_____

_____

_____

_____

_____

_____

_____

_____

_____

_____

_____

_____

_____ .

3. What would motivate you to become a saver rather than a spender? How much of your take-home pay
    (amount or percentage) do you think you should and could save? How might you plan to make sure you save
    at least part of any salary increase, promotion/raise, or bonus into a savings or investment program?

_____

_____

_____

_____

_____

_____

_____

_____

_____

_____

_____

_____

_____ .

IT'S NOT EASY SAVING GREEN

This "simple" task of planning, saving, and investing is not as easy as I make it seem. It takes lots of effort and hard work, but the time and effort are more than worthwhile. Once you start the habit and do it for just a few months, it can stick with you your whole life. It becomes background noise—you no longer even notice it unless you make a real effort—it just happens.

   If saving and investing were easy, everyone would be saving and investing—but they're not, so maybe it's a bit more complicated than it seems.

2

What's in It for You?

If you can't see a reason (or several reasons) to do something, you aren't going to even consider the idea. So let's take a look at the many topics this book will cover.

What's in it for you? A road map to lifelong financial and personal success. What is financial success? According to one young adult:

> Financial success is when you've reached a point where you and your family are able to live comfortably without having to worry about money. I think that once this point is reached it's time to share it with others. Personal success is when you are truly happy with your life and you are able to look back on your life with fondness.—Libby M., a young working adult in Denver.

CHAPTER 5

The Highlights: What's in This Book for You?

You can learn a lot about money, investments, credit, loans, life, school, and much more in this book. Some of the key topics you'll learn about are:

- Money
- Credit
  - Loans
  - Credit cards
- Interest and inflation
- The time value of money
  - Compounding
  - Simple interest
  - Rule of 72
- Taxes and planning for them
- Managing your money
  - Checking accounts
  - Getting and using credit and loans
  - Repaying debt and loans
  - Credit and your credit score
- Protecting your credit and your identity
- Paying for your education
  - Traditional sources of funding
  - Alternative sources of funding
  - Maximizing your chances of getting financial aid
- Managing your money—making and using a budget
- Building your savings and starting an investment program
- Understanding, obtaining, and managing insurance
- Building a financial plan
- Blending two incomes and lifestyles
- Understanding company- or employer-provided benefit plans
  - Retirement
  - Health/medical
  - Disability
  - Education funding
  - Vacation and holidays

- Planning for major purchases without breaking the bank
- Combining two households
- Retiring in style
- Starting and running a business
- Balancing life, work, money, and credit

Not all of these areas are going to interest you right now, but sooner or later you're probably going to want to know a bit about almost everything in this list. An informed consumer is a prepared consumer.

3

A Brief History of Money and Credit

Money is a surprisingly new invention—it came about when bartering became too difficult and people became more mobile. For bartering to work, you need a number of things to converge:

- Everyone involved in the barter operation has to come together with the same goals, at the same time, and be in the same place.
- Each person has to have something someone else wants or needs, and then the wants and needs have to mesh.
- The value of the items must be agreed—there is likely no set value.

It is simply easier to have something with an assigned value that everyone agrees to, hence we have money. Sure beats carrying around cows and pigs, and shoes and jackets, and pots and plates, hoping you'll have something someone else wants and they'll have something you want, and you can agree the rate of exchange.

THE PROBLEM WITH BARTER

How many shoes equal three pots and two plates? That's the age-old problem with barter. And what if you don't want or need shoes, but that's all the pot-maker has to barter with?

How do credit cards and loans work? Why is a good credit rating important? Libby, a young working adult (in the banking industry), explains it this way:

Credit cards allow you to purchase items, when you may or may not have the money at the time, with someone else's money. This then puts you in debt to the person who lent you the money. If you do not pay off your bill on time, you are then charged a usage fee [interest] each time you fail to pay in full. This is how credit card companies make [some of] their money.

Car loans are also a type of debt, although you do not have to pay your bill [balance] in full every month to [prevent] the bank or person responsible for the loan from taking the car from you. Also, because you are paying off the car [loan] over time you must pay interest, much like if you don't pay your [credit] cards off every month.

Credit ratings are important because they determine if you are eligible for more credit and loans, like loans for a home. Defaulting [not paying] on your payments of existing loans and credit cards hurts your credit [rating] making it hard to get more of either [loans or credit cards].

Money: A History

A Brief History of Money

Long before there was money as we know it, there was barter and trade. Of course, it was hard to carry the "right" items so you could barter or trade for something if you happened upon the "perfect" club or animal hide! So people began assigning value to small, easy-to-carry items such as beads, shells, gold, and so forth.

Eventually, the size or weight of these portable items of exchange was standardized, and coins as we know them began to appear. Coins have been around for thousands of years.

Paper money was still a long way off—no one wanted something that had no substance or value in its own right. When paper money finally began to be used regularly (only a few hundred years ago), it was usually tied to something with recognized value, for example:

> **Did You Know?**
>
> **The term "bit" refers to the way a coin (generally a $1, $5, $10, or $20 gold piece) was cut into eighths to pay smaller costs?**

- The British pound sterling (silver and gold)
- The silver and gold certificate dollars (silver and gold)
- The Dutch florin or guilder (gold)

It wasn't until the middle of the 20th century that the U.S. dollar was cut loose from the "gold standard." Until then, you could (in theory) take your gold and silver certificates to certain banks and exchange them for actual gold or silver. Many coins were also made largely of silver (until the 1970s).

The leap of faith to currency backed only by "the full faith and credit of the United States government" was actually an amazing move at the time. Of course, few people truly doubt the value of our currency, which is a good thing since otherwise we could never have credit cards.

Practical Exercise

Try and paint a picture of your life today if there were no money. Imagine buying the things you need and want and having to trade or barter with the things you have available. What do you think your skills and resources would be worth in a barter economy? What could you trade to a music shop owner for DVDs and CDs? How would you acquire the home entertainment center? What do you have that someone would value in exchange for a car—even a used clunker?

Credit: A History

A Brief History of Credit

Credit is something few of us would want to be without, yet until the 1960s or 1970s few Americans had credit cards. MasterCard, Visa, American Express, Discover, Diners Club, ATM cards, debit cards, and so forth are everywhere now, but it wasn't always that way. Many people had department store credit cards, and the local mom-and-pop stores might extend credit occasionally, but that was about it. It was cash or check, or you didn't get the goods or services.

Times have certainly changed. Now it seems every bank and credit union in the world issues its own major credit cards, and there are few places in the world where you can't use a credit card to pay for almost everything, and get cash from machines, too.

Credit cards used to be pretty difficult to get, and the credit limits were generally low—a few hundred dollars, maybe $1,000 or so. Now they are everywhere; you've probably received one or more offers to get a major credit card already. There are a few credit cards with no spending limits at all.

Managing credit is a real challenge—it's not free money, and new users of credit cards don't always truly understand that. Learn to use credit wisely and the world can be a fun place with lots of great bargains. Use credit poorly and you will quickly find yourself trapped in a nightmare with no easy way out.

Credit comes in many shapes and forms, but the two types you are most likely to see are loans and credit (or debit) cards.

Practical Exercise

Repeat the exercise from the "History of Money" text (chapter 6), but think in terms of credit cards and loans:

Try and paint a picture of your life today if there were no credit. Imagine buying the things you need and want and having to trade or barter with the things you have available. What do you think your skills and resources would be worth in a barter economy? What could you trade to a music shop owner for DVDs and CDs? How would you acquire the home entertainment center? What do you have than someone would value in exchange for a car—even a used clunker?

_____

_____

_____

_____

_____

4

What Affects the Value of Your Money?

Before we get into the details of managing credit and managing money, let's take a look at two things that

- drive the cost of borrowing
- affect the performance of investments, and
- determine the way salaries are set.

What are these two powerful factors? *Interest* and *inflation*.

Interest and inflation affect all aspects of managing money, investments, income, and credit. They affect the amount of your raises, the amount of your tax deductions, the "real" cost of borrowing, and so on.

Your parents probably talk about how "cheap" food or housing or education was when they were your age. Yes, things cost far less 20 or 30 years ago, but people earned far less money too. As costs and salaries rose, so did the prices of most things. This increase was due to inflation.

In "real" terms—meaning after the effects of inflation are taken out of a price or cost or salary—not much has changed. In fact, some things have fallen dramatically in price, especially things that are high-tech in nature. The best way to judge the "true" cost of something is to see how many hours you have to work to make enough money to pay for the item or service. That figure has probably changed very little in the past hundred years.

CHAPTER 8

Interest

Interest is the "reward" you get for lending someone or someplace (such as a bank, through your savings account) money. It is also the "penalty" you pay for borrowing (owing) money.

Without interest (or dividend) payments, the value of bonds, certificates of deposit, and savings accounts would never increase beyond the actual amount of money you put in them. Then no one would want to invest money in these "fixed income" investments. It would be easier and just as productive to keep your money on a shelf in your closet!

Without interest charges, there would be less money to be made in credit cards, mortgages, or other loans—so banks would have no reason to lend money to anyone.

Interest affects almost anything to do with money or credit. Interest also affects the cost of doing business for companies since they often depend on borrowing to meet cash flow, payroll, and other financial needs.

Interest impacts both sides of the money equation—the money you save or invest and the money you borrow or owe.

Interest and Credit Card or Loan Payments

The higher the rate of interest on a credit card or loan payment, the more your charged items or loans are going to cost you. Why is interest charged in the first place? There are a number of reasons, but here are the main ones:

- Lenders are in business to make money, whether from your credit card balance, loan balance, checking account overdraft balance, or other money you have borrowed. If you owe money to a business, that business is very unlikely to let you use their money without charging you for the privilege. This charge is called interest.
- If you have borrowed money (or charged something to a credit card), the person or place that lent you the money has lost the use of the money. To make up for this, they charge you interest—it makes up for the lender's inability to use the money.

CREDIT CARDS AND DEBT

Think about this: If you charge your purchase of a new DVD-R, someone has to pay the merchant—you haven't given the shop cash, but the shop still expects to be paid.

If you don't pay with cash but use a credit card, the lender (the place that issued your credit card) has to pay on your behalf, using *their* money. The credit card company is counting on you to pay them back. To help cover their costs, make money to pay salaries, and cover other expenses, they charge you fees and interest.

If someone pays your debts—by lending you money in the form of a car loan, for example—and you don't pay it back, who owns the item (car)? If you think you do, you are mistaken. The person or place that lent you the money owns the item. If you have made some of the payments, you own part of the item—but the lender can still force the sale of the item (such as your car) or take it back if you don't make payments on time.

Interest and Credit Cards

When you use a credit card, you are charged interest after a certain number of days, or maybe even right away.

Most credit cards have a "grace period." This is the time between charging something and having to pay the amounts you've charged before interest is assessed. If you always pay your balance in full before the "due date," you probably won't be charged interest.

If you don't pay your full account balance on a credit card by the due date, you are going to be charged interest. Every credit card company has a way it calculates interest, but the most common is to calculate $\frac{1}{12}$th of the annual interest rate, then multiply that percentage times your "average daily balance."

Example: If you have a credit card balance at the end of your billing cycle and don't pay the full amount, here is what most credit card companies are going to do. First, they will calculate your "average daily balance." The actual method can vary slightly, but here is a rough idea. If you charge $600 on the first day of your billing cycle, and don't charge anything the rest of the month, and there are 30 days in your cycle, your average daily balance is $(30 \cdot 600) \div 30 = \$600$. If your annual interest rate is 18%, your monthly interest rate is 1.5% (18% $\div$ 12 months = 1.5%).

In this simple example, you will owe 1.5% $\cdot$ $600 or $9.

> **Prepaid credit cards, secured credit cards, and debit cards don't charge interest because they never have a balance—the amount you "charge" is deducted immediately from your account.**

If you charge additional amounts through the month, your average daily balance will be higher. If you charged an additional $600 on the 15th day of your billing cycle, you would have an additional $600 balance for half of a month. This means your average daily balance would be:

$$[(\$600 \cdot 30) \div 30] + [(\$600 \cdot 15) \div 30] \text{ or } \$900.$$

You would then owe 1.5% $\cdot$ 900 or $13.50.

If you don't pay your credit card balance in full every month, your average daily balance will vary, but it will *never* go away. Adding interest charges makes your average daily balance even higher.

In the example above, if your average daily balance is $900, and your minimum payment is $15, you will still owe $898.50 at the beginning of the next month ($900 + $13.50 in interest, minus $15 in payments). That means your average daily balance at the beginning of month is already high, and anything you charge will be added to that amount. It takes a very long time to pay off hundreds or thousands of dollars of credit card debt at a few dollars per month.

Interest and Loans

Interest you will owe on loans is calculated in many ways.

If you are paying interest on a car loan, your payments are structured in such a way that paying a bit extra has surprisingly little effect on the total amount you will end up paying.

If you are paying interest on a line of credit, such as a home equity line of credit, it is to your advantage to pay more than the scheduled payment amount. This type of loan is very similar to a credit card balance, so interest is calculated on your average daily balance.

If you are paying interest on a home mortgage (first or second mortgage), paying more than your scheduled payment will help reduce the total amount of interest you will pay. If you actually stay in the house long enough to completely pay the mortgage, paying a bit extra each month can shave years off the total amount you will pay. If you only live in the house for a few years, you will have a much larger ownership share in the house when you sell it.

MORTGAGE INTEREST

How much interest do you actually pay on a mortgage if you only make the scheduled payments? If you have a $200,000 30-year mortgage at about 5% interest, you are going to pay about $1,050 per month in principal (the amount you borrowed) and interest. In the first few years only $150–$250 per month goes toward your principal repayment.

Over a 30-year period you are going to pay about $378,000 in principal and interest: 12 months/year • $1,050/month • 30 years. That means almost half of the money you paid will go to pay interest charges.

Interest and Adjustable Rate Loans

Many loans, including home loans and credit card balances, are "adjustable rate" loans. That means if certain conditions are met, the interest rate you are charged can go up or go down. If your rate goes up, you are going to be paying more money for interest charges and less money for debt repayment, unless you increase the amount you pay each month.

What might cause your interest rate to rise?

- A general rise in short-term interest rates—meaning "The Fed" has announced an increase in its interest rates
- A history of late or missed credit card or loan payments on your part
- A history of exceeding your credit limit
- A history of late or missed payments of any sort—these can be used by the credit card and loan companies or other lenders as justification for raising your interest rate on unrelated loans and credit cards

Comparing Loan Options

Before you take a loan (from a bank, car dealer, mortgage lender, or other lender) it is very important to compare "apples to apples."

If a car dealer is offering a "no-interest" or very low interest loan, you need to see if there are any "catches." For example, if you are paying more for the car to get the lower interest rate, what is your total cost going to be over the loan period? If you pay $20,000 for a car at 1% interest or you pay $19,000 for the same car at 3% interest (both 48-month loans), which is the better deal? Answer: The second choice. In the first choice you end up paying $425 per month and in the second choice only $420 per month. The interest rate on the first option is lower, but the selling price is higher, so your total payments are higher.

Anything you do that affects your credit rating—good or bad—can raise or lower the interest rate on all your adjustable interest rate payments. Bouncing checks or missing payments on your electric bill or having a car wreck/auto insurance claim can all hurt your credit rating and affect the interest rate you pay on other things. These same actions that cause your adjustable interest rates to rise can result in the interest rate on new loans and credit cards to be higher too.

If you are thinking about "consolidating" credit card debt to lower your payments, here are a few things to look at:

- Is the interest rate (often advertised at 0% or 2% or something similar) only offered on balance transfers from another card?
- What is the interest rate on *new* purchases? It may be quite high.
- How long does this special interest rate last?
- Is there an annual fee with this new credit card?
- Is there a fee for balance transfers?
- How long is the grace period?

USING CREDIT CARDS TO CONSOLIDATE DEBT

If you get a new credit card to consolidate the debt on higher rate credit cards, don't forget to cancel the old credit card, and do so in writing. Failing to do this leads to at least two big problems.

Problem #1: Keeping the old card leads to the temptation to use it and run up even more debt.
Problem #2: The more "available credit" you have, the lower your credit score may be. Why? Because there is a risk you will use all your available credit and not be able to pay all the money back.

Think about this:
If you had a credit card with a $1,000 limit and you had a balance of $800, then got a new card with a $2,000 limit, and transferred the balance from your old card, what happens? You now have your old card with a $1,000 limit and no balance (no debt), and a new card with a $2,000 limit and $800 in debt. Before you got the new card, you could only charge an additional $200 ($1,000 limit − $800 balance). Now you can charge an additional $2,200. Unless your income and/or overall financial situation have improved drastically, you are a much bigger risk than before—you can incur far larger debt that you might not be able to repay. By canceling the old card you can't charge as much ($1,200 instead of $2,200) so you are a bit less of a risk. This helps your credit score.

If you are planning to use an adjustable-rate home loan, here are some things to keep in mind:

- Beginning in 2004, short-term interest rates started rising again. If your home loan is tied to a short-term index, your interest rate is going to rise too.
- Your interest rate may be able to rise as much as 2% in one year. That doesn't sound like much, but if you were paying $1,000 per month at 6% and your interest rate rises to 8%, you are going to have to find another $300 per month or so.
- It is not likely your interest rate will fall in the next several years, but it is very likely it will rise.

Practical Exercises (Answers in Appendix C)

1. List four things that are affected by rising interest rates.

    _____

    _____

    _____

    _____

2. List three things that are affected by falling interest rates.

_____

_____

_____

3. How can you compare loan terms "apples to apples"?

_____

_____

_____

4. Martha has a debit card. Her checking account balance is about $450. She wants to buy a new four-in-one stereo/DVD-R system that costs $475. What is going to happen when she tries to charge the system with her debit card?

_____

_____

_____

_____

_____

_____

_____

_____

_____

_____

_____

_____

_____.

CHAPTER 9

Inflation

Inflation determines the "real" cost of the things you buy and the "real" rate of return you earn on your savings and investments.

Inflation is not a bad thing and it's not a good thing. Sometimes inflation can be high and sometimes low, and other times it is possible to have deflation (when "real" prices fall) or stagflation (when prices and costs go nowhere in particular).

The goal of savers and investors is to earn a "real" rate of return on their money that keeps them ahead of inflation (and taxes). If you can reach that goal, your money is growing in "real" terms.

WHAT CAUSES INFLATION?

In very simple terms, inflation results when there are too many dollars chasing too few goods and services. In other words, people have too much income and too much available credit, so when they go out to buy things they have to compete against everyone else. This causes prices to rise.

The main tool we have to "fight" or manage inflation is short-term interest rates. If the cost to borrow money gets too high, people will think twice about using credit or loans to buy things. As a result, the cost of many items stops rising and may even fall.

If long-term interest rates get too high, the cost of things such as homes may fall because fewer people can afford the payments on a 30-year mortgage.

Coping with Inflation

How do you know if you are staying even with or getting ahead of inflation?

1. If your salary is not rising, you are probably falling behind. If you're getting a "cost-of-living" raise or adjustment, you are probably keeping even with inflation. If you are getting performance-related raises or bonuses in addition to cost-of-living adjustments, you are probably staying ahead of inflation.
2. If you are putting all your money (after paying your expenses) into a checking account, you are probably falling behind. If you are putting all your money into a savings account, certificates of deposit (CD), or many types of bonds, you are probably keeping even with inflation.
3. This is where it gets interesting. . . . If you are investing your money in a mix of stocks and bonds and CDs, and building a fund in your checking or savings account to cover emergencies and large expenses, you are probably staying ahead of inflation, at least in the long run.

Here's how to estimate how you are doing with your investments and savings, to see if you are doing the "right" things to stay ahead of inflation (and taxes):

Inflation and Taxes and Your Money

Example: Assume inflation is 3% per year and taxes are 20% on interest and 10% on capital gains (more on these later).

1. If you put $1,000 in a savings account and earn 2% per year, are you going to beat inflation?

   Answer: No. Why? Simple—3% inflation is more than 2% interest, so your money will lose value in "real" terms every year. Inflation (3%) is 50% more than the interest (2%) on your account value. In addition, you will owe 20% for taxes on the interest you earn each year—that's 20% of $20 worth of interest.

2. If you put $1,000 in a CD or bond paying 4% per year, are you going to beat inflation?

   Answer: Yes, but jut barely. Why? You are earning more interest than what you lose in "real" terms due to inflation (earn 4%, lose 3%). But you also have to pay 20% of your interest earnings as taxes. So you have to pay 20% of $40 for taxes. That is $8, so your net increase in value is $32, or 3.2%—barely more than inflation.

3. If you put $1,000 in a stock mutual fund (more on these later) and average 8% per year in capital gains, are you going to beat inflation?

   Answer: It certainly looks that way. Why? You are certainly earning a better rate of return (capital gains) than you are losing to inflation. In addition, the taxes on capital gains are lower than on interest earnings. So you earn (on average) $80 per year, and pay 10% of that in taxes. That leaves you with $72 per year. Inflation is only 3% and you have $72 or 7.2% increase in value, so you are potentially well ahead of inflation.

Practical Exercises

1. What would happen to your lifestyle if your raises were only half the rate of inflation?

   _____

   _____

   _____

   _____

   _____

   _____.

2. Is inflation a "bad" thing, a necessary thing, or even a "good" thing? Explain your position using examples.

   _____

   _____

   _____

   _____

   _____

   _____.

CHAPTER 10

The Time Value of Money

Money "loses" value over time, unless you can do something to ensure it holds its value or even increases in value. Inflation ravages the value of money; interest (or capital gains or dividends) helps preserve and increase its value.

Compound Interest versus Simple Interest

The best way to increase the amount of money you will have in the future is to invest as much as you can comfortably afford into investments that pay interest or have capital gains, and allow you to "reinvest" the interest or capital gains so you get paid on a growing amount of money, not just your original investment.

Not all investments allow this "compounding." Most bonds, whether from a government, business, or any other place, do not allow compounding of the interest they pay. Stocks don't really allow compounding of the dividends they pay either (dividends work much like interest). In both examples, you get a check for the interest or dividends on some regular basis. If you don't reinvest this money, you may actually lose money in "real" terms.

Most investments do allow compounding. Here are some examples:

- Savings accounts—the interest can be allowed to accumulate and you earn more interest on the accumulated interest each year.
- Money market and regular checking accounts—these work like savings accounts.
- Mutual fund accounts—these accounts grow as the value of the stocks and bonds in them grow. This is what is called "capital gains." In addition, these accounts often pay "dividends" (much like interest) and you can use these dividends to buy more shares of the funds. This allows your entire investment to take advantage of compounding.

Saving and Investing Now Rather Than Later

One of the best ways to take advantage of compounding is to start small while you're young. Here is an interesting example of what can happen if you put a few thousand dollars a year in an investment starting with your first full-time job (age 22) and continuing for 43 years, compared to waiting until you are 37 and saving twice as much until you turn 65. Look at how much money you could potentially have!

Table 10.1. The Time Value of Compound Returns

	Amount Invested per Month	*Average Total Return (Dividends and Capital Gains)*	*Amount Saved/ Value at Age 65*
Start age 22, end age 65	$167	8%	$86,172/ $747,316
Start age 37, end age 65	$334	8%	$112,224/ $417,021
The difference	$167/month	Same	$26,052/ $330,295

So the person who started saving at the outset actually put far less money away (about three-quarters, or 75%, as much) and ended up with far more (about 80% more) at retirement. And if you start saving at age 18, or even 16, the numbers are even better!

Mutual fund companies have lots of great "self-educating" materials you can order.

The Rule of 72

How does the time value of money work? First of all, it is based on compound interest—that's interest on both the interest earned and the money you invested. This leads to a simple "rule" we'll look at in just a moment.

Do you know how long it takes to double your money? If you can do it at an online casino or a betting track, more power to you. If you have to do it the old-fashioned way—by earning and investing it—here is a quick and easy way to estimate the time it takes to double a sum of money.

How Money Doubles

If you invest a sum of money and don't touch it, and reinvest everything that sum earns, it will take 72 divided by the total return you are earning to double your money.

Example:

1. If you invest $1,000 today, leave it alone, reinvest the proceeds, and earn a total return of 8%, how long will it take to double your money?

   Answer: About nine years. Why? According to the Rule of 72:

   $$72 \div 8\% = 9, \text{so it takes nine years to double your money.}$$

   Now let's look at the flip side—you don't know the total return, but you know how long you want to invest your money.

2. If you invest $1,000 today, leave it alone for ten years, and reinvest the earnings, what total return do you need in order to double your money?

Answer: About 7%. Why? According to the Rule of 72, if you divide 72 by the total rate of return, you will get the number of years to double your money. Using basic rules of mathematics, here's the equation:

$$72 \div \text{total rate of return} = \text{years to double, so}$$
$$72 \div \text{years to double} = \text{total rate of return.}$$

WHAT IS "TOTAL RETURN"?

Most investments (at least in mutual funds and retirement plans) include both interest-paying components such as CDs and bonds, dividend-paying elements such as stocks, and elements that result in capital gains (growth in the actual price of the element) such as mutual fund shares, stocks, and certain bonds.

I asked several young adults to explain the value of compounding, and here's what they told me:

Kai Ge Y., a teenager in Denver, said, "Compound interest is the growth of money from the interest and original [balance] from the previous month. It's better to start off young because compounding will grow exponentially in the long run."

Libby M. described it this way: "Compounding interest allows for your money to grow faster. If your savings earns a percentage on your money slowly over each month you are mot making nearly the same [as] if it is compounded, where interest you've earned can grow more interest over the year if it is compounded quarterly.

"Saving at [beginning at] 22 is *much* better because your money has a chance to grow and earn interest for 20 years. Starting to save at 42 your money doesn't have a chance to grow as much [as long]. Also, so your money stays in savings accounts it grows faster the longer it's been there because there is more and more money to earn interest."

Examples and Case Studies

Here are a few examples of the interest and inflation topics we just finished, and then a few problems for you to try on your own.

Example #1: John has a credit card that charges him 24% interest per year on his unpaid balance. He charges $500 on the first day of his 30-day billing cycle, and another $600 on the 20th day of his billing cycle. He isn't able to pay the charges in full before the end of his grace period. How much interest is John going to be charged?

Answer: His average daily balance has two parts since he made two charges this month. The $500 charge on the first day of his billing cycle is going to give him an average daily balance of $500. His $600 charge on the 20th day is going to add $200 to his average daily balance for a total average daily balance of $700.

Since the interest rate is 24% per year, John is going to owe 2% for this month, times the average daily balance. That means he will be charged 2% • $700 or $14 in interest for the month.

Why is only $1/3$ of the second charge added to his average daily balance? Because John didn't charge the $600 until he was $2/3$ of the way through the cycle. That means he only carried the $600 charge for $1/3$ of the cycle, so only $1/3$ of the charged amount is used to calculate the rest of his average daily balance. He charged the $500 items on the first day of the cycle so the full $500 was carried as a balance every day of the 30-day cycle.

Example #2: John only plans to make minimum payments on his card (starting with his original balance in Example #1) for the next three months because he is broke. If he pays $20 each month and doesn't charge anything else, what will his average daily balance be each month?

This is easier than it sounds, but you will need a calculator.

Answer: At the end of the first month, John will owe $600 + $500 (his original balance) plus the $14 he owes in interest, less the $20 he paid. So he owes $1,114 − $20 or $1,094 at the end of the first month.

Throughout the second month John had an average daily balance of $1094. He didn't add to his debt but he didn't reduce it much, either, and carried the full amount every day of the month. So he now owes $1,094 • 2% for the second month's interest, or $21.88. Since he is only planning to pay $20, he is actually going to fall a little bit behind. He now owes $1,094 + $21.88 or $1,115.88 at the end of the second month, less the $20 he is paying. So John enters the third month owing $1,095.88

Throughout the third month John had an average daily balance of $1,095.88. Since he owes 2% interest on this amount, John now owes about $1,117. If he again pays $20, his balance is $1,097 at the end of the third month.

So, John has paid $60 but only reduced his credit card balance by $3.

Example #3: Alana plans to invest $11,000 her grandmother gave her. She has explored some options and has chosen the XYZ Mutual Fund as her investment option. Although she knows the past performance can't predict the future, she is comfortable with the objectives and investments in the fund. For the past 25 years, the total return of XYZ Mutual Fund has averaged 9%. If Alana is fortunate enough to average 9% as her total return, how long will it take her to double her $11,000? How long will it take to double her money a second time? If Alana is 21 now, how old will she be by the time her money doubles a second time? A third time?

This example can really show the value of compounding.

Answer: If you use the Rule of 72, you get 72 ÷ 9% = 8 years. So, at the end of eight years, Alana could have about $22,000—at age 29. If she stays the course and doubles her money eight years later, she could have about $44,000—at age 37. Add another doubling and Alana is now 45 and has about $88,000. Not too bad considering what she started with.

Example #4: Which loan is the better deal—a car loan at 5% that costs $400 per month for 48 months or a car loan at 3% that costs $325 per month for 60 months?

Answer: Let's look at the total of all payments:

Loan #1: 48 months • $400 = $19,200
Loan #2: 60 months • $350 = $21,000

It certainly appears the person buying the car with what appears to be a lower interest rate is actually paying more for the car!

It pays to do the math—the second car's financing probably wasn't such a good deal, although the lower payments are nice.

Example #5: Is Michaela, Andrew, or Luis going to have the best chance of coming out ahead with their investments after taxes and inflation? Assume inflation is 3.5%, taxes on interest are 25%, and taxes on capital gains are 15%.

Michaela keeps most of her money in a bank savings account earning 2.5% but always puts 20% into a mutual return that has usually averaged a 10% total return.

Andrew invests 30% of his money in bonds earning 4% and the rest in mutual funds that have averaged a 9% total return.

> It pays to know when your credit card cycle ends, especially if you have a balance. This lets you make a charge at the end of the cycle instead of the beginning and reduce your average daily balance, if you don't plan on paying the full amount due.

LOAN (BUY) VERSUS LEASE

When you are considering leasing a car (or having your parents do it for you), take a look at the total cost to buy the car. Lease payments are much lower than the payments you will have to make when you buy the car and take a loan. But at the end of the lease period you have to either get another car and keep making payments, or come up with the money to buy the car.

The total of all your lease payments plus the money you'll have to spend to buy the car at the end may be far more than if you had simply bought the car in the first place.

Another problem with leased cars—you have to return the car in stellar condition, with all "normal wear and tear" items fixed. That means you have to replace the tires and windshield in most cases, plus fix any dings, dents, and scratches, and maybe even have the car detailed.

To make matters more expensive, you also have to pay (about $0.30–$0.36) for each mile you drive over the contract limit, but you don't get a credit for driving less than the limit. Unless you have a business that makes money and you are able to deduct the costs of a lease, leasing rarely makes sense.

For most young adults, leasing is a way to get a fancier car than they really need or can afford, and simply delays ever paying off a loan for a car. The long-term costs of leasing are unbelievably high for most people—even business owners.

Luis invests all his money in a mutual fund that has unpredictable total returns—some years it loses money, other years it has a total return of 15%.

Answer: There really isn't quite enough information to decide in each case.

Michaela's savings account is losing money due to inflation before even considering the bite of taxes, but her mutual fund is beating inflation and the tax bite. She probably is just keeping even.

Andrew is definitely keeping ahead since even the bonds are breaking even or doing a bit better.

Luis is in a difficult spot. His investments are losing a lot some years and gaining a lot other years. You really don't have enough information to decide in his case. Over the long run he may do okay, but the jury is out.

Practical Exercises

1. Patrick is determined to double a $10,000 bonus in no more than five years. What total rate of return will be needed to reach this goal? Do you think this rate of return is likely? Why or why not?

   _____

   _____

   _____

   _____

   _____

   _____

   _____

   _____

   _____

   _____.

2. Briana has decided to invest her money primarily in government bonds that pay 4% interest. She hates the thought of losing any money. If inflation is 3% and she owes 20% of her interest earnings as taxes, what are her "real" earnings this year. Assume Briana invested $10,000 in her bonds.

_____

_____

_____

_____

_____

_____

_____

_____

_____.

3. If you earn 5% simple interest on a $1,000 investment, how long will it take to double your money? If you earn 5% compound interest on $1,000, how long will it take you to double your money? Remember, simple interest does not earn "interest on interest" so the Rule of 72 doesn't work.

_____

_____

_____

_____

_____

_____

_____

_____

_____.

5

What Is Credit? How Do You Manage Credit?

Credit, especially in the form of credit cards, is frighteningly easy to get. If you are a college student or have a full-time job, you have probably already had several offers show up in your mailbox in the past few months. Amazing, since you have no track record making credit card payments and little or no steady income the past few years.

The credit card companies learned from other places like tobacco companies—get you hooked at the earliest possible age.

Have your older teenagers or adult children ever applied for a credit card or loan? Have they received offers in the mail that they accepted (with or without your knowledge)? How have they handled credit? What did they do right/wrong? One parent answered:

Both teens have cards (MasterCard from the Young Americans' Bank). They get multiple offers in the mail daily and are instructed to shred them immediately. They handle the cards well. We showed them how to save receipts, check those against the statement, use the 1-800 number to keep track of outstanding balances.—Devyn N.

CHAPTER 11

Credit and Loans

What Is Credit?

Credit consists of two main things: credit cards and loans. Each of these is "awarded" to you based on your proven or anticipated ability and willingness to manage money and handle responsibility.

GETTING CREDIT

Getting credit is almost too easy—in fact, it *is* too easy for many people—no matter what their age. Misusing credit can cause a number of problems. Bankruptcy, a poor credit score, a bad credit history—these are some of the problems, but they can fade and be overcome with the passing of time. The other thing misused or mismanaged credit can lead to is the loss of your reputation and your good name. These two things are very difficult to ever fully regain.

Credit cards come in several forms. The most common are traditional credit cards, secured credit cards, and home equity line of credit cards. ATM and debit cards are like credit cards in some ways, but very different in most ways, so they are covered in the section about writing checks.

In the previous section about inflation and interest, you learned some of the ways loans and credit cards can be affected when you have to manage and repay them. Now let's look at some of the many features, benefits, cautions, and disadvantage of borrowing money.

> **If you don't manage your credit and loans, they will soon be controlling you and your life. Money worries are not fun.**

Loans come in many shapes and forms. Most of them are essential to a 21st-century lifestyle, and all forms need to be managed carefully or they will get you in more trouble than you can begin to imagine.

Here are some of the main forms of loans you are going to encounter—if you haven't already.

What Are Loans?

If you're going to college, or recently graduated, you are probably learning quite a bit about student loans. If you are trying to buy a car, there's yet another type of loan to think about. If you are in a position to be thinking about buying your first home, there are mortgages, second mortgages, and home equity lines of credit to consider. And there are a few other types of loans such as payday loans, bank overdraft protection, and unsecured loans out there, too.

Student Loans

Unless your parents saved a bundle for your education or you're a successful child actor or you got lots of scholarships, you are probably staring student loans in the face. Either you're trying to figure out how to get them or you now have to repay them.

If you're looking for student loans, where can you go? One of the biggest source of student loans is Sallie Mae—the Student Loan Marketing Association. Make sure you check out their Web site at www.salliemae.com.

When you get to the section about paying for college, you'll learn a lot more about loans, as well as how to qualify for as much money as possible to help pay for school.

Car Loans (New and Used)

Okay, you've found your dream car, and the only way you're going to own it is to finance it. Maybe you can borrow the money from your family, or maybe your family is buying the car for you. Problem solved.

For many of you, a gift of a car or a loan from Mom and Dad is simply not an option. That means getting someone or something else to lend you the money.

> Keep in mind the federal government is not very tolerant of people who do not pay their student loans back—if you fail to make your payments, bad things can happen to you, and your ability to get future loans of any kind may be ruined. At a minimum, your credit history and score will not be pretty sights. You may also be denied certain jobs or security clearances.

FINANCING A CAR PURCHASE

There are almost as many financing options and loan designs for car loans as there are types of cars. Choose wisely or your car will be worth less than what you owe if you decide to sell while you're still making payments.

If you decide to lease your car, this is still a loan. The difference between a lease and buying a car is much like renting a home with an option to purchase (or renting to own) and buying a home with a mortgage. Leasing may be the only thing you can afford, but at the end of the lease, you don't own the car and you have to spend a lot more than the car may be worth to buy it or fix it up to meet the dealer's standards if you want to return it.

If you have been working (maybe a part-time job) for several years, and have always paid your bills on time, not bounced a check, and are at least 18, you *may* be able to get a car loan on your own. If you have a credit card and have managed it wisely, your chances of getting a loan are pretty good, assuming you have a steady income and have been at the same job for a year or two.

If you have good credit, a steady job, and want to get a loan, what are your choices? The two main options are:

• A bank or credit union loan
• A loan from the car dealer

If you're buying a used car, a bank or credit union may not want to lend you money. New cars are easier to finance (get a loan for). A car dealer will often handle both new and used car loans. Often so-called dealer financing is actually handled through a subsidiary (such as Ford Credit or VW of North America).

The other major source of car loans is to have a co-signer. If your parents, another family member, a boss, or a responsible friend is willing to sign the loan with you, you can usually get a loan. This is because the place lending the money has two ways to collect if you don't pay—they can go to the co-signer(s) or take away your car. The loan is considered to be "secured"—in this case by the car itself, so the lender can take your car away and sell it. Co-signers are also liable for the payments, so the lender can let you keep the car and demand payment from them.

Payday Loans

Payday loans are a *very* bad deal. The interest rate is phenomenally high—20–30% per year, or more. In addition, you usually pay fees to get this "loan," and you have little or no "grace period" after you get paid; you must repay the money right away. Companies and people who offer these so-called loans prey on the less-educated and poorer segments of our society. Please don't become a victim.

> If you are very responsible with your checking account and your job is relatively secure, you might set up an automatic payment (called an electronic funds transfer or EFT) to ensure your payments are always made on time. In some cases, this approach may even help you get a loan in the first place.

CRITICAL INFORMATION

If you default on your loan payments with a co-signer involved, you are probably going to wreck your credit history and score. If your co-signer defaults, both of you will have damaged your ability to get credit in the future, *and* you will lose your car or whatever else the loan was for. If the co-signer was a friend or relative, you may lose his or her goodwill and friendship. If your boss co-signed your loan, you may lose your job.

Home Loans (Residential Mortgages)

If you are a recent college graduate or have been working full-time for several years or maybe a newlywed with two incomes, you may be in the enviable position of being able to buy a home while you're still in your early 20s.

Of course, this is only possible if you meet some stringent conditions. Here's what you'll need to do to buy a home (and get a mortgage) or prepare to buy a home in the future:

- Take very good care of your credit rating and score. That means *always* paying *every* bill on time, never taking on more credit cards than you can handle, and reviewing your credit reports annually (more on that later).
- Save for the down payment. If you can't put at least 20% down, you are going to be paying private mortgage insurance (PMI) for many years to come. It's expensive, and it's *not* tax-deductible.
- Talk with a mortgage lender or broker well in advance of looking for a home. Find out what you can afford and how to get the best interest rate possible. These specialists may also be able to help you finance your mortgage in such a way as to avoid the need for PMI even if you can't put 20% down. Ask for referrals and interview at least five lenders and brokers. Get a detailed breakdown of expected costs—they can vary by a factor of 100% or more.

Bank Overdraft Protection

Bank overdraft protection is a special type of loan. Unless you write a check for more money than is in your account or try to use your debit card for a purchase that exceeds your account balance, you will probably never use this feature.

How does the overdraft feature work? Normally you have to apply to your bank to have a "line of credit"—generally a few hundred dollars—approved. This means your credit history will be checked. Then if you accidentally or occasionally write a check for more money than is actually in your account, the bank will cover the check—up to your overdraft protection limit. You will also be charged substantial fees for this benefit. However, you will avoid bouncing a check—an important consideration.

CHECK 21

With the advent of a new law called "Check 21" banks now get electronically scanned copies of the checks you write. These scanned checks are sent to your bank, often within minutes or hours of being written, so there is little or no "float" and many people are unintentionally bouncing checks.

When renewing a health club membership in January of 2005 I found out just how efficient Check 21 can be. I wrote a check for my fee, handed it to the clerk, and waited for my receipt. Instead of a simple receipt I got my actual check back, plus what looked like a credit card slip. I had to sign the slip and the transaction cleared my account as if I had just used an ATM. On the other hand, banks can still "hold" checks in your deposit for a number of days, depending on the type of check and whether it is in-state or out-of-state. Unfair, but that's the current law.

Line of Credit

Business owners and homeowners often rely on a line of credit. This is a predetermined and approved amount of money the person or business can access via a credit card or check. Personal lines of credit are usually "secured" by the equity (value) in a home or other property. Business lines of credit are usually based on cash flow and track record.

If you have excellent credit, you may be able to get a personal loan that is not tied to any form of collateral (home, car, boat, etc.). The interest rates with this form of loan are quite high since there is more risk to the bank; if you don't pay, it is hard for the bank to get its money back.

Practical Exercises

1. Explain "credit" to someone who has never applied for a loan or had a credit card.
2. Give examples of where/when you might use the following types of credit:

   • Payday loans _____

   • Line of credit _____

   • Home equity line of credit _____

   • Unsecured personal loan _____

3. Think of, and then list, three steps you might take to make sure you don't get in too much debt because of your use of credit:

_____

_____

_____

_____

_____

_____

_____

_____.

Credit Cards: The Nitty-Gritty

Credit cards are the most readily available form of loan/credit, and they can get you into trouble so fast your head will spin. They are incredibly easy to get, and even easier to misuse.

Why is it so easy to get one or more credit cards when you're still a student or newly employed? Here are two typical situations for you.

First situation: You're young, you have a part-time job, and you're a student. Why would *anyone* want to give you a credit card?

Second situation: You just graduated from high school or college, got a good job, and the credit card companies are stuffing your mailbox with offers.

First of all, no one is *giving* you anything. The credit card companies are actually *taking*, not giving. Yes, really. They are taking away some of the control you have over your money and your future. They are taking your freedom to make informed spending decisions. They are taking away your chance to have a debt-free future. They are potentially taking away your good name and future credit history, and possibly ruining both. They may even be hurting your parents' or spouse's financial situation.

I know what you just read sounds like scare tactics, but too often bad things happen to young adults with credit cards. But the good news—it doesn't have to be that way.

> **Have you ever said, or thought, this: "What do you mean I don't have any more credit—I still have my credit cards, don't I?"**

What Are Credit Cards?

Contrary to popular belief—a belief held by people of all ages and income status!—credit cards are not intended to be a symbol of free money or a ticket to unlimited consumption.

Credit cards are little pieces of plastic with a magnetic strip on the back. That strip holds lots of information, and is the way the card is identified and processed.

PROTECT YOUR CARDS

Be careful how you carry your credit cards, ATM card, debit card, student ID cards, and any thing else with a magnetic strip. Don't put strips next to one another. They can scramble each other's magnetized brains and not work when you need them. Don't put anything magnetic near them either, like that cute little key chain with the magnet at the end, or the screwdriver you used around something magnetic last week. Don't set your credit cards on or near the little pads that demagnetize the sensors in books, CDs, DVDs, clothes, and so on. These boxes are nondiscriminatory and will cheerfully demagnetize your credit cards, ATM cards, ID cards, and so on.

Using a credit card is your "promise to pay." You signed a pretty lengthy agreement when you applied for the credit (or debit or ATM) card. You probably didn't read the agreement—who does?—but you signed it anyway. You agreed to pay on time, use the card responsibly, safeguard the card, surrender it if the card company demanded it, notify the company if the card were stolen or lost, and on and on. You signed a legally binding contract, and failing to live up to it is not a good idea. The fact that you didn't read it or misplaced it or whatever does not get you out of the contract terms.

Credit cards provide the merchant with more security than do checks. As long as the merchant processes your card properly (generally part of the "swipe" processing), he or she is usually off the hook if the card turns out to be stolen or bogus. The user of a stolen or bogus card is liable for a lot, though.

You get a certain amount of protection against unauthorized use of your credit cards. Even if you don't know (or fail to report) your card was stolen, you are usually only liable for the first $50 in charges. If you report it before it is used, you are usually not liable for any charges. If the card is an ATM or debit card, the rules are often different, so make sure you talk to your banker and understand your liabilities and responsibilities.

AVOIDING IDENTITY THEFT

It may sound complicated, what with all the reports of identity theft and ads and commercials showing a 75-year-old woman getting tattoos or a 20-year-old guy buying a Cadillac (when the cards actually were stolen). But the reality is this—a bit of caution and care goes a very long way and quickly becomes second nature. If you wouldn't leave your car keys somewhere or with someone, act the same about your credit, debit, and ATM cards. You'll probably never have a problem if you follow those simple precautions. Be at least as possessive and careful with your credit cards as you are with your car.

Who Needs Credit Cards, Anyway?

The answer? Almost everyone. It's difficult or impossible to write a check for an expensive purchase any more. Things cost a lot, and few people want to carry that much cash around. Getting a loan to buy a new laptop is time consuming and may not even be possible, but the cost of the computer probably falls well under the limit on your credit card.

It is almost impossible to rent a car unless you have a major credit card. A debit or ATM card is not enough. It may also be hard to get the phones turned on in a hotel room unless you have a credit card to guarantee the charges.

COMPANY CREDIT CARDS

You may have a company credit card, but it is likely to be in your name. That means you are ultimately liable for the charges. Never use a business credit card for personal purchases. That practice can get you fired—for cause.

Make sure to file your expense reports right away so you get reimbursed in time to pay the credit card bill. If you don't get reimbursed in time, at least make the minimum payment—it's your credit history on the line. Company credit cards, properly handled, can lead to a great credit score and be a credit history booster for you. Poorly managed they are like a "kiss of death."

Credit cards can also help you if the merchandise you bought is defective, if the airline cancels the flight you charged, or if you canceled a reservation (held with the card) but the hotel billed your account anyway. Read your credit card agreement—it's filled with cool features.

Well-managed credit cards can go a very long way toward establishing your credit history and building a good credit score (more on that later).

If you ever plan to buy a house, the time to start building *and* protecting your credit history and score is now. At the same time, the mistakes you make today will stay on your credit record for a long time—often as long as seven years.

When you're evaluating credit cards and interest rates, and just trying to learn their ins and outs, check out www.bankrate.com. It's a very useful website for anything that involves interest rates, and credit cards certainly do that!

According to www.bankrate.com's Lucy Lazarony, purveyors of plastic are eager to hand their cards to college students, and those cards can be useful tools. But they're also a way to get into trouble, so proceed with caution.

Case Study: How to Get a Credit Card

Martha just arrived at Loyola University. As part of her registration, she was in a presentation about students and managing money. On the way out, there were tables with representatives from the three largest banks in town. These reps were giving out information about their checking and savings accounts. There were some great deals on these accounts, so Martha chose one of the banks and signed up for a checking account. Easy.

Then the banker asked her if she wanted a credit card to cover "those little things that make college life more fun." Martha had grown up watching her parents make significant use of their credit cards, and have even been allowed to use their cards on occasion. So, of course, she said "Yes!"

What do you suppose happened over the next few years? Was Martha like Alex or perhaps like Phoenix?

Practical Exercises

Develop two scenarios—one like Alex and one like Phoenix—for how Martha used her credit card for the next few years (refer back to chapter 4 to remember which was the "Saver" and which was the "Spender"). Compare her actions in each scenario. You might want to make a side-by-side comparison in a two-column table.

Scenario 1—Managing credit like Alex

_____

_____

_____

_____

_____

_____

_____

_____.

Scenario 2—Managing credit like Phoenix

_____

_____

_____

_____

_____

_____

_____

_____.

Chart 12.1. Side-by-Side Comparison

Getting and Using Credit Cards

I have applied for a credit card and have received mail for one also. I've done everything pretty good with the credit card. Made every payment on time in full. I have exceeded my limit once.—Kai Ge Y., a teenager in Denver

Why Is It So Easy to Get Credit Cards?

Credit cards are readily available because students and newly employed graduates are "easy sells" with both pent-up demand and a "need" to buy. They have an income or other access to money. They also often have parents who will pay the bills rather than allow their children to get into financial trouble. Credit card companies know these things.

"As long as you're a full-time student, you can get a card," according to Gerri Detweiler, author of *The Ultimate Credit Card Handbook*. Credit card issuers know your parents will bail you out if you run up large card balances or fall behind in your monthly payments. Check out your options. Find the best credit cards and rates *before* you sign the application.

CREDIT LIMITS AND MINIMUM PAYMENTS

Be very careful about exceeding your credit limit. Doing so may cause the credit card company to raise your annual interest rate. Be equally careful to always make at least the minimum payment, and preferably much more, on time every month. If you are late or don't at least pay the minimum charge, you are going to be hit with a penalty—as much as $20–35 each time. Your credit rating will take a hit, and your interest rate could go up dramatically.

And another thing—no matter how large the credit limit (the max you can charge or have as a balance) a credit card company offers, you probably should only accept a few hundred dollars for the time being. It's too easy to say "charge it" and graduate in debt well over your head; this is especially true if you also have student loans.

There are a number of different types of credit cards you should know about:

- Secured cards
- Traditional cards
- Bank debit cards
- Check guarantee cards
- Preloaded cards

Secured Credit Cards

These are not true credit cards because you can only charge a limited amount and you have to keep that full amount in a separate (savings) account. The issuer of the credit card is not at risk because it can tap this account if you don't pay your bill in full and on time. At the same time, this type of card can help build your credit history if you make the payments on time.

One of the target markets for this type of card is people who have had past credit payment problems or bankruptcies. As long as you manage your use of credit properly, you will probably never need this type of card.

These cards have a "credit limit"—the amount of money you deposit to "secure" the card.

It is a good idea to avoid these cards because they charge high fees and tie up a lot of your money.

Traditional Credit Cards

These are the cards you are probably getting offers for in the mail. These cards have a credit limit—the limit is the amount the card issuer believes you (or your parents!) can repay.

The traditional credit card lets you charge up to the limit on the card. As you pay back the amount you have charged (the amount you have *borrowed*), that portion of your credit limit is available to you again.

Most credit cards have a "grace period." This means you don't get charged interest on the balance right away. Instead, you have a certain number of days after the statement "closing date" to pay the full balance. If you do this, there is no interest charged. This is one of the things many people really like about credit cards.

HOW THE CREDIT CARD ISSUER MAKES MONEY

Since you don't pay interest during the grace period (as long as you pay the balance in full before the end of the grace period), how does the card issuer make money? Simple. The card issuer charges the company accepting your credit card 3–7% or so of each sale. So the issuer can get paid several times for the same charge:

- Once when the merchant pays the 3–7% fee
- Once when you pay any interest charges
- At least once when you pay other fees (annual fees, fees for exceeding your credit limit, late payment fees, and so forth)

Debit Cards

Debit cards do just that—when you use the card, the entire purchase is immediately subtracted (debited) from the account associated with the card. Most debit cards are associated with checking accounts (or savings accounts). They can be used as ATM cards, but the reverse is not always true—ATM cards are not necessarily debit cards.

Debit cards may or may not work in some places the same way as credit cards do. For example, since the limit for a debit card is the balance of the account that it is associated with, you can't use it to rent a car (although you can use it at the time you return the car to pay the bill).

It is very difficult, but not impossible, to exceed your limit on a debit or ATM card, so these are easier to get than traditional credit cards. Generally, there is no interest charge since the cost for the items you "charge" or the cash you get from an ATM is instantly deducted from your account.

Check Guarantee Cards

These may or may not be ATM cards. They are more powerful than pure ATM cards and generally function much like debit cards.

Because these cards can be used to guarantee your check won't bounce, you may have to set up an overdraft account. The merchant still pays the card issuer the same 3–7% of your purchase.

Preloaded (Prepaid) Cards

These are different from secured credit cards. They are "single-use"—once the amount you have allocated to one is gone, there is no value to the card. You can throw it away or take it to the bank and have it reloaded. People who travel often (especially overseas) use these cards since if they lose one they only lose the remaining value on the card. These cards often will function as ATM cards.

There is no interest rate since you are spending your own money. The merchant still pays the card issuer the same 3–7% of your purchase.

Students and Credit Cards

Credit card companies are targeting young adults of all ages, and you could be next. Who are these issuers of credit cards looking for?

- You, if you are a high school student who's 18, or close, and working part-time
- You, if you are a new high school graduate with a job
- You, if you are a college student
- You, if you're none of the above but can get someone to co-sign the application

Credit card issuers want to extend credit to you, and credit cards can be very valuable tools when you're starting out and your cash flow is not as regular or great as you'd like. But you can get into incredibly deep waters very quickly if you don't manage these cards responsibility and actively.

At the same time, getting a credit card is virtually a rite of passage for new graduates, newly employed young adults, and college students. You may even have gone to your mailbox and found at least one credit card offer waiting for you the first week of college.

> **Is it easy to get credit? Consider this statement from a young working adult:**
>
> **"I have applied for credit cards through my bank and never through the mail because I feel safer at this point with my own bank. Although I have gone over my limit I've never been charged for this because I pay *all* my cards off every month (my two credit cards and three store credit cards)."**
> **—Libby M.**

Protect Your Credit Cards

In many ways, your credit cards are more vulnerable than cash left on your bed or on a seat on a bus. If someone steals your cash, or it blows away, you've only lost that amount. It may be a lot of money, but it is a limited amount.

If someone gets your credit card, ATM card, or debit card, he or she can take far more than a few dollars. They can spend up to, and even beyond, your entire credit limit. They can use your card, along with a few other bits of information (such as the information on your student ID) to *become* you. They can also use your cards and ID or driver's license to get more credit in your name, change your address, and so on—but more on this in the section on "Protecting Your Identity."

Ten Rules of Credit/Debit/ATM Card Protection

In addition to keeping your cards physically separated from one another, here are a few steps to take.

1. Don't leave your credit cards lying around.
2. Don't leave your charge slips (receipts) lying around. Some states require merchants to leave off all but the last four digits of your credit card number, but this is only in a few states. If someone gets your number, he or she is 80% of the way to being able to use your card. If you use your card outside the United States, your full card number will almost certainly be on your receipt, and you're a long way from home.
3. Don't let your card out of your sight in places like restaurants and stores. People have been using a handheld magnetic card reader to collect the data from your card—skimming—(including all the information from both sides of the card) then making a duplicate and charging up a storm until the card is reported stolen. Worse, they often wait for weeks or months so you have no idea when or by whom the card was copied.
4. Don't loan your credit card to *anyone*.
5. If you are going to charge something by telephone, only do so if you initiated the call.
6. Never give anyone your personal identification number (PIN). Watch for "surfers" when using ATMs. These are the people who lurk a few feet away or in a nearby car and use binoculars or other means to get your PIN.
7. Don't throw your ATM receipts away. Use them to balance your account. Don't drop them on the ground or use the trash can by the ATM.
8. If the ATM grabs your card and won't give it back, get someone to go for help. Don't leave the machine unless you absolutely have to. A favorite scam is to put some glue in the ATM, let the machine "swallow" your card, wait for you to leave in disgust, and then they pry your card out after you've gone. By combining this technique with "surfing," the scammers now have your PIN and your card, and you will soon have no money.
9. Never give your credit or debit card number or other information out on a nonsecure website. Look for the locked lock at the bottom right corner and "https" (not just http) at the top (in the browser bar) before you enter any personal data or credit/debit card information.
10. Never carry cards you don't need. Keep the others in a safe place (not on your dresser or in your jewelry box or in your car's glove box).

Avoid Credit Card Trouble—It Will Find You Soon Enough, Anyway!

Manage your credit cards wisely and they can be one of the greatest inventions ever. Manage them badly and they will haunt you for years to come.

You've probably heard the old sayings:

- "Caveat emptor"—meaning "Buyer beware."
- "Pay me now or pay me later."
- "There's no such thing as a free ride."
- "What goes around, comes around."

All of them are so true when it comes to credit cards.

Buyer Beware

When you get a credit card, you are buying the right to use a lender's money, but you have to pay for this right—in the form of interest on your balance (the amount you owe) and higher prices since the lenders charge stores when you use a credit card. You can also end up paying, a few dollars at a time, for food you ate years ago, clothes that no longer fit, or a DVD you can't even find anymore. So, buyer beware.

Pay Me Now or Pay Me Later

If you don't pay cash now, or pay the credit card bill (the balance) in full when the bill is due each month, you are going to be paying later. In some cases you are paying much later, and much more, since at minimum payments it can take many years to pay off a single charge. And, if you keep charging, you may still be paying for that sorority party dress when you're 32!

There's No Such Thing as a Free Ride

If you think credit card companies are offering you credit just because they are nice guys (or gals), think again. Credit cards are not free. *The fact you still have the cards does not mean you still have money*! Everything you buy is marked up in price to allow for the cost of using credit cards (since credit card companies need to make money too).

Since many people charge things they have no way to pay for, and credit card companies have to pay even though you haven't paid them, the prices in stores reflect this. Finally, many people see bankruptcy as a way to get out of credit card bills they can't pay. Those costs get passed on to you, too. That CD you paid $15 for might only have cost $10 if there were no credit cards, or if everyone paid in full, on time, and no one declared bankruptcy. But it ain't going to happen in your lifetime.

What Goes Around, Comes Around

If you don't pay your bills on time or if you miss payments, you are going to pay the price—maybe in the form of higher interest rates, lower credit limits, harder-to-get mortgages, or less than the best deals on auto loans. You may have a harder time getting affordable auto insurance or getting that dream job, or you might find your life otherwise impacted in the next year or two.

Why Give Students, New Graduates, and New Employees Credit?

You have little or no income. After all, you're a student, or you just graduated and started working. The attitude of the credit card companies seems to be "no income, no problem." Why?

College students and new graduates are notoriously loyal. They have lots of wants and "needs," and if someone gives them a chance to fill some of these wants before they have the income to pay, they remember. Credit card companies know about this loyalty, and count on it. If you get through the first few years without getting into serious credit trouble, you are going to remember who gave you your chance and keep that card. You are less likely to shop for lower interest rates, higher credit limits, and so forth.

Credit card companies are confident your parents will bail you out if you get into serious payment difficulties. Even if your parents didn't co-sign the credit card application, the credit card companies know from experience your parents probably won't hang you out to dry.

Colleges and universities make a lot of money from allowing credit card companies to come on campus and be the "preferred" credit card offerer. These credit card companies may provide funds for new turf in the football stadium, help upgrade lab facilities, or help defray other costs that give them great visibility and benefit the school. According to Robert Manning, author of the book *Credit Card Nation*, those deals now pay the nation's 300 largest universities nearly $1 billion a year.[1]

Why Bother with Credit Cards?

If you use a credit card responsibly, it plays an important role in your entire future financial life. It takes good credit to get more credit, and even better credit to get mortgages, leases, or loans on high-end cars, and lines of credit. The best way to build this good credit is to start small and manage well. If you always pay your credit card bills on time, you have one of the best credit references a young adult can ever want.

The flip side, though, is the damage a poorly managed credit card can do. If you run up balances you can't pay, make payments late, and miss payments, the mistakes you made at 18 or 20 or 23 are going to haunt you for many years. It is said experience is the best teacher. True, but you can learn just as well from good experiences as bad ones.

Manage Your Credit Card Use

Start small. Try a single card with a $500–$1,000 limit, and if you're a student, make sure your parents know about the card. Pay the entire balance each month if you can; if not, pay a lot more than the minimum, and put the card away until you have paid off the balance (the freezer is a good place to store it).

Use your first credit card for necessities and emergencies. Necessities are school expenses, maybe gas for the car, work clothes, and similar items that support your education or ability to make a living. If it's consumable, like pizza and pop, or something that will look good at the frat house (like a new baseball hat or sequined top), it's not a necessity or an emergency.

Here are some of the uses to which you might be tempted to put your credit card. Take a few minutes to think about each possible use, then mark whether the use would be good or bad, wise or unwise, or just plain ugly.

Table 13.1. You Decide—Good, Bad, or Ugly?

Emergency, Necessity, or a Poor Use of a Credit Card?	*Wise or Unwise Use?*
Textbooks	
Pizza for the team after a big win	
New jeans to replace the ones with a hole	
Weekend in a hotel at an away game	
Airfare home for Thanksgiving	
Bus pass to get to work	
New blazer, tie, and Dockers for a job interview	
Dress for sorority formal	

1. Robert Manning, *Credit Card Nation: The Consequences of America's Addiction to Credit* (New York: Basic Books, 2000).

If a lender gives you a credit card with a $500 or $1,000 or $2,000 limit, that doesn't mean you can afford to max out the card. The payments are going to be murder. If you can only make minimum payments, it would take over 12 years and more than $1,100 in interest to pay off a $1,000 balance if the annual percentage rate (interest) is 12%. And that assumes you don't add to the balance at the same time you are trying to pay it off.

And if You're Late or Miss Credit Card Payments?

What happens if you miss a payment or make one or more payments late? Even if you make up all the payments, it's too late—the damage is done. Your credit may be seriously hurt, if not mortally wounded.

At best you are going to have to pay late fees that can easily run $20–$35 per occurrence. You may see your interest rate raised. It is even possible your card will be canceled.

If your credit rating is affected, it's going to be harder and more expensive to rent an apartment; get utilities, cell phone service, Internet service, or cable TV; get life, home, renter's, or other insurance; get a loan to buy a car or get approved to lease a car; and you may have a harder time getting a number of good jobs.

Insurance companies, employers, lenders, utility companies, and many other entities you depend on can, and do, check your credit history before they will work with you.

HELP OR HURT YOUR CREDIT RATING

While carrying a manageable credit card balance and making regular (greater than minimum) payments can actually improve your credit rating and score, making less than the minimum, making only the minimum payment for months at a time, getting new cards and rolling over the balance, or making late payments can really hurt you.

When Credit Card Troubles Loom

If you are over your head and can't even make minimum payments, or can only make minimum payments for the foreseeable future, you are in credit card trouble. Talk to your parents, or if that isn't an option, talk to the professionals at your local CCCS—that's the Consumer Credit Counseling Service. Here's their toll-free number: 800.355.2227. Their services are free and just might save your future credit rating and ability to buy a house or car.

More on CCCS

There are CCCS offices around the country. To find the one nearest you, do an online search for "Consumer Credit Counseling Service" (in quotes).

Two of the things CCCS seeks to do are help you deal with creditors (the people and places to which you owe money) and avoid bankruptcy. How do you know you are in, or approaching, serious financial trouble? Here are some signs (from www.cccservices.com).

Have you experienced:

- Not wanting to answer your phone in fear of it being a bill collector?
- Late fees or penalties on your credit card statements?
- Creditors calling you at home or even at work?
- Not knowing which bills to pay out of each paycheck?

- Family squabbles over money matters?
- Applying for other credit cards to take cash advances to pay the others?

If so, then it is time to call an organization like CCCS—before you have to declare bankruptcy. The cure is painful, but in the end you'll be healthier and more financially savvy than before.

Caution: Beware of people or places saying they will "repair" your credit, help you get out of debt for a fee, or negotiate with the places and people to which you owe money—for a fee. All the "credit repair" places do is challenge every negative thing in your credit report. While the challenges are being investigated, the negative items are "suspended" or marked so the place you are trying to get credit from may give you credit. This is a fraudulent approach and will ultimately (and quickly) get you into even more trouble. With the exception of CCCS and a few other places in your state, the places that offer to handle your payment problems and deal with your creditors (the people/places to which you owe money) for a fee are bogus.

WHEN YOUR DEBTS ARE OUT OF CONTROL

By now you know how important your credit rating can be. To keep your credit status healthy, you need to keep up with all your payments. If you start to fall behind, contact CCCS immediately.

CCCS can't get you out of paying your debts. But the counselors can help work out payment arrangements with your creditors—the people and lenders to whom you owe money—and help you avoid future problems. A note—if you use the services of CCCS or a similar entity, you are almost certainly going to be required (or forced) to give up your credit cards.

Practical Exercises

1. Explain each of the following types of credit/debit cards and when they make sense to have and use:
   - Secured cards
   - Traditional cards
   - Bank debit cards
   - Check guarantee cards
   - Preloaded cards
2. Explain the grace period.
3. What can the CCCS do for you if you get into financial trouble and can't pay your bills?
4. What is "skimming"? What can you do to prevent this happening to you?
5. List three uses for a credit card that are "wants" rather than "needs."

_____

_____

_____.

CHAPTER 14

Managing Credit Cards and Avoiding Becoming a Fraud Victim

Manage Your Credit—Keep It from Managing You

Here are some ways to get a handle on your use of credit before credit gets a chance to control you:

- Any form of credit—credit card, car loan, overdraft protection, mortgage—is a loan. You have borrowed real money, and you have to pay it back or face very unpleasant consequences. The money you borrow is not yours to keep—it is only yours to pay back.
- Always get credit for a specific purpose and use it for that purpose only. For example, if you get a credit card for gasoline, it usually can only be used to fill up the car. If you get a general card for school necessities, don't start using it to enhance your wardrobe or take all your friends out for drinks.
- Plan to pay your bills in full most, if not all, of the time. If you can't do this, *always* pay more than the minimum. Never, ever skip a payment, even if the credit card company offers you the chance to do so. If you are at or close to your credit limit, put your card on ice—literally, if need be. The freezer is an excellent place to let your overworked credit cards chill out for awhile.
- Don't get another credit card because the one(s) you have is at the limit.
- Never use a credit card for cash advances—the charges are horrendous.
- Never use one credit card to make the payments on another credit card.
- Never get a second credit card until you can manage the first one, and always earmark the second card for a specific purpose. For example, if you take one or two trips a year you might use your second card just for those expenses.
- Shop around for the best deals. Cards can have both high interest rates and high fees, and short (or no) grace periods. The costs can add up quickly. Check sites such as www.bankrate.com.
- Be careful if you get a card that gives you airline miles. The annual fee can be $80 to $120 or more. For most young adults, airline mileage cards are not a good deal. One possible exception—if you have the money on hand to pay your tuition and fees, you might charge these expenses to get airline miles, but *only* if you have the money in hand to pay the bill in full when it comes.
- Always read every credit card agreement and all amendments. Always read the fliers that come with your bills. The terms can be changed with very little notice; if you have been missing payments, paying late, or running up high balances on this or other cards, your terms may change from one month to the next. The terms on balance transfers can change—if you are late on a payment, for example, the interest rate may skyrocket.
- Try to keep your total credit card debt payments to no more than 10% of your take-home pay each month. Your take-home, or net, pay is the amount you actually get after taxes and other deductions—it is rarely the same amount as what you earned. This does not mean pay the minimum amount on your credit cards to keep your debt payments at this level. This means pay the bill in full almost every month (if not every month).

- Make sure you keep the credit card company informed of your address. If for some reason you know a payment will be late, call the toll-free number (look on an earlier statement) and let the company know.
- If you are not using a credit card, close it by telling the issuing company *in writing*. You need to notify the issuing company to close the account and cancel the card. Credit ratings can be hurt if you have too much available credit—even if you aren't using the cards.
- Review your credit reports once each year. If you are denied credit, you can get these reports for free; otherwise, they are available for about $10 or so apiece.

AVOIDING CREDIT CARD CANCELLATIONS

If you are going to put a large or unusual expense on your credit card (such as tuition or a trip overseas), call your card company ahead of time and let them know your plans. Otherwise you may find your card has been canceled. Although this cancellation is to protect you, that isn't much consolation when you can't pay your tuition or buy books or pay the bill at that hotel in Prague.

To get copies of your credit reports, go to the credit bureaus' websites and follow the procedures. Over the next few years, a requirement is being phased in across the country to provide you with a free copy of each credit bureau's report on you—once a year. Here are the Web sites for the three main credit bureaus:

- www.experian.com
- www.equifax.com
- www.transunion.com

These websites actually have a lot of useful information. You can get the telephone number to opt out of having your personal information sold to credit card issuers and other lenders. You can also put your file on a "fraud watch"—an excellent idea if you have ever lost, or had stolen, personal items such as your driver's license, credit cards, checkbook, mail, passport, or Social Security card. Both the opt out and fraud watch services have a time limit of two or three years in most cases, so you need to renew them every so often.

FRAUD WATCH AND OPT OUT

There are two benefits you can use to reduce the likelihood of theft, fraud, or other credit problems caused by people who mean to hurt you. Take advantage of these two credit bureau features—fraud watch and opt out.

A fraud watch simply instructs any place where you apply for credit to call you on the telephone number you list with the credit bureaus and verify you actually are the person applying for the credit card, loan, or whatever.

An opt out reduces the likelihood your credit score and payment information will be sold to places that want you to amass large numbers of credit cards and debt. It also reduces the amount of junk in your mailbox! You can permanently opt out of many credit card offers by calling 1.888.5OPTOUT or going to the web site www.optoutprescreen.com. This is an excellent step to help your credit score and reduce the likelihood of these offers being stolen from your mailbox.

An additional note: Some states require that you be able to semipermanently block inquiries to the credit bureaus. There is a cost, and you have to manually "unblock" to allow lenders to access your credit history, again at a cost (about $10 for each access/block). If you have been an identity theft victim, this is a very useful tool.

A final consideration—always put your personal telephone numbers (landline and cell phone) on the federal Do Not Call list. You can do this by going to www.donotcall.gov and filling out a form for each number. After three months, most telemarketing calls will stop, and you can go to the same website and file a complaint against any place that does call you on those numbers. You can't put business numbers on this list. To get both the fraud watch and opt out features, contact any one of the main credit bureaus

- www.experian.com
- www.transunion.com
- www.equifax.com

and follow the links on the website.

Fraud and Credit

Credit repair is a form of fraud you will encounter very soon, if you haven't already. As soon as you start looking for a house or new car loan (or lease), you are going to become ever more aware of all the places using lines such as:

"Credit Problems? *No* problem …"

"We can erase your bad credit! 100% guaranteed."

"We can remove bankruptcies, judgments, liens, and bad loans from your credit file, *forever!*"

"Create a new credit identity—Legally!"[1]

All because people want the highest credit score possible so they get the best loan rates—and instead they get ripped off.

Here are some things you need to know:

- Accurate negative credit information cannot be erased. If a credit repair company tells you that it will be able to remove negative information from your credit report, the company is not telling you the truth. Only two things can be changed: information that is actually wrong, or information that is more than seven years old (no bankruptcy) or 10 years old (for bankruptcy information). Only time can repair a poor credit report.
- It may be illegal to try to hide bad credit. Some credit repair schemes promise you that they can "hide" bad credit by helping you to establish a new credit identity. If you pay a fee for such a service, the company may direct you to apply for an employer identification number (EIN) from the Internal Revenue Service, and to use the EIN in place of your social security number when you apply for credit. You may also be instructed to use a new mailing address. This practice, known as file segregation, is a federal crime.[2]
- You can take certain steps to repair your own credit report. Contact your creditors when you realize that you cannot make scheduled payments. Your local CCCS or equivalent can help you work out a payment plan and a budget. These groups are nonprofit agencies and charge little or nothing in fees.

Anything a credit repair company can do, you can do for yourself.

1. Source: http://www.consumersgroup.com/crimewatch/credit_repair_scams.htm
2. Source: http://www.consumersgroup.com/crimewatch/credit_repair_scams.htm

Case Studies

Example #1: Felipe and the Campus Credit Card Mess

Felipe just started at State U and the very first day he found two credit card offers in his campus PO Box. Boy, was he excited! The first one was a MasterCard with a $500 limit, and the second was even better—a Visa card with a $1,500 limit.

The first thing that came to Felipe's mind was, "Why am I getting these credit card offers? I'm just a poor student who barely found enough money to pay for school." The second thought that he had was, "Wow! I'm just a poor student who barely found enough money to pay for school. This is my lucky day. Now I can buy a laptop, CDs, DVDs, go out to eat, and even buy some cool stuff for my dorm room."

What lies ahead for Felipe?

Answer: No one can say for sure, but Felipe was last heard from when he had to get a job at the local ice cream parlor and cut his school hours to part-time. He had to make enough money to pay his ballooning credit card bills, and he was so busy worrying about his debt load, he forgot to worry about his class load. He lost his scholarships because of unacceptable grades and dropped three of his six classes.

Without an income, the poor college student had no way to make even minimum payments on the credit cards. Unlike many students in his position, Felipe knew if he declared bankruptcy it would stay in his credit history for seven to ten years, and that would ruin his chances of buying a house or flashy new car for at least that long.

Smart guy, that Felipe!

Example #2: Choosing the Right Credit Card

As you just learned, credit cards come in many forms. Some of these forms look like credit cards but really aren't. Others are true credit cards and can get you in a lot of trouble.

Winnie just graduated high school where she studied culinary arts. She landed a terrific job with a posh restaurant, making $32,000 a year. Now she is setting up all her accounts—checking, savings, and so forth—and is considering what kind of credit and debit cards to get. Based on the facts that she isn't making a whole lot of money, needs to buy a car, doesn't like to carry lots of cash, and plans her purchases carefully, what would you suggest she do?

Answer: Winnie probably needs a debit/ATM card since it is so hard to write checks these days. She might also start with a preloaded or prepaid credit card, or a very low limit ($500 or so) credit card. High-limit cards are a big risk, even though Winnie sounds pretty responsible. She's never had to manage money before.

Example #3: Missing Payments

Alicia graduated from Private U with honors. She landed a cushy job as a Wall Street analyst with a six-figure income. Wow—lucky girl! Of course, four years as a poverty-stricken student took their toll on Alicia's self-esteem. No new clothes, a used beater for a car, a hand-me-down DVD/CD/TV system, and so on.

Now she has the money to *live*! And that's what she did, until she got into payment troubles. How could this happen on 100K+ a year? Easy—let's take a peek inside Alicia's mind and checkbook.

Alicia went hog-wild with her spending—making up for lost time. Given her income level, it's no surprise she was offered a "no limit" American Express Card to go with her $5,000 limit Discover card, MasterCard, and Visa card.

As soon as she got the cards she went shopping. Now she owns a complete Bose audio/video/home entertainment system, $10,000 of new clothes and shoes, over 500 DVDs and CDs, and has booked a first-class, two-week trip to Europe. As you can imagine, her cards are tired and maxed out.

She also decided against sharing an apartment—after all, she was rolling in the dough.

Since Alicia needed a car (she's too snooty for the subway), she leased a new Jaguar XJE. Imagine what the payments are for that? Not to mention insurance, garaging, and gas.

Did I mention Alicia paid for her Ivy League education with loans? And now the banks want to be paid back. . . .

Alicia just found out she can't make even the minimum payments on everything. How can this be? She makes over $8,000 per month! What should she do? A bankruptcy now would be a financial and personal disaster!

Answer: Alicia forgot to read the sections on taxes and money/financial management! After taxes she is only taking home about $5,000 each month. Sounds like a lot, but her Manhattan apartment costs $2,300 a month (including utilities), her auto lease is $900 per month, insurance adds $200 per month, the garage costs another $300 per month (that's $3,700 committed already) and she still has to eat, pay for entertainment and personal expenses, pay her student loans, and make at least minimum payments (about $500 a month) on her credit cards!

Alicia has a problem or three. She should immediately get either a roomie or a cheaper apartment, and get out of her lease on the car. The subway costs a fraction of what her Jag is consuming. She is an excellent candidate for the CCCS—now, before her money woes overwhelm her.

Practical Exercises

1. You just got your first two credit card offers in the mail. You are going to school on a combination of savings, money from your family, loans, a scholarship, and a work-study program. The first card has a limit of $500 and the second a limit of $1,200. What should/would you do?
2. List five ways you can manage your credit and explain why each one matters to you. Choose ways that you think you could stick with.
3. List examples of emergency, necessity, or a poor use of a credit card and explain why you classify each as you did.
4. Explain in your own words why it is so easy for young adults to get credit. Why is this a good (or bad) thing?
5. Name and explain three different types of loans and their uses.

Practical Problems (Answers Given in Appendix C)

1. What is the biggest difference between a loan and a credit card?

   _____

2. List at least five things you should do to protect and manage your credit cards and credit rating.

   _____

   _____

   _____

   _____

   _____.

6

Protecting Your Credit, Yourself, and Your Credit Rating

Your ability to get credit (your credit) is essential to most aspects of living in society today. People don't carry cash. Many merchants (stores) refuse to take checks. Paying cash for a car (even a used one) is beyond most people's means. So they need credit.

Once you have credit (cards, loans), you need to take care of it so it will take care of you. Doing this will help make you even more "creditworthy" because you'll have a good credit score, reflecting how you handle your bills, debts, and other obligations.

CHAPTER 15

Protecting Your Credit

What, exactly, is "credit"? If you look it up in the Merriam-Webster Online Dictionary (www.m-w.com), here's the definition:

Main Entry: **¹cred·it**
Pronunciation:'kre-dit
Function: *noun*
Etymology: Middle French, from Old Italian *credito,* from Latin *creditum* something entrusted to another, loan, from neuter of *creditus,* past participle of *credere* to believe, entrust.

The subentry for consumer credit is even more interesting:

Main Entry: **consumer credit**
Function: *noun*
Etymology: credit granted to an individual especially to finance the purchase of consumer goods or to defray personal expenses

But what does all that technical jargon really mean?

Credit refers to whether or not you can borrow money, and whether or not the place you want to borrow from wants to lend you the money. It all comes down to how likely the potential lender thinks you are to pay everything you owe in the agreed time, on the agreed dates, and pay the full amount due. This is your "creditworthiness."

How does a lender determine your creditworthiness? By looking your past history—your ability to manage money, pay your debts, and plan your finances.

> **The Past as a Predictor of the Future**
>
> As with many aspects of money and finance, what happened in the past is no guarantee of what will take place in the future. Nonetheless, what transpired in the past is the best indicator of what is likely to happen in the future. As the saying goes, "History repeats itself."

The Role and Importance of Being "Creditworthy"

Although the past is far from a guarantee about what will happen in the future, often it's all decision makers have to go on. Colleges look at how you did in the past—high school and test scores—to try to determine how well you will do in the future. Selective high schools look at how you did in junior high and on standardized and state tests. None of these factors is an ironclad guarantee of what will happen in the future. But—they're all the schools have, and these indicators are right more often than they're wrong. So, they get used a lot, and carry a lot of weight.

Employers also look at the past in an attempt to predict the future. They look at your school performance and your part-time work history to try and decide how you will perform if you're hired.

You may be a late bloomer, but when it comes to things that affect your credit history, the old saying "better late than never" simply doesn't hold true. Maybe you know you can do better—on tests, in class, in managing your finances and credit—but if you've messed up, it's going to take a lot of effort to recover.

Case Study

Mikki is looking for a job with the CIA. She knows she will have to prove she is very responsible, and that the CIA investigators will look into her background, including her finances, to make sure she is not in financial trouble (or likely to get in over her head). She has had two credit cards all through college and always made at least minimum payments. In fact, most months she paid more than the minimums. Right now she owes about $500 on the one with a $1,000 limit and $1,200 on the one with a $2,000 limit.

As part of her job interview process Mikki wants to get several new outfits to impress potential employers, even though she has a nice black suit and a green wool dress. Mikki happens to have a lot of clothes—one of the main reasons she owes $1,700 on two credit cards. She also wants to take a quick trip to Mexico to celebrate her upcoming graduation and relax before finals get underway. Of course she plans to charge the clothes and the trip. Mikki is also very busy with classes and a part-time job and tends to charge more and more of her meals at the local restaurants, or charge ready-to-heat foods at the local organic grocery store.

The CIA or any other potential employer who looks at Mikki's spending habits is going to be concerned. To have $1,700 in debt is a lot for a 21-year-old student. If she runs up even more bills, potential employers (and insurance companies) are going to get really concerned. She may be considered a risk since she could find herself needing money, fast, to keep paying her debts.

If Mikki really wants to be considered for certain jobs (and stay out of financial hot water), she really needs to start paying off her credit card debt and living within her means. Fewer meals out, fewer new clothes, and certainly no trip to Mexico!

CHAPTER 16

Managing Your Credit

Credit: Who Cares How You Manage It?

Hopefully, you care; if you don't, here are some reasons to reconsider your position.

The Importance of Good Credit and Good Scores

Good credit matters and bad credit hurts. If you're looking for your first job, trying to get a lease on an apartment, or checking out car insurance rates, the quality of your credit—your credit history and credit score—can be the difference between getting what you want or not getting it at all.

    If your credit history is not up to snuff, several things can happen, and none of them are very pleasant.

    First, you might find an offer of employment withdrawn, especially if you need a security clearance or will be handling money. One late or missed payment could change your entire job outlook. You might still get a job offer, but not for the job you had in mind. Think about it—would you want to trust your bank accounts to a bank whose manager is irresponsible with his own money? Would you want someone with money troubles to have access to your personal information? Would you want to trust someone with military or government secrets if she might sell these secrets because she needs money to pay her debts?

The Importance of Paying on Time

If your credit records show you are often late or miss payments on credit cards or loans, or bounce checks, it is going to be hard to get an apartment, even with a good job. If you skip a car payment or are late paying MasterCard or Visa, what reason does a landlord have to think you'll care if you pay your rent on time?

    The same need for timely payments applies when you try to get utilities—cell phone, landline, Internet, electric and gas, satellite or cable, and so forth. If you can't make credit card payments on time, you will probably have to put down large deposits or get your parents to co-sign your applications.

    In addition, to drive a car you need insurance. Many insurance companies routinely check your credit rating and score before they will quote you a rate and issue a policy. If your score is below a certain level (and this varies with the insurance company), you are either going to pay more or be refused altogether.

> **Credit and Your Job**
>
> Worrying about your credit history isn't a silly concern, it's often a "national security" concern. You may remember the Aldrich Ames case and the damage he did to our national security, all so he could have a bit more money than his government job paid. He gave away the names of people in Russia working for the CIA and cost them their lives.

Finally, credit card companies, loan companies, lenders, insurance companies, and many other places are looking for reasons to deny you credit, or make you pay more to get credit or a loan. Sure, as a student your mailbox was flooded with offers for credit cards, car leases, and loans of all sorts. But that was because the companies making the offers had (probably) checked out your parents too, and were pretty sure your parents would bail you out if you got into financial trouble. That was before you kept missing payments and your parents wouldn't pay the bills for you. Sound familiar?

When you are young—say, under 25—your credit rating is just being built, and you are not going to get the breaks your parents do, but you can still make a big difference by doing a few simple (but often painful) things:

- Always pay your bills—utilities, loans, and similar—on time or early. Pay the full amount due.
- Don't routinely mail payments to arrive at the end of the grace period. If a payment is due on the 15th and late after the 25th, payments that arrive after the 15th are okay, but don't help your credit history. You are labeled as a chronic "late-payer," even though you made the second deadline. Paying after the 25th is a very bad idea, and will seriously wound your credit score. Even once after the second (late payment) date is going to hurt you for years to come, and twice will make it almost impossible to get credit or a loan unless you pay sky-high rates.

What Affects Your Credit Score and Rating and the Interest Rate You Pay?

What can hurt your credit rating and credit score? After all, you're young and haven't had time to get into much trouble, have you? Maybe no, maybe yes.

- What can hurt your credit rating and score?
- What can cause the interest rate you pay to go up?
- What can cause your credit cards to be canceled?

There are many factors than cause any one, two, or all three of these undesirable events to occur. Here are the main causes of nasty things happening to you because of the way you handle credit and your credit cards, loan payments, checking account, and bill payments.

Late Payments

Being late on a loan or credit card payment even once is going to hurt your ability to get future loans and credit at good rates. Being late twice is much worse—you may not be able to get many types of loans or credit at all.

Routinely paying during the grace period (the 10–25 days after a payment is first due) is not a good thing. If this is your approach, you are likely to see the interest rate charged on any monthly credit card balance(s) rise.

Making only partial payments is a big problem. If you make a partial payment that is less than the required minimum payment, you are going to run into problems. Before taking this approach, it is very worthwhile to speak with a certified, not-for-profit, consumer credit counseling service (such as the Consumer Credit Counseling Service).

Any of these situations can cause adjustable rates such as those on credit cards to rise. They can also cause your car to be repossessed. Your credit cards may also be canceled by the company(s).

WHEN DEBT TAKES CONTROL OF YOUR LIFE

Picture this—you routinely make late payments on your car loan and on your Visa and MasterCard. In fact, the last two months you skipped all three payments so you could go skiing at Alta/Snowbird or Stowe this weekend.

You just found out you're in the running for a promotion at work. To celebrate, you invite seven of your co-workers to a martini lounge for drinks and cigars—your treat. At the end of the evening, you offer your Visa and it's refused for being over the limit. No problem, you say, and give the server your MasterCard. That card is refused, too. Finally, after much ribbing and eye-rolling, your friends come up with the money to cover the bill.

You head to your 11-month-old sports car, and it's not where you left it. In fact, it's not anywhere to be found. You look all over the parking lot, and decide it's been stolen. You try to call the police, but your cell phone doesn't seem to work anymore. Funny, it worked just fine earlier today! When the police finally come, they tell you your car has apparently been repossessed, and give you a ride home.

Sound funny? Funny, but too often true. No car, no credit cards, no cell phone, no friends, and probably no promotion when the word gets around (and it will).

Going Over the Limit

If you try to buy something and your credit limit is $1,000, and your unpaid card balance is $800, and the item costs $300, you are "going over the limit." You already owe the credit card company $800 against the agreed-upon $1,000 you could borrow, so if you charge another $300 you have spent $100 more than the credit card company was willing to risk on you. You may be allowed to exceed your limit this one time, but it's going to require approval and it might hurt your credit rating.

The credit card company agreed to risk a certain amount of money on you. That is the limit on your credit card. If your unpaid bills—your balance—and the amount you want to charge go over the agreed-upon amount, the credit card company is going to worry you are "living beyond your means" and are taking on debt you can't or won't repay.

The simple solution? Know exactly how much you have charged each month and how much you have paid, and balance those amounts against your credit limit. Don't even try to go over the agreed limit. Always pay at least the minimum required payment, and try to pay more. Your best choice? Pay every credit card balance in full every month.

CREDIT LIMITS

Try thinking of your credit limit this way: When you have a checking account, you have a certain amount of money there. When you make a deposit, it is much like making a payment on a loan or credit card. You have more money available to you after you've made a deposit. If you try to write checks for more than the amount of money you have, your check either "bounces" or it is cashed against a "line of credit"—your overdraft amount. You probably don't have overdraft protection, so a check for more money than is in your account is going to bounce. This is a bad thing and may hurt your credit score.

In the case of a credit card, the process is the same. You can charge goods and services up to the limit of your card. To restore part or all of your credit card limit, you have to pay the credit card company to reduce your balance. If you try to charge something and you have not reduced your balance by enough to allow the new charge, you are either using a version of a line of credit (if the credit card company agrees) or you are "bouncing" the charge (if the company doesn't agree to let you make the purchase). Both can be very bad for your credit history and score because they show you are not able to manage money, don't pay your bills, and/or are spending more than you should.

Having Too Much Credit Available

Yes, you really can have "too much credit."

It's really tempting to accept every loan and credit card offer that comes along. Instant gratification is nice, but very costly in both the short and long run. It's not just the number of credit cards you have, it's how much you can charge if you "maxed out" each one. When a lender, credit card company, employer, insurance company, or many other places look at whether to hire you, lend you money, give you (more) credit, or give you insurance, they look at how much you could borrow and whether you could handle all the payments. After all, each place wants to make sure you can pay the money you owe them, or aren't a risk to crash your car to get the insurance money, or won't sell company secrets to support your lifestyle!

A VICIOUS CYCLE

Think about this: One of the biggest reasons people "sell out" their country is to get the money they need to support a lavish lifestyle. These people may have gone into debt, or may simply want more than their salaries cover. If you ever saw the movie *The Falcon and the Snowman* or followed the Aldrich Ames spy scandal, you saw what happened when people got addicted to "the good life" without the means to pay.

Credit cards are just as risky. Stories appear almost daily about someone who had five credit cards, charged them to the max, couldn't make the payments, so they applied for five more cards. Then they charged the payments for the first five cards on the second five cards, until the second set was maxed out, and so forth. It's a vicious cycle, and bankruptcy doesn't solve the underlying problems.

Why not just declare bankruptcy when times get tough? After all, you're young, you have years to recover, and you have your whole life ahead of you.

About Bankruptcy

It's too easy to "declare bankruptcy." People declare Chapter 13 bankruptcy and think they can walk away from all their troubles and their debts, and start over with a clean slate. Although this is partially true, there's more to bankruptcy than meets the eye.

- Bankruptcy stays on your record for *at least seven years*. It will be difficult to get credit cards or a car loan, and almost impossible to get a home loan during that time.
- Certain debts, such as student loans and taxes, are virtually never forgiven.
- Your car may not be safe—it can be taken if it is deemed excessive for your situation, if it hasn't already been repossessed.
- If you have a mortgage, you can lose your home.
- If you're trying to rent a place, you're going to have a hard time.
- You'll probably need substantial deposits to get your utilities hooked up. Many utilities are disconnected for nonpayment.
- You will have a very hard time getting some of the modern "necessities" of life such as a cell phone, Internet service, and satellite or cable TV. No one will trust you, and these services will likely be disconnected when your bankruptcy filing notice is posted.

- It is difficult to get many jobs, such as police officer, military officer, firefighter, insurance agent, stockbroker, or attorney, if you have a bankruptcy in your files.
- Many of your expensive "toys" may be confiscated—the home entertainment system, dirt bike, and so forth.
- Your friends may not think much of you, and will insist you pay cash when it's your turn.

Why Do Credit Card Companies and Other Places Care about Your Credit?

Credit card companies and other entities that count on you to pay your bills on time are looking at risk factors. They believe that if you are behind with your payments to one company you are more likely to fall behind with other companies. Insurance companies believe you are more likely to make a bogus claim or pad an existing claim if you are having financial difficulties.

Car loan companies, banks, and other lenders charge people with less favorable (and shorter) credit histories more for a car loan than they charge people with long histories of never missing a payment.

If credit card companies like what they see in your ability to manage credit on existing cards, they often offer you *more* credit. Why? There are fees for every credit card transaction—the place selling the goods or services has to pay your credit card company 3–7% of every sale. The more you can charge, the more money the credit card company can make, provided you pay your bills. But one negative entry in your credit report can send your interest rates soaring.

Credit and Auto Insurance

Increasingly, insurance companies believe there is a link between paying your bills on time and your attitude toward driving. So they are tying your insurance rates, and even your ability to get car insurance, to your credit and payment history.

Statistics show several things. First, young drivers are far more likely to be involved in an auto accident than most other drivers. Second, there appears to be a connection between your credit history and your driving habits. According to a study by Conning & Co. (an insurance research and asset management firm), 92 of the 100 largest auto insurance companies use credit data when looking at new business. In fact, many of these insurance companies actually require you to sign a waiver that allows them to get a copy of your credit reports every year, and they use this information to set your renewal rates.

The Insurance Information Institute (www.iii.org) collects data about which drivers are more likely to file insurance claims. Their findings? Drivers with poor credit ratings file 40% more claims than drivers with the best ratings. So if your credit history and score are less than stellar, you could pay more for auto insurance—even higher rates than the under-25 bracket already pays. How much more? Maybe 20–50% more, according to Clarence Smith, assistant vice president at Conning & Co.

INSURANCE AND YOUR CREDIT HISTORY

Insurance companies may review your credit reports and history when you initially apply for a policy, then periodically review your history. Some insurance companies look at your information at renewal, some more often, and some never look. Some states don't allow credit information to be part of the insurance issue process, but that is changing. Note that life and disability insurance companies also look at this information—more on this in the chapter on insurance.

The Casualty (property loss) Actuarial Society did a study and found something very interesting. If you have a clean driving record but a poor credit history, you are more likely to make a claim than if you have moving violations or accidents with a good credit history. This can have a very significant impact on your insurance rates.

WHY DOES CREDIT HISTORY AFFECT AUTO INSURANCE RATES?

Think about it. When people have a problem making payments on credit cards, they probably have budget or cash-flow problems. If these people have maxed out their credit cards, and maybe are looking for more cards to continue living beyond their income and means, it could be very tempting to stage an accident for the insurance money, or exaggerate the damage from an actual accident, in order to get more money to support their lifestyle.

Credit Scores

You've probably heard the term "credit score" before you ever picked up this book. Credit card companies, loan companies, bank lenders, and mortgage lenders use these scores. Insurance companies get a version of these scores, called "insurance scores," from the credit bureaus. These scores are related to the information in your credit file. They are calculated using information provided by any several sources.

How is an insurance score different from a credit score? As a young adult, the difference is very important, because it looks at something you haven't had time to build: stability. You are moving often—to and from school, to your first full-time job. You are getting an apartment, and probably won't stay in your first one very long. You may be changing your telephone number because you want to switch everything to your cell phone and wireless Internet. So you are probably going to pay more just because you are young and getting established. Don't complicate matters by loading up on credit cards and debt and taking out huge car loans.

CREDIT AND INSURANCE SCORES

Consider Page, who graduated high school, got a good job at the local factory, and married Colby (who works at the same plant) two years later. Now they've been out of high school for four years and are still working at the same place. They've been in the same apartment Colby had, and they've always paid their bills on time.

Then look at Mica and Stone. They both went straight to college, but transferred out-of-state after two years. Now they've graduated. They are getting married and moving to another state to take their first jobs. They have had credit cards all through college, and occasionally been late on a payment. Mica went over the limit twice, too. Both couples have been out of high school for the same amount of time.

Which couple is likely to have the better credit score and get better insurance rates?

What Matters When You Are Looking for Insurance?

Stability and credit history affect your insurance rates (and even your ability to get insurance in the first place). If you are changing jobs, making big lifestyle changes, or having problems paying bills (credit or cash flow problems), you may need to stay with your current insurance company for now. If you're going to change, read the fine print before you sign. If you are signing an authorization to get credit or other personal information, beware—your insurance rates could be adversely affected!

What can you do to improve your credit score?

Avoid Credit Score Problems

Make a list of all your regular payments and accounts. Use the table that follows.

Table 16.1. Sample Credit Card and Loan Payment Record

Account Type, Number, and 800 Number	Payment Due Date	Credit Limit or Balance	Current Balance	Date and Amount of Last Payment
MasterCard 1234-5678-1234-5675 1.800.555.1314	25th of the month	$1,200	$800	9/21/05 $150
Visa	15th of the month	$900	$150	$200
Car loan	1st of the month	$17,000	$17,000	$400

Use the preceding example to build your own payment record. The information will be used again when you start to develop your personal budget.

Table 16.2. Your Credit Card and Loan Payment Record

Account Type, Number, and 800 Number	Payment Due Date	Credit Limit or Balance	Current Balance	Date and Amount of Last Payment
MasterCard # Telephone:	____ of the month			
Visa # Telephone	____ of the month			
Car loan	____ of the month			

If the due date of a credit card or loan (except your mortgage or rent) is on a date when you are usually low on cash, call the lender and get the due date changed. This is easier to do than you think.

The payments in the table we just looked at are spread out across the month. This can be a good thing if you get paid every week, but not so good if you get paid once a month. It's best to have due dates shortly after you get paid. Then you know you have the money, and the bills are due before the money sits in your checking account for several weeks tempting you to do something else with it!

Pay your bills as soon as they arrive. It's not a good idea to play with grace periods. Many bills such as your cell phone and some credit cards don't have a grace period. Your cable company may not have a grace period either, and late payment could cut off "Survivor" and your Internet service in one fell swoop.

You might want to set up an automatic deposit of your paycheck and an auto-pay for your regular bills such as rent or mortgage and insurance. This avoids late payments and can do wonders for your credit history and score. Just make sure you write down the amounts of the auto-payments so you don't bounce checks!

Case Studies

Our old friend Phoenix has had it. Too many people calling demanding payments, credit cards being canceled for nonpayment, no place willing to lend more money or issue a new card, the new car repossessed, and things are only getting worse. There's no money to pay the student loans or the rent. Phoenix's employer has announced everyone has to take a pay cut of 15% or there will be lay-offs.

Phoenix has decided the only way out of a bad situation is to declare bankruptcy. Alex is trying to persuade Phoenix to do whatever it takes to avoid bankruptcy.

What might Alex suggest?

Answer: It's hard to tell someone else to take drastic financial steps, and that's what Phoenix needs to do. The best favor Alex can do is offer Phoenix a shoulder to cry on and the telephone number of the local nonprofit credit counseling office. Alex could even go along to the first meeting with a counselor to lend support.

Phoenix really should try to avoid bankruptcy for a number of reasons—here are several of those reasons:

- For the next seven to ten years it will be difficult at best to get any loans or credit cards.
- Employers may refuse to hire Phoenix for some jobs, especially in the military, government, or defense contractor fields.
- It's embarrassing and word does get around.
- Auto and home/renters' insurance can become very expensive. Life insurance, too.

Practical Exercises

1. What can hurt your credit rating and score?
2. What can cause the interest rate you pay to go up?
3. What can cause your credit cards to be canceled?
4. Name at least three problems you may encounter in the future if you declare bankruptcy.

_____

_____

_____

Identity Theft

When it comes to identity theft, there's no time like the present—to protect yourself, that is. Preventing identity theft is a major component of managing credit, as you shall soon see!

Why Would *Anyone* Want to Become You?

You're young, you have the world in your grasp, and you probably have a clean record. When you turn 18 or 19, even any bad things you did are usually erased from your record. You are just starting to build a credit history. You probably haven't defaulted on a loan, declared bankruptcy, or built much of a credit history yet.

You are a virtual clean slate.

Who wouldn't want to be you, or at least the "you" that has a clean driving record, Social Security number (SSN), criminal history, and credit report?

The answer? There are tens of thousands of illegal immigrants, thieves, and general lowlifes out there who need or want a new identity so they can:

- Get a job
- Get a driver's license
- Get insurance
- Bring their families to this country
- Shop till they drop
- Take expensive vacations
- Get into colleges

In essence, there are people who need to create an identity to do the things you take for granted. If they can become you for a day, or a week, or a month, or much longer, they can do all these things. Of course, you are the one who suffers. You are the one who gets a wrecked financial, personal, work, and credit history. You are the one who has to spend hundreds of hours and thousands of dollars to clean up someone else's mess. And there is no guarantee the same thieves, or others just like them, won't continue to use your information.

The best solution to this problem is a ton of prevention. Prevention takes time and effort, but is not anywhere near as much trouble as cleaning up later.

Who Has the Need to Have Your Personal Data?

Not as many people as you might think. Unless the situation involves money (such as financial aid or getting paid at work), or an entity that needs to verify your credit history, the odds are there is no need for the place to have your

Social Security number (SSN). While there are no guarantees that someone can't rip off your identity without having your SSN, an SSN and some other information goes a long way—the wrong way.

Here is a list of many of the places that have a need and a right to have your SSN and other personal information. They also have a legal obligation to safeguard this information.

Places That Can Require Your SSN and Other Personal Information

- Credit bureaus: This includes Transunion, Equifax, and Experian, plus several smaller bureaus. Hint: To see the names of some of these other bureaus, read the fine print on the back of your credit card applications. The names of the credit bureaus that the card issuer uses are listed there. So is a lot of other useful information.

CREDIT APPLICATIONS

Always keep copies of both sides of credit card applications. This includes applications you fill out at department stores, gas stations, car dealers, and anyplace else.

Take a yellow highlighter and read through the fine print on the back of the application. Mark such things as the *grace period*, *payment due date*, *privacy policy*, *penalties and fees*, *credit bureaus used*, *contact information*, and anything you have questions about. Call the card issuer to get any questions you may have answered *before* you send in the application.

Since your copies of the applications are going to have your SSN on them, store these applications in a safe place. Your dorm room or a room in a shared apartment is *not* a safe place unless you keep your personal stuff in a locked place—one that is secured with a combination lock, not a key. Too many people come and go from communal living quarters, and not all of them are trustworthy. It's unfortunate, but true.

- Banks, credit unions, and savings and loan companies where you have accounts: These places need your information, including your SSN and probably a copy of your driver's license, so they can identify you and report account interest earnings to the Internal Revenue Service (IRS).
- Investment accounts: If you have retirement accounts, mutual funds, money market accounts, savings bonds, stocks, or other investments, you *must* provide the organization with your SSN.
- The IRS and your state Department of Revenue: The IRS and your state Department of Revenue need your SSN to track your tax payments, refunds, and generally match up money paid in your name.
- Other federal and state agencies: If you are paying into a pension plan (the military or others) or making Social Security contributions, these places will have your SSN. Deal with it.
- Employers: Because these places pay you and make your tax payments, they *must* have your SSN. They *should not* use your SSN as your employee number, or allow the group insurance benefits providers to use this number as your identifying number.

> **Any time you sign an application, authorization, release, or other form, get a copy of all the pages, and keep it filed in a safe place.**

- Financial aid organizations: These places need to verify income and assets (yours and your parents') and report certain information to the state and federal governments so they need your SSN.
- Insurance companies: If you are applying for an individual insurance policy (health, life, renter's, auto, homeowner's, disability, and so forth), the insurance company has a right to get your SSN and verify your creditworthiness. You will get a release and authorization form to sign—read it carefully and keep a copy.

- Mortgage and other lenders: Since you are applying for credit and paying interest that may be deductible, the lenders for mortgages, lines of credit, auto loans, and other loans *must* have your SSN to do a credit check and report interest payments to the state and federal governments. Of course, they also use your SSN to report late and missed payments to the credit bureaus, too. Nothing you can do about that except always pay on time.
- Any other places you apply for credit: Department stores, gas stations, and many other places issue credit cards. If you apply for one, the issuer will require your SSN so your credit history can be checked.
- Driver's license bureaus: While these places *should not* put your SSN on your driver's license, they can require you to produce your SSN card when applying for a license. Of course, this means they can note and file your SSN. This has proved to be a big problem in many cities since staffers have collected and sold this information (along with blank driver's license forms).

Places That Do Not Need and Should Not Ask for Your SSN

Most people know their SSN, and it is a long enough number to provide unique identification around the world. It is also a standardized number—nine digits—so it lends itself to computer coding as a standard field. Many other numbers are not standardized—each state has a different form for driver's license numbers, and insurance companies have their own format for policy numbers. Banks have standardized routing numbers, but the account numbers are different at almost every bank or other savings institution.

These are some places that may ask for your SSN. They do not need the number (even if they tell you "That's how the computer is set up") and should give you an alternate number.

- Universities and colleges and other schools: Outside of financial aid departments, your school rarely has a need for your SSN. You certainly *should not* be identified in your student records by your SSN. You *should* have a separate student number.
- Health and other group insurance companies: Many health insurance companies want to use your SSN as your identifying number because it is easy and unique. You have a right and an obligation to refuse to allow this. Your employer has *no* right to provide this information without your consent. Health and other forms of group insurance do not perform a credit check on individuals so they have *no* need for your SSN (or driver's license number or passport number).
- Professional, trade, business, or other organizations: Unless these places are paying you—say, for a presentation—they have absolutely zero need for your SSN, driver's license number, or passport number.
- Grocery stores and other places you write checks: Sometimes these places ask for your SSN. *Do not* give it to them. All a merchant should need to run your check through the system and verify funds is the check itself. It is possible they may ask for your driver's license number and telephone number. Giving those out is your choice. You can always refuse, take your check back, leave the items, and walk out—maybe the clerk will call you back and say they don't really need the information.
- Any place that accepts your credit card and wants additional personal information: If a store clerk wants to look at your driver's license to verify your signature on a credit slip that is a *good* thing. If the person wants to write down any numbers (SSN, passport, telephone, driver's license) that is *bad* thing. Walk out—taking the credit slip with you and leaving the merchandise.
- Courses and workshops: If you have a professional license or just take a course at a local college or other place, these places have no need for your SSN. Your professional license number is sufficient, not matter what the record keepers try to tell you. They don't need your SSN. Ditto places you take general or academic courses.

A CASE IN POINT

Many states have a third party manage the continuing education requirements for their professional license holders (insurance, nursing, financial, law, real estate, accounting, and so forth). Recently one of these third parties contracted with another entity to run the course recording process. Up until that time, course attendee information could be maintained and filed by license number.

The new entity *requires* SSNs and will not/cannot accept license numbers. This is a very *bad* thing. Why? Because the SSNs of tens of thousands of professionals are now in the hands of course providers and the recording entity—and neither place needs this information. In addition, both the providers and the recorders have other personal information about the professional license holders—addresses, full names, telephone numbers, e-mail addresses, and so forth. And there is currently only one very difficult work-around to continue to use license numbers.

Can you spell "identity theft"? This is an example of convenience being allowed to overrule personal data security, and you're going to run into it again and again. Be aware, be careful, and be protective of your information. Question authority!

Reduce the Risk of Your Identity Being Ripped Off

Be very careful about where and with whom you share any personal information. If you did not initiate the contact (by telephone, written request, snail mail, or e-mail), do not give out personal information.

Never respond to e-mails from places you do not know. Anytime a place asks for a password to one of your accounts or wants any number (telephone, SSN, account, etc.), call the company directly and ask what is going on. You may find you are being "phished."

Take advantage of the national Do Not Call (DNC) list (www.donotcall.gov). Go there *now* and register your personal telephone numbers (landline and cell phone). You can't register a business number, but that shouldn't be a concern at this point.

Don't carry unnecessary personal information with you—that means your SSN card, for example. Unless you travel out of the country on a regular basis, don't carry your passport, either.

Never leave your wallet in your car, or lying around in your room or apartment.

Don't leave your purse, laptop bag, or briefcase slung over a chair or lying in your office or in your car. If you live with a roommate, don't leave these items or your wallet out in the open. Things seem to sprout legs and go for hikes in direct proportion to the number of roommates and guests you have in your place.

> **I have a friend who was in the Navy, and proud of it. In fact, he is so proud he uses one of his dog tags as a key chain. This is a very bad idea. The dog tag has his name, date of birth, and Social Security number. All someone needs to do is note the information if they get a glance at his key chain and his identity is stolen.**

Safeguard Your Identity and Documents

Never leave things of value lying around. This is a simple, and often overlooked, action. Money is not the only thing of value that thieves want. Identity thieves want copies of your credit card and mortgage applications. They want copies of your automobile loan and purchase records. They want your birth certificate, passport, SSN card, military discharge papers, and driver's license. They want the credit card applications that come in the mail.

You need to develop the habits of protecting your valuable information and safely destroying or storing the papers you no longer need or don't want.

At Home or in the Dormitory

Shred everything that has your name, address, telephone number, SSN, or other personally identifying information you don't need or want to keep. Shredders are the single best piece of hardware you can buy to protect yourself and your identity.

Use the shredder—not the trash.

Keep important papers, your wallet or purse, and your laptop out of sight.

Be very careful using wireless Internet connections or unencrypted Internet connections (look for https in the URL and the "locked" lock at the bottom right of your screen).

Be equally careful what information you store on your PC and laptop. Consider using a password for initial system access and don't leave your computer on when you are not around. Booting up only takes a few minutes.

Put spyware, firewall, adware, and antivirus software on your computer and use them. Never open attachments from unknown people or places. Update your protective software at least every week.

Set your cookies to reject all but "per session" cookies. You can use the Internet Tools settings to manually configure to accept other first-party cookies from your mail services and other sites that require password access. Never click on ad banners.

Get a safe deposit box. Use it. It will be the best $20–$30 you ever spend. Make sure you keep the key with you. Consider having your parents or spouse on the account so they can get into the box if need be. Put your passport, SSN card, birth certificate, military papers, diploma, and any documents with raised seals in the box. Put any jewelry you don't wear at least once a month in here. Put all your jewelry in there when you are traveling. Don't put your original will in there—a copy is fine.

When Traveling

Use a money pouch or money belt for your money, credit cards, tickets, and passport. Wear this pouch under your clothes.

Get in the habit of *not* touching your pockets or money pouch/belt to see if it is still there. That is tantamount to shouting at a pickpocket, "Here's where I keep everything of value—just look where I keep patting myself!!!"

Keep copies of all your cards, passport, travel documents, and other valuable papers in two places: With a person back home who will accept a collect call from you, and in your e-mail account (scan and send the stuff to yourself).

Guard your laptop. *Do not* leave it with anyone—people have been known to surf your hard drive and download data or load malicious software (or worse).

Don't flaunt your wealth. To many people, even in this country, you look fabulously wealthy. In other countries, they will think you are King Midas or Britney Spears, just because you have a bit of jewelry, clean clothes, and nice luggage. Leave the earrings, rings, necklaces, bracelets, and expensive watches at home. If it glitters or gleams, don't take it.

Don't let your backpack or daypack out of your sight and grasp. That means hooking the strap around your leg and keeping the bag against your leg.

If you travel with a laptop, consider carrying it in a daypack rather than a laptop case. It's a bit less obvious that way.

Make sure you collect everything when you are leaving the security screening area or airline lounge!

At Work

Hopefully, your employer has implemented the safety and security processes I outline for your home/dorm. But here are a few more things to do . . .

Put your purse, briefcase, or similar items out of sight or take them with you.

Lock your file cabinet when you are not in the office—even if it's just a trip to the restroom or coffee machine. This is a good place to put your purse, laptop, valuables, and so forth, as well.

At School

See the comments about the home/dorm room. You have to be extra careful because you probably have one or more roommates and they have friends and there are lots of strangers in and out of your room or apartment. Some people have light fingers or unfriendly agendas—unfortunate, but true.

Out and About

Don't leave your laptop or purse or backpack or daypack hanging on a chair or lying near your feet. Hook the strap around your leg and keep the bag against your leg.

Don't throw out credit card slips—not all places give you a copy with the first 8–12 numbers blanked out. Ditto receipts from ATMs.

Be aware who has your credit cards. "Skimming" is the latest trend—the server or clerk takes your card out of your sight, then returns a few minutes later with your credit slip for you to sign. Unbeknownst to you, he or she also had a little handheld card reader in the back and made an electronic copy of your card. A few weeks or months later, your card starts showing lots of charges that you did not make, and you have no idea where the theft occurred because you still have your card. This is not a big issue if you are at home—just call the card issuer (the number is on the back of your card) and they will cancel your card and send a new one and you shouldn't be liable for more than $50 or so in charges. However, this "skimming" is a *big* problem when you are out of the country—and then it's much harder to get a new card.

"Phishing"

If you get an official-looking e-mail from your bank or any other financial place, or from your ISP, be very careful. Banks *do not* ask for financial or personal information via e-mail, and ISPs do not verify information such as passwords via e-mail. These places are trying to get enough information about you to create an identity for someone else.

General Steps You Should Take to Protect Yourself

Get off as many lists as you can. This includes catalogues you don't want, credit card mailings you don't want, and so forth.

How can you do this?

Set aside an hour once every two years and do the following:

- Go to any of the three major credit bureau websites (www.equifax.com, www.experian.com, and www.transunion.com) and do the following:

- ○ Copy the addresses and contact instructions for the Direct Mail and Telephone Soliciting databases (Direct Marketing Association or DMA).
- ○ Copy the telephone number to "opt out" of credit card solicitations from lists provided by the credit bureaus themselves.
- ○ Follow the instructions to get on a "fraud watch" if you have *ever* had any personal information lost or stolen (credit cards, driver's license, mail in general, passport, birth certificate, SSN or SSN card, and so forth).
- Write to the DMA at both the telephone and mail solicitation addresses and request your name be removed from their databases.
- Call the "opt out" telephone number and follow the steps to get your name off the credit bureaus' mailing lists.
- Register your personal landline and cell phone numbers with the national Do Not Call list (www.donotcall.gov).
- Call each catalogue company to get off their mailing list. There is a toll-free customer service number on the back of the catalogue—call it and give the telemarketer the information he or she will request.
- Call each credit card mailing and do the same as for the catalogues. Make sure to shred or carefully burn the application when you are done with the call. Do not throw the application in the trash!

> **Share this credit protection information with your family and friends. Following a few simple steps could go a long way toward eliminating identity theft, unwanted telephone calls, and junk mail!**

Case Study

Derek lost his wallet a month ago. He thinks another student took it during a party his roommate hosted. Inside were his driver's license, several credit cards, $25 in cash, two blank checks, and even his Social Security card. Because there wasn't a lot of cash, Derek didn't report the loss to the police or put a fraud watch on his credit information at the credit bureaus.

Derek is trying to buy a new car. He has a good job, has always paid his credit cards in full and on time, never bounced a check, and has a good driving record. He pays his student loans on time, too. Until now, Derek has been financially savvy. But the loss of his personal information is about to really bite him—harder than he ever imagined.

When he gave the car dealer's sales manager his Social Security number and personal information to get the loan approved, Derek was eagerly anticipating driving off the lot in a new Honda Element. Imagine his surprise when, ten minutes later, the manager of the dealership came in and said, "Derek, why didn't you tell me about the five new credit cards you just applied for, and the other new car you just bought?"

Derek was flabbergasted. He hadn't applied for any new cards and certainly hadn't just bought a car!

What happened?

The person who took his wallet either used or sold the information (or both) and one or more thieves immediately began to pretend they were Derek. One of the things identity thieves do immediately is start applying for credit in the victim's name—stealing the identity—and then using the new cards until they are at their limits. They also try to get other loans, such as for a car, and then never make payments. Instead, they drive the car until it is either identified as stolen or repossessed. They often divert your mail to their address by filing a change of address. This lets them do even more damage.

Even college students can be hurt by identity thieves. Take the steps you can to protect yourself. Never carry your Social Security card unless you need it that day (at a bank or new employer's office, for example). Immediately report to the police any stolen items that include identification of any sort (license, Social Security card, passport).

Let the credit bureaus know right away that potentially damaging material has been stolen and put a "fraud watch" on your account. Watch your mail for missing items (bills, statements, etc.). Watch your credit card statements carefully for unusual purchases.

Practical Exercises

1. What do you consider the three most important things you can do to protect your credit?
2. What steps do you plan to take to avoid becoming a victim of identity theft?
3. What is "phishing"?
4. When can a place or person request your SSN?
5. What places/people should not request/need your SSN?

7

Life Is Very Taxing

Taxes are an unpleasant, but necessary, fact of life. Without the revenue from taxes, cities, states, and the federal government would not be able to

- Build interstate and other highways
- Maintain an air traffic control system
- Provide programs for the elderly and poor
- Review and regulate drugs
- Manage water safety
- Subsidize colleges and universities
- Provide student loans and grants
- Support museums
- And much, much more.

CHAPTER 18

Taxes, Deductions, and Your Income: The Basics

Getting your first job, even a part-time one at a local store or service business, is exciting. You are meeting new people, learning new skills, and earning your own money.

Unfortunately, not all the money you earn is actually yours. There are many places waiting to take a share. Later we'll look at what benefits and retirement plans can do to the amount of money you actually have to spend, but let's start with taxes.

So what kind of taxes and deductions do you need to be concerned with? Starting out, your taxes are fairly simple and straightforward, as are your deductions.

> **Staying out of tax trouble is a good idea. It's tempting to cheat on taxes, or hide income, or do other less-than-bright things, but it's bad practice. The Internal Revenue Service—the IRS—is not stupid. Keep in mind the nine scariest words in the English language: "I'm from the IRS and I'm here to help."**

Dependents and Standard Deductions

While you are still living at home, your parents are probably going to keep deducting you as a dependent on their tax return. In fact, as long as they are paying the majority of your bills and expenses (such as tuition), they are likely to continue to declare you as a dependent on their tax return. You do get certain deductions for yourself, and these don't impact your parents' tax returns.

Once you are out on your own, you get to take both the dependency exemption and the standard deduction. Yes, you are your own dependent! The amounts of these deductions change (generally increasing) from year to year. In 2005, the dependent/personal exemption amount per person was $3,575 and the standard deduction was $4,850. These deductions reduce the amount of income on which you must pay taxes.

Table 18.1 shows dependent exemptions and standard deductions for the next several years.

How do you decide how many dependent exemptions to claim? We'll look at this in more depth later, but the worksheet you use is a Form W-4. Samples of most of these forms are included in Appendix B.

To get the most up-to-date information and tax forms, visit www.irs.gov.

Table 18.1. Standard Deduction and Dependent Exemptions

Year	Standard Deduction	Dependent and Personal Exemption
2005	$4,850—single $9,700—married	$3,575—single $7,150—married
2006	Same—but may be increased	Same—but may be increased
2007	Same—but may be increased	Same—but may be increased

Key Definitions

Not everything is taxed, and some things are taxed in different ways. As a result, our tax code is messy at best. Here are a few definitions you'll want to make sure you understand.

Taxable

If some form of tax is owed on something, that "something" is taxable. Examples of things that may be taxable (by the federal, state, or local authorities) include

- Your salary
- Your interest and dividend income
- Your capital gains
- The value of your car
- The value of your home
- The value of your boat
- The things you buy or sell

Some of the taxes you will pay are:

- Federal withholding (income) tax
- State withholding (income) tax
- FICA—that's the infamous Social Security and Medicare taxes
- Local and city taxes
- Use and head taxes
- Property taxes
- Sales taxes
- Dividend and interest income taxes
- Capital gains taxes (short and long term)

Tax-Free

This is the ideal form of income in many people's minds. What you see is what you keep. Unfortunately, it is easy to confuse "tax-free" from its distant cousin "tax-deferred."

Some of the things in life that are tax-free are:

- Your income if you live in state with no state income tax (but you still pay the feds—and that's the biggie)
- The increase in value when you sell your house—as long as you've lived in the house for two of the past five years and the amount you net is no more than $250,000 per owner.
- Certain pension payments in some cases (but that's years away).
- Many inheritances, at least at the federal level and at least until the beginning of 2011.

Tax-Deferred

This is the one that gets people in trouble. There is a huge difference between never owing tax on something and not owing taxes right now.

When taxes are deferred, it is usually to create an incentive to get people to save money. But the various government entities want their money sooner or later. Here's what happens to this money.

When you do something with your money that is tax-deferred, such as contributing to most retirement plans, you don't pay income taxes on that money—until you take the money out to use it. You do pay Social Security taxes (6.2%) and Medicare taxes (1.45%) on the money—now. Since the government (federal, state, local) have agreed to forgo current taxes on the money, they expect you to do several things:

- Leave the money to grow for a number of years (usually until you are at least 59½).
- Pay the taxes when you take the money out, just as if it were regular income. This is true even when someone retires. After all, the money *is* regular income (plus growth, interest, capital gains, and so on).
- Pay the taxes if you take the money out before you retire, and pay a significant additional penalty for taking the money early.

> **If you take money out of a tax-deferred investment, such as a 401(k) or deductible IRA, you can expect to lose 35–50% of the money in taxes and penalties, unless you are at least 59½.**

You don't pay Medicare and Social Security taxes on the money; that has already been done.

The government wants people to save for retirement because Social Security is not enough—even if private investment accounts are allowed and used. Social Security was never intended as a retirement plan; it was meant to be a supplement to other retirement plans and people's own savings. The government wants you to save for your own retirement so they make it as painless as possible (by deferring the taxes so your income doesn't fall as much) and encouraging you to stick with it by making it *very* expensive to take money out before retirement.

Practical Exercises

1. When you are still living at home, what deduction or exemption do you normally *not* take?
2. Why do you forgo this deduction?
3. The employer's contribution to your pension or retirement plan savings is often referred to as "free money." Why is it called "free money"?
4. What is the difference between tax-free, tax-deferred, and tax-deductible?

_____.

_____.

_____.

CHAPTER 19

Taxes, Deductions, and Your Income: The Details

Most of your life to date has been spent as someone else's "dependent." Even if you earned most of your spending money or paid your way through college, you were probably still a "dependent" in the eyes of the IRS. That meant your parents "took you as a deduction" on their tax return. Once you are on your own, that changes—you become your own dependent and you get both the dependent exemption and the "standard" deduction. If you itemize your taxes, you give up the standard deduction and keep records of lots of things we'll cover later in this section.

Taxes and Deductions and Benefits—While You Are a Dependent of Your Parents

As a dependent (of your parents) with a job, you are entitled to the standard deduction ($4,850 for a single person in 2005). You can also take the dependent exemption, but then your parents cannot do so. Since you probably aren't making a lot of money, and so are in a lower tax bracket than your parents, it makes sense for them to declare you as a dependent.

DEDUCTIONS AND EXEMPTIONS

While you are living at home or at college and your parents are earning far more money than you are, you can take the standard deduction, but let your parents continue to declare you as a dependent and take the dependent exemption. If you chose to take the dependent exemption, your parents cannot do so. This is rarely a good idea. When you fill out your W-4, you should indicate that you have "0" dependents.

In all likelihood, you are still covered by your parents' medical insurance, or else by a medical insurance program at school. You probably can't contribute to a company retirement plan (but you can, and should set up and contribute to a Roth IRA—more on that later). Life is fairly easy from a tax and benefits perspective, but that is about to change!

Taxes and Deductions and Benefits—Once You Are on Your Own

This is truly the heart of this chapter. You will learn about taxes, deductions, planning, benefits, retirement savings, and decision making.

When you start a job, there are many decisions to be made, and you'll see lots about that in Part Eight. In the meanwhile, let's look at a generic pay stub. You might not see all these entries on your first job's pay stub, but you'll see them sooner or later, unless you decide to skip benefits and retirement savings (not a good idea).

When you accept a job, you are told what the salary or hourly pay rate will be. Wouldn't it be nice to get the entire amount to spend for living expenses and having a good time?

As most of you already know, what you get (your gross or total salary or pay) is not what you see (your net or take-home pay). Many entities have their hands out for a chunk of your earnings. One of those "hands" should be your own, in the form of retirement savings and your share of certain insurance benefits.

Sample Earnings Statement

What does a "pay stub" look like? For starters, it doesn't look much like the "stub" you may use to record information when you write a check. That's because so much more information has to be included on your pay stub or earnings statement:

- Income
- Deductions (retirement, insurance, charity, cafeteria plan, section 125 plan, automatic payments and savings, etc.)
- Taxes (federal, state, local, Medicare, Social Security)
- Accrued vacation days
- Accrued sick leave days

Let's take a look at a pay stub my CPA gave me, based on a real employee at a real company. We'll look at each entry in detail in the rest of this section. Your pay stub won't look just like Table 19.1, but the basic elements will be there.

What do all these deductions, taxes, and abbreviations mean? First of all, you may not have all of these items, especially when you get your first job. Not all states or cities have an income tax. Not all employers have, or will let you immediately join, a 401(k) plan or have savings deducted from your check. United Way or other charitable contributions are entirely voluntary. The disability insurance (DI) and medical and/or dental insurance contributions are voluntary, but if you don't pony up you don't get the insurance. And the Section 125 Plan is also voluntary.

Jenna gets paid twice a month, so her pay period covers 15 or 16 days. The "Code" indicates she is paid a salary, not an hourly rate. Jenna has a very good job, since her "Rate" is $96,000, meaning she makes $96,000 per year. She worked 86-2/3 hours this past pay period. Her salary in this pay period was $4,000. The final column, "YTD," will show the total of each deduction for the year-to-date. Since this is the first pay period of the year, the amount is the same as the "Withheld" (for taxes) and "Amt" (for insurance and benefits) columns. Jenna gets paid the day following the end of the pay period (the "Date" at the top of her pay stub).

If Jenna Jones decides not to (or can't) participate in the voluntary deductions (Section 125, 401(k), DI insurance, medical insurance, savings program, and United Way), she will have a lot more take-home pay, but a lot less financial security.

One thing this earnings statement doesn't clearly show is that some of Jenna's deductions are taken out before income taxes (so she pays less tax) but after Medicare and Social Security taxes. Note the asterisk next to each pre-tax deduction (tax-deferred).

Effect of Taxes and Deductions on Each Item in Your Pay Stub

It's pretty obvious that taxes and other payroll deductions have a big impact on the amount of money you actually take home—your net income or net pay.

Table 19.1. Sample Earnings Statement

Employee Name	Employee ID	Social Security Number	Date	Accrued Vacation Days	Accrued Sick Days	Pay Period
Jenna Jones	2345JJ	123-XX-XXXX	01-16-2007	22	15	01-01 to 01-15 2007

Earnings				Taxes			Deductions		
Code	Rate	Hrs	Salary	Code	Withheld	YTD	Code	Amt	YTD
Salary	96K	86.67	$4000	Soc Sec	226	226	*401k	300	300
				Med	53	53	*Sec 125	150	150
				Fed	250	250	*Med Ins	50	50
				State	125	125	DI Ins	10	10
				City	25	25	United Way	50	50
							Auto-save	300	300
							Net Pay	$2461	

*Denotes pretax-deduction—made before income taxes, but after Social Security and Medicare taxes are calculated.

Table 19.2 summarizes the federal income tax brackets and rates and Social Security/Medicare tax rates for 2005. These brackets and rates are adjusted slightly most years.

Many, but not all, states have a state income tax. This takes another 2–8% or so of your income after all deductions, credits, and exemptions have been subtracted.

Some cities, counties, or other government entities may also impose an income tax.

Definitions: Taxes, Credits, Exemptions, Deductions

There are taxes, credits, exemptions, and deductions that determine your total taxable income for federal and state income tax purposes. These things *do not* affect your Medicare or Social Security tax amounts.

Taxes: The federal government and many states levy (charge you) tax on the money you earn. They also charge taxes on the money you don't earn—interest, capital gains, and so forth. Both normally allow you to reduce your income with certain exemptions and deductions. In addition, you can reduce your actual income tax obligation with certain credits (if you qualify).

Table 19.2. Federal Tax Brackets and Rates (2005)[1]—Single Filer

Tax Rate	Income Range
☐ Federal Tax	Applies to all income *after* all deductions, credits, and exemptions
10% of	$0 to $7,299.99
Plus 15% of	$7,300 to $29,699.99
Plus 25% of	$29,700 to $71,949.99
Plus 28% of	$71,950 to $150,149.99
☐ Social Security Tax[2]	Applies to all income *before* deductions, credits, and exemptions
6.2% of	$0 to $90,000
☐ Medicare Tax	Applies to all income *before* deductions, credits, and exemptions
1.45% of	Every dollar you earn

1. These rates are from the 2005 IRS tax tables. You can find these on www.irs.gov or at the back of your 1040 series tax packet.

2. Note that your employer matches the amounts you pay for Social Security and Medicare taxes.

Credits: There are many credits. These don't simply reduce your taxable income—they reduce your taxes, dollar for dollar. The two you are most likely to encounter are the "Child Credit" and the "Earned Income Credit."

Exemptions: If you have family members, you are entitled to a certain number of "exemptions." This is a way to ensure the right amount of tax is taken out of your check each pay period. It is never a good idea to take too many exemptions because you'll end up owing tax, but don't take too few, either—a refund just means you gave Uncle Sam an interest-free loan for as long as 16 months.

There is a certain strategy to calculating the number of exemptions, and it ties into the standard deduction and other types of deductions. If you are taking the standard deduction you normally want to choose "2" for the number of exemptions on your W-4 that you fill out when you start a new job. That's because the amount of the standard deduction is just about equal to two exemptions. If you put "0" you are going to get a fairly large tax refund, as the chart you'll see shortly shows.

Deductions: Everyone who pays taxes is entitled to some sort of standard deduction. There are different amounts depending on whether you are single, married, married filing separately, or head of a household (no spouse, just kids). The examples here are usually for a single person, but a quick visit to the IRS's website (www.irs.gov) will net you the information you need to calculate things if you are not single.

In many cases you are going to find the standard deduction (for 2005, $4,850 single, $9,700 married) to be more favorable than if you kept track of all your expenses and "itemized" your deductions. As long as you don't own a house, or pay lots of property and car taxes, or pay lots of state taxes, and/or buy lots of stuff that has sales taxes, you probably won't be able to itemize and exceed the single/ married standard deductions.

> **Getting Tax Advice**
>
> Even though you are just starting out, it pays to talk with a CPA or other tax professional so you understand your entitlements to reduce your taxes. The more you know about taxes now the less trouble they are likely to cause you in the future.

But it never hurts to run the numbers with a tax professional, especially if your state has a high sales or income tax, if you bought a fancy car, or if your state has high personal property taxes (like California and Colorado, for example). And if you bought a house, you almost certainly will want to itemize.

So what happens if you don't take the "right" number of exemptions? See Table 19.3.

Table 19.3. The Impact of Too Few Exemptions: For a Single Person

Income	No Exemptions	Two Exemptions
$36,000	Total tax withheld by employer: $5,665	Total tax withheld by employer: $3,963
	Total standard deduction and personal exemption from tax table: $4,850 + $3,575 = $8,425; this is the amount you get to subtract from your income before figuring your taxes	Total standard deduction and personal exemption from tax table: $4,850 + $3,575 = $8,425; this is the amount you get to subtract from your income before figuring your taxes
	Total tax actually owed by employee: $3,042	Total tax actually owed by employee: $3,042
	Refund: $2,623	Refund: $921

Of course, getting a check for $2,623 is nicer than getting one for $921, but to get that bigger check, you have to lend the entire amount to the federal government *interest free* for months—from the beginning of one year until almost the middle of the next year. Do you really want the government to have your money that long?

If you had taken $1,800 (the approximate difference in the zero- versus two-exemption refund amounts) and invested the money each month, you could have about $1,940 by the time the IRS got around to sending you your refund check for $921. So you would have $2,860 or so instead of $2,623 or so. That means it cost you about $225 to lend your money to the IRS.

Is that really what you want to do with your hard-earned money?

Impact of Social Security and Medicare Tax

Let's look at this tax first.

People tend to lump these two taxes together, but they are two separate taxes.

Medicare taxes (1.45%) are collected on every dollar you earn, with no limit and no deductions. Social Security taxes (6.4%) are collected on the first $90,000 you earn in 2005 (the amount used as the "Social Security base" rises each year).

Medicare taxes fund your eventual participation in the Medicare health benefit system, generally at age 67. Social Security taxes fund various Social Security payments—retirement is only one of these—over your lifetime.

Even if your deductions, credits, and exemptions offset all of your earned income, you still owe the combined 7.65% for Medicare and Social Security taxes. Your employer, by the way, pays the same amount on your behalf. If you happen to own the company, you end up paying a whopping 15.3%!

So, if you earn $36,000 a year, you are going to pay 7.65% of it (or $2,754) to the federal government. No way around or out of that.

Impact of Federal Income Taxes

As the chart "The Impact of Too Few Exemptions: For a Single Person" shows, your federal tax liability (assuming you take the personal exemption and standard deduction totaling $8,425) will be about $3,042. Not too bad, really—that's only about 8% of your gross income, if you make $36,000 a year.

The Total of Federal-Level Taxes

Between federal, Social Security, and Medicare taxes, you owe about 15.65% of your total income in taxes. That's really not too bad—about $242 each pay period (assuming you are paid twice a month, at that same $36,000 per year).

If this was all you had to pay, you'd be in good shape—you'd still have $1,258 each pay period.

Of course, life is never that simple or that cheap!

Impact of Other Deductions from Your Pay Check

There are a number of other expenses to consider when figuring how much you'll really have to live on—your net or take home pay.

Here's a fairly complete list:

- State taxes
- Local/city taxes
- Head or use taxes
- Retirement plan contributions
- Voluntary short-term disability insurance contributions
- Voluntary long-term disability insurance contributions
- Voluntary life insurance
- Health insurance premium—employee portion
- Other voluntary deductions (specialty insurance, loan payments, savings bond purchases, United Way contributions, etc.)

All of these expenses or deductions are taken out of your pay *after* the Social Security and Medicare taxes have been subtracted. Some of these expenses are taken out before federal and state taxes are calculated, and some after federal and state taxes are calculated.

The main expense that comes out before other taxes are computed is your contribution to the company-sponsored retirement plan.

Some expenses can be either before- or after-tax deductions depending on how your employer has set things up. This includes short- and long-term disability and your share of your medical/health group insurance premium.

The other expenses are almost always paid from your income after federal, state, and local taxes are calculated.

How Much Tax Do You Owe? What's Your Take Home Pay?

Assuming the twins make $36,000 per year and take the standard deduction, Table 19.4 shows the impact of Alex's and Phoenix's choices:

Table 19.4. Alex the Saver vs. Phoenix the Spender

	Alex	*Phoenix*
Semimonthly take-home pay	$1,500	$1,500
Social Security & Medicare taxes	7.65% • $1,500 = $115	7.65% • $1,500 = $115
Retirement plan contributions	10% • $1,500 = $150	$0
Deductible health insurance contribution	$50	$0
Net taxable income	$1,300	$1,500
Other deductions	Disability: $25	None $0
Total federal-level taxes due:	$212	$242
Total take-home pay	$948	$1,143

As you can see, Phoenix's habit of refusing to plan for the future or emergencies is coming through loud and clear. Phoenix has a lot less deducted from each pay check—but also pays more taxes.

By putting $300 ($150 × 2) each month into the company retirement plan, Alex will probably never have to increase the amount saved for retirement or even think about retirement. By participating in and contributing to the company health insurance plans, the majority of Alex's medical bills will be covered. If Alex is suddenly hurt in a skiing or boating accident, the paycheck will continue, thanks to the disability insurance deduction. That's a lot of assurance for not too much money.

STARTING NOW INSTEAD OF LATER

It really is easiest to start a retirement plan as soon as you are able. There are three reasons for this:

- Being newly out of school, you are used to having very little so when you suddenly have a lot it is easier to give up 10–15% to not have to think about the future too much.
- You get to take the maximum advantage of the time value of money—the value of compounding.
- Your employer usually matches the money you set aside, so you get free money. There's an example shortly that shows how valuable this employer matching contribution can be.

If Alex continues to save just $300 per month for the next 40 years (at 8%), and Phoenix continues to do nothing, look at the difference at retirement (Table 19.5).

Table 19.5. Saving $300 Per Month for 40 Years vs. Saving Nothing for 40 Years

Alex—$300/Month	Phoenix—Nothing
Total amount saved: $144,000	Zero, nada, nothing, zilch
Value of compounding: $903,302.35	Zero, nada, nothing, zilch
After 40 years: $1,047,302.35 (approximately, before taxes)	After 40 years: Zero, nada, nothing, zilch

There are two "hidden" benefits to Alex's savings—the employer probably matches at least 3% of the salary, or $90 each month, and Alex's contributions are made before income taxes are taken out, so the take-home pay is reduced by less than $300.

Adding the Employer Matching Contribution for 40 Years

If Alex's employer matches contributions with 3% of total salary, that is another $90 per month. If this match continues unchanged for the next 40 years, Alex will have an additional $314,190 to add to the $1,047,302. That makes a nice start to a great retirement—$1,361,492—assuming the level of contributions stays the same and earns about an 8% return.

In reality, a saver like Alex will probably increase the amount saved over the years, in both retirement and non-retirement accounts, including the very valuable Roth IRA, and will have pots of money with very little effort.

Phoenix—the spender—will have to flip burgers at a fast food joint to supplement Social Security unless he or she makes some *big* changes early on.

Practical Exercises

1. Name at least eight kinds of taxes or other deductions you might find have come out of your paycheck.

_____.

_____.

_____.

_____.

_____.

_____.

_____.

_____.

2. What is the difference between total (gross) pay and take-home pay?

_____

_____

_____

_____

_____

_____

_____

_____

_____

_____.

3. Your employer offers you the chance to be part of the company group health insurance plan. There is one catch—you have to pay 25% ($100 per month) of your premium. What do you feel are the pros and cons of paying or not paying this money?

_____

_____

_____

_____

_____

_____

_____

_____

_____

_____

_____.

CHAPTER 20

Basic Tax Planning

Taxes are something no one really wants to pay, but they are the price of living in our society. You get a lot of benefits from your tax dollars. At the same time, there is no reason to pay more than you owe, or to give the government (state or federal) an interest-free loan.

A little planning and information go a long way to reducing your tax burden. Here are some tips you can probably use.

1. Go to the www.irs.gov website and poke around. There is a lot of useful information there.
2. The IRS website has a "tax calculator" you can use to determine how many exemptions you should list on your W-4 to keep from paying too much in taxes. Enter "tax calculator" in the search field on the IRS website and follow the steps.
3. Work with a professional tax advisor at least long enough to understand whether you should itemize your deductions or take the standard deduction.
4. If you are married and have children, you may be eligible for some very valuable tax credits—talk to a professional.
5. If you live in a state with no income tax, keep receipts for everything you bought so you can get the maximum sales tax deduction if you itemize.
6. There are times that are better than others for buying a home—you get certain deductions and these deductions may be worth more—get you a bigger tax savings—in some years than others.

Taking too few exemptions (or none, for that matter) just to get a bigger tax refund check is rarely a good idea. You are far better off increasing your exemptions to the point you don't get a refund and putting the extra money into a retirement plan, Roth IRA, emergency reserve account, and/or other investments.

Avoid trouble in future years by keeping copies of all your tax forms and supporting documents for seven years. This includes your copies of the actual 1040 form, state tax forms, and all attachments (schedules) and forms, such as 1099s and W-2s.

8

Getting (and Losing) a Job

There are statistics galore about how many jobs (and different careers) you are likely to have over your working life. Even if you get one job and keep it your entire life (not likely!), you need to plan to get *that* job. Most people born in the second half of the 20th century can expect to hold five to ten jobs, or more, in two or three different career fields. In addition, virtually no one is exempt from lay-offs and firings and down-sizing and right-sizing and consolidation and mergers. That means you may be on the "finding" and "losing" sides of the job search several times in the next few years.

From teenaged clients at the Young American's Financial Center:

1. How many years do you expect to spend working in your chosen career?
2. How many "careers" do you think you will have?
3. What is your current career choice?
4. Why this career?
5. At what age do you want or expect to be able to retire?
6. How many years do you think you will spend in retirement?

1. Until retirement. 2. One. 3. Media Production 4. It's a passion, not a job. I enjoy production. 5. 60. 6. 20 years+ —Derek N., 15

I expect to work at least 35–40 years in a career of my choice. I hope to have the experience of more than one career; however, I currently do not have any real plan or direction for a career in any specific field. I hope to be able to retire at an age close to 60, but do not know where my career(s) will lead me.—Kris Z.

1. Until retirement. 2. One [career]. 3. Sports broadcasting. I thoroughly enjoy sports. [I expect to retire at] 60, [and be retired at least] 20 years.—Vanessa N., 17

I expect to spend four years in college studying business. I believe I may have a couple of jobs after college but will soon settle down. I've always wanted to do something in business because it's very important but I don't know in what specific field. I hope I will be able to retire at an early age as an option but I want to work for as long as I can. I don't want to retire.—Kai Ge Y.

And a young working adult answered this way:

My current career choice is working with [a bank] as a program assistant. Although I wouldn't classify this position as a career, I do hope to find my niche somewhere within this organization. Once I do find my "career" I would expect to work at least five years. From there I expect to have about five career changes at which point I hope to retire at 65–67 years old. As for my time in retirement I think that's for time to tell.—Libby M.

CHAPTER 21

Finding the "Perfect" Job

How do you define the "perfect" job? Is there really any such thing? While nothing is ever exactly what you plan it to be, you can still come close if you actually *have* a plan for your job search.

THE PERFECT JOB

Here's one definition of a "perfect" or "dream" job: When you wake up in the morning and usually look forward to going to work, are able to sleep without worrying about your job, don't think much about work during your time away, and make enough money to cover your budget and some of your dreams, then you have as close to a perfect job as you're likely to find. Sure, there will be some days when you absolutely, positively don't want to get out of bed, especially to go to work. There will be times you want to quit right now. On these days, promise yourself you'll get up *this time* and go to work, or wait until tomorrow to tell someone you want to quit. Twenty-four hours later, things almost always look a lot different. If things are just as bad the next day, and the bad feeling lasts for more than a week, it's time to talk to someone outside work about the situation.

Don't blow off steam to people at work—every office has its snitches, and you don't want to become the "snitchee." Give it a few weeks of talking to an outside professional and then start looking for other alternatives—quietly, and not on the office computers!

When you started looking at colleges, were you methodical or did you take a haphazard, scattered approach? I hope you were at least somewhat methodical, because that approach is just what you'll need to use in your job search.

Getting Started in Your Job Search

Whether you're looking for your first part-time job, your first job after graduation, or planning to change jobs (or careers), it really pays to have a plan of attack.

You've probably heard the statement, "Plan on spending at least one month for every $8,000–10,000 you expect to earn each year." This is really a true, although general, statement.

Think about it: If you are graduating college at the end of next semester, that means you have about four months, plus the remainder of this semester, to find a job. If it's October now, and you graduate in early to mid-May, that's only about six or seven months. It's no coincidence the recruiters show up on campus in October and November. If you expect to earn $45,000 or so, and it takes a month per $8,000 of salary, you do the math.

The same applies if you are looking for a part-time job when you turn 16, or want a job for the summer after each year of college, or are going to work full-time after high school. In order to start an $8.00 per hour job (the equivalent of about $16,000 per year full-time), you need to start looking about two months *before* you turn 16. If you are looking for a $12.00 per hour job for the summer, that's the equivalent of about $24,000 per year, so you'd better look over the winter and spring break holidays. And if you are looking for a $18.00 per hour job after high school, you are planning to earn about $36,000 per year, so you need to start looking no later than the winter holiday break.

Where Are the Jobs?

In order to mount a methodical job search, you need to know where the jobs are. Let me assure you 95% (or more) are *not* in the want ads. So, where are the jobs?

Most jobs are never advertised. In fact, most job "openings" don't really exist. Instead, a potential employer has a number of areas where more effort is needed, and they find the people with a mix of skills and then fill these "openings." So how do you get yourself into this pool of skilled people?

Think "out of the box" and put yourself in the employer's shoes. People want to work with, hire, and spend time with people they know, like, and trust. So you need to be one of these known, liked, and trusted people, or get referred by a known, liked, and trusted person or source.

So, when you are searching for a job, here are the "hidden" ways to get in the door:

- Talk to your family, neighbors, classmates, and current employer about the type of job you are looking for. These are the people with the connections to help you get in the door. They know about the jobs that are never advertised, and they know the people who make the interview and hiring decisions. This is called *networking* and is a skill that will serve you well your entire life.
- Haunt the online job boards.
- Consider talking to professional recruiters if you are in a unique or high-demand field.
- Visit company websites and go to the "About Us" and then the "Jobs/Careers" tab.
- Talk to your on-campus placement office staff.
- Make sure you can outline, in 30 seconds or less, what you are looking for in a job. This is called an "elevator speech" because you should be able to give the speech to a complete stranger in the time it takes to go a few floors in an elevator.

Websites

There are hundreds of job search websites out there. You need to become an expert at searching the right sites in the right ways or you will experience information overload!

Learn to do key word, industry, and job title searches. Don't just look at all the jobs in a given area. If you are an aerospace engineer, and like to write, you might search for "aerospace, engineer, writer, writing, technical, proposal" rather than just "aerospace engineer."

Make sure you read the entire job posting, and comply with all the requested procedures. Here's an easy way to make sure you don't overlook any stated requirements:

- Use the copy-paste feature to copy the "requirements" part of the job description into a blank document.
- Use this pasted material to create the (almost always) required cover letter. You can cut and paste and address each listed item in a short paragraph in the cover letter.
- If you are applying by e-mail, you now have the cover letter that forms your actual message. Make sure the formatting you used looks okay in the e-mail before you send it.
- Now all you have to do is attach your résumé (or paste it if that's what the employer wants).
- The final step? Create a folder called "Job Search—Month" and save a copy of the job posting and your cover letter (for each job) in it.

Never, ever do anything related to a job search from your employer's computer system. Many companies have "tracking" software in place and you could easily get fired. The same applies to any other personal use of company computers.

If you don't want the boss to know your personal business, then don't do it at work. One exception to this is your company's intranet—if there is one. Once you've been in your current position for a year or two, you should be regularly looking for ways to move up in the company, and a new job at a higher level is ideal.

Here are some of the most popular websites:

- www.monster.com
- www.hotjobs.com
- www.dice.com
- www.careerbuilder.com

To get more ideas, ask your school counselors and placement offices, and ask your fellow students and employees. Do a Web search, too. There are lots of "boutique" job search sites that aren't advertised outside a particular industry.

To Register or Not to Register

Most of the job/career search websites want you to register, post your résumé, and take e-mails from their advertisers. I advise you to *not* do any of these things. In fact, you should make sure your system doesn't accept anything but "per session" cookies from these places, and regularly run spyware and ad aware programs.

Posting your résumé is not a good idea—you never know who will see it. Your boss might be patrolling the sites looking for people like you . . . and then it is known you are job-shopping.

Other Services on Job/Career Search Websites

Most of the websites that are geared toward job seekers also have features such as salary surveys, company information, city information, and résumé creation services. These are very worthwhile as starting places to get useful information.

Working with Recruiters ("Headhunters")

If you have a few years of experience in your field, or you are a specialist or expert in an area (such as a type of software, SAP, Oracle, or machine tooling), you might find recruiters contacting you. The same is true if you have a security clearance. You may also want to approach these "headhunters" when you are considering making a career or job change.

Many recruiters take a roundabout approach to seeing if you are open to new opportunities—they ask you if you know "anyone" who might be interested in a particular job or company. What they usually want is for you to say, "No, I can't think of anyone, but I might be interested. Tell me more." That is fine. If you are tempted to give out someone's name, never do so without that person's permission. You could get that person or yourself into a lot of trouble and out of a job.

Keep in mind not all recruiters work or get paid the same way. How they get paid is not your problem, though, so avoid the ones who expect you to pay for their services. That is the hiring company's problem.

Creating Your Résumé

You need to have a résumé and you need to keep it current, even when you are in love with your present job. Companies merge, go out of business, lay off people, hire terrible new managers, and so forth, so you could be looking for a job tomorrow. And the average person in his or her 20s today is probably going to work in several careers and a dozen jobs or companies before retiring.

It never hurts to be prepared.

Dos and Don'ts

Here are some things you *must* do:

- Make sure your résumé is letter-perfect. Some people are grammarians and will see nothing but red if they see a typo or grammatical error. Then it's off to the reject pile with your résumé.
- Make sure your résumé is easy to read—lots of white space, simple sentences, and short words.
- Make sure your résumé is written in the first person. After all, it's your time to shine.
- Keep it to one page. You are going to have lots of time to build a two-page résumé.
- E-mail your résumé to several different ISPs to see what the bullets and formatting look like after a few servers have handled the document. You may be rudely surprised.
- Have more than one version of your résumé if you are looking for different types of jobs.
- Use a cover letter every time you send your résumé (even via e-mail) and use the cover letter to add the details that are unique to the position for which you are applying.
- Update your résumé at least every six months, every time you get a new position or promotion, and whenever your focus or objectives change.
- If you put an "objective:" on your résumé, it should be specific. Better to leave that item for the cover letter so you aren't always having to change your résumé.

Here are some things you should *not* do:

- Don't use fancy paper—clean white printer paper is fine. Your résumé is going to get photocopied and/or e-mailed anyway.
- Don't use fancy fonts or bullets—they can get really messed up when you e-mail or scan the résumé.
- Don't use colored ink or paper. They don't copy, scan, or e-mail well.
- Don't put personal information (hobbies, sports, etc.) or "References available upon request" on your résumé.

Style and Format

Keep your résumé simple. Don't try to "wow" the prospective employer. You are relatively new to the job scene and employers know this. If you blow smoke, the hiring managers will quickly figure you out.

The Importance of the Truth

How important is the truth? Unbelievably so, given the ease of verifying information.

Here's what happened to an acquaintance of mine who "stretched" the truth a little bit. It made the local papers and even ran in some other states.[1]

When Alan saw the posting on the city website for a Manager of Contracts, he knew he was a perfect fit. He had all the skills and met all the requirements posted—except the four-year college degree. So he decided to apply and "fudge" just a bit. Instead of his résumé reflecting that he attended, but did not graduate from, a four-year college, he wrote the text in such a way it appeared he actually had a business degree from a Midwestern college. He did take a number of relevant business courses but dropped out after four years without getting his degree.

When the local press investigated Alan's background, they were acting on a tip from a person who had also applied and lost the job to Alan. Sour grapes, maybe, but Alan also lied by omission.

The end result? He lost the offer of a $75,000 government job (and its great benefits) and was pilloried in dozens of newspapers. Alan eventually moved to another state.

The irony of it all? Alan was very well-qualified for the job, and according to the job posting, relevant course work and work experience could substitute for the college degree—both of which Alan had in abundance!

It is so easy for a potential employer (or a college, for that matter) to verify almost anything you claim. Google searches, background checks, and so forth make it easy. Don't even think about lying, or stretching the truth, whether by commission or omission.

Selecting References

References are one of the many ways employers try to verify your personal, educational, and work data.

Before you offer someone's name as a reference, you should do several things:

- Get that person's permission!
- Make sure you have correct, complete contact details for the reference—name, telephone number to be used, time to call, mailing address, and e-mail address.
- Make sure that person is going to say good (and truthful) things about you and your work.
- Give the reference some talking points about your best skills and traits.

When Your Grades Aren't So Good . . .

Finding a job when you are in school or newly graduated is hard. If you didn't get the best grades, you need to have a very good reason—employers will want to know why.

If you simply goofed off, you are going to have to try to make up for this by having excellent references and acing the interview.

If your grades suffered because you had to work to help pay for college, make sure that is very clear in your résumé. Work experience is worth a lot to potential employers, especially if it only affected your GPA by a half point or so. Your cover letter is a good place to emphasize that "I worked as a waiter, 20 hours a week, at the same restaurant during my entire college career. As a result I was able to pay 75% of my tuition and cover the rest with student

---

1. Names and some details have been changed.

loans." The employer can read between the lines—you are hard-working, reliable, and don't hop between jobs. Yes, your grades aren't so hot, but you are a proven worker.

Interview: Dress the Part

You may be a poor college student, or the working attire may be business casual, but that doesn't mean you get to dress down for your interview. If you aren't sure what to wear, ask a counselor. Or call the company human resources department and ask. No jeans, no shorts, no midriffs, no sleeveless tops, and no ultra-short skirts or spike heels, please!

When You Land That First Job

Many things should go without saying, but you're entering a new world, so here are some tips that will become second nature in no time:

- Write thank-you notes to everyone who took the time to talk to you (at the employer's office) and help you get the interview (at school, other contacts).
- Make sure you bring all requested information and documents with you the first day. That means proof of the right to work in the U.S.—your passport or your Social Security card and driver's license, for example.
- Make sure you bring a check (marked VOID) so you can sign up for automatic deposit of your paychecks.
- Have a copy of your transcripts and résumé.
- Be at least 20 minutes early.
- Consider doing a site "reconnaissance" the day before so you know which road to turn on, how long it takes to get there, where the Human Resources (HR) building and your work building are, where to park, and so forth. This is a great stress-reducer.

What Happens Your First Week

A lot goes on during your first day and week at any new job. You're going to have lots to read, lots to sign, and decisions to make. Preparation is critical because some of the decisions you make may not be changed for months, if ever.

Choosing Benefits

You are going to have to make a number of decisions about employer-sponsored and other benefits. The specifics are covered in several other sections of this book (see taxes, investments, and insurance). You'll have to decide whether you want to take health insurance (absolutely, even though it may cost you some bucks!), join the retirement plan once you're eligible (absolutely, as with health insurance), and whether you want to buy disability insurance (another good idea, but it's rarely paid for by your employer).

You'll also need to let the HR people know how you want to get paid—by check or payroll deposit. Payroll deposit is a good idea. There are forms to fill out (see the tax section and Appendix B) so you don't pay too much or too little in taxes.

Getting into the Routine

Every company is a bit different, and it always seems overwhelming your first few days or weeks. Seek out someone who has only been there a year or two. They will remember what it was like to be in your shoes, and you'll be amazed at how confident they are. In a month you'll be almost as sure of yourself, hard as it is to believe right now.

Getting and Managing Your First (and Future) Paychecks

Most companies pay "in arrears." That means you get paid for last week's work at the end of the following week, or the past two weeks at the end of the following week. It makes for a grim first month—no money coming in—so be prepared.

The tax section gives you more information about what comes out of your paycheck and why, but here's a rough idea to avoid a shock when you get your first check:

Assume about 30–40% of every paycheck will be taken for taxes and your contribution to health insurance. If you are making $3,000 per month and are paid twice a month, here's what to expect.

If your first day is the 1st of the month, and you get paid twice a month, you will probably get your first check on the Friday following the 15th of the month. Since you get paid twice each month, you will get $1,500, less taxes and other items. If your taxes are 30% and your health insurance contribution is $50 each month, you will only get $1,025, not $1,500. That's because 30% of $1,500 is $450, and half of $50 is $25, for a total of $475 in deductions from every paycheck.

Dealing with Problems

Life is full of issues and problems. Even if you love you job, there are likely to be things you are less-than-thrilled about. Sometimes situations can become major problems.

Be very careful about burning bridges.

Co-Workers

You don't get to choose your co-workers but you still have to work with them and get things done. There will always be some people you simply will not like, but that's too bad. You should not quit a job just because someone in the next cubicle made you mad, or didn't contribute his or her fair share to a project.

One of the worst things you can do is become known as a "complainer," so you have to be positive in your workplace dealings, but there are times when you need to work through your supervisor and/or HR to resolve issues.

Bosses

Not all bosses are like Donald Trump in the show *The Apprentice* but not all bosses are easy to deal with, either. The same considerations apply as with co-workers. Be very careful if you complain about the boss to anyone at work—there are snitches everywhere.

If the situation is careening out of control, and talking to your boss does not work or is not an option, go to HR. Be prepared to be made uncomfortable by HR and by your boss, though. If the situation is bad, you may have to look for another position in the company or go somewhere else.

Case Study

Marcus, a soon-to-be graduate of a prestigious culinary institute, is just starting to think about what he'll do after graduation. He used a very focused, methodical approach to choose his culinary arts program, and plans to tackle his job search the same way.

Marcus is a regular at the campus career assistance and placement office. He's the first to sign up for interviews when recruiters come to campus, even if he doesn't think the job is a fit. He wants to find out as much about the industry as possible, and he figures talking to people in the business is a good way to start. Besides, he believes (rightly) that if he makes a good impression the recruiter will remember him when a more suitable position comes up. He even bought a nice suit from an upscale resale shop to ensure he makes a good impression at his interviews.

Marcus also works part-time for a catering company and has made sure he gets to rotate through all the areas of the business—serving, cooking, cleanup, sales, and marketing. Now he knows that business pretty well. He also worked at a top-notch restaurant in town, first as a busboy, then a host, then a waiter, and finally as a sous chef-in-training. He also took the time to learn a bit about the financial side of the business. He made some great contacts in the business world at these jobs—he's a very likeable, pleasant, but focused fellow.

One of his business contacts has invited Marcus to attend a number of events that attract lots of business owners from all types and sizes of businesses. This is giving him great contacts for his job search.

Of course, Marcus devotes at least an hour a day to searching the job sites and e-mailing queries and letters and résumés out. He also devotes an hour to following up on his e-mails and contacts, and always writes a thank-you note to anyone who takes the time to talk to him or help him or interview him. Can you imagine the impact of a hand-written thank-you note in today's impersonal electronic world? Of course, Marcus makes it a point to collect business cards so he has a great database of potential referral sources and contacts.

Marcus may not get a job tomorrow, but he has an excellent chance at getting the type of job he wants and ensuring there is "move-up" potential. He is almost certain to get a much better job—in terms of roles, responsibilities, satisfaction, and pay—than most of his peers. He is doing just about everything he can, and doing these things in the right way at the right points in time.

Practical Exercises

1. Find and check out at least three job websites that specialize in areas of interest to you. Skip the big sites like www.monster.com, www.dice.com, www.hotjobs.com, and www.careerbuilder.com and see what you can find that is less visited and more suited to you and your goals.

    _____

    _____

    _____

    _____

    _____

    _____

    _____

_____

_____

_____

_____

_____.

2. Write down your job search strategy, using the approach in the case study to get ideas if you need them.

_____

_____

_____

_____

_____

_____

_____

_____

_____

_____

_____

_____

_____

_____

_____

_____.

CHAPTER 22

Losing Your Job/Changing Jobs

The old days when someone went to work at a company and expected to retire from the same company 40 years later are long gone. Your parents' generation started the job-hopping and merger mania, and the Information/Internet Age virtually guarantees you will be even more mobile and flexible.

You can lose your job for a number of reasons, so it pays to prepare for any or all possibilities. How do people lose their jobs?

- Voluntarily—taking a new job, volunteering to be laid off, quitting
- Involuntarily—being laid off, being fired, through disability

Planning for the Inevitable

Leaving Voluntarily

If you make the decision to leave to take a new job, take a leave of absence, or simply quit, you are on your own. You have to have the resources to cover your expenses (and your health insurance) until you start another job and have an income and benefits again.

If you are offered the choice to take a severance package—a form of lay-off—you will get some financial help from the company. You may or may not be able to apply for unemployment benefits once your severance package runs out.

Leaving Involuntarily

The most common reason someone leaves a company involuntarily is through lay-offs. Even if you are laid off, most employers are under no obligation to offer a severance package. You get paid for unused vacation days, possibly for sick days, and that's it. Then you have to apply for unemployment benefits if you don't have a new job.

If you are terminated for cause you may not be able to collect unemployment benefits. Each state is different. It pays to have the resources to pay your expenses for several months so you can get by for six or eight months without a job.

When You Think You Were Wrongfully Terminated

Talk to your state's Department of Labor. Every state is different in its rules and procedures.

Keep notes and records of conversations, e-mails, and so forth, especially if your work situation is heading south.

Filing for Unemployment

Your state Department of Labor is a good source of information. If you are eligible for unemployment compensation, your HR department may tell you, but it may not. Finding out is up to you.

Starting the Search Again

Once you are unemployed, you can stay that way as long as you can afford to live without a job. However, if you are collecting unemployment compensation, there are limits on part-time work and requirements to actively seek a new position. You have to prove you are looking—with written materials and contacts at companies.

Managing Your Resources during Unemployment

No one expects to become unemployed, but it is going to happen, and probably sooner rather than later in your career.

In other sections of this book there is financial information you need. One of the most ignored, yet important, things you need to do is build a cushion for emergencies. For every month you expect a job search to take, you need at least half of a month's expenses. As long as you are eligible for unemployment benefits, that money should cover the other half month. If you have three months' expenses set aside, this gives you about six months to find a new job before your money runs out.

Some things have to go when you're not working. Credit cards are the first thing to put away. Put them in the freezer if you must, but do everything in your power not to use them. You're going to feel blue and may be tempted to "charge it" to make yourself feel better—but all you'll be doing is digging a very deep hole.

Take a hard look at your expenses—you'll find lots of things to cut. Don't buy books and magazines—haunt your local library. Skip meals out—entertain your friends at your house with a potluck supper. You'll be amazed at how much "fat" there is in your spending.

Don't cut everything, though. Maybe you can go from DSL to dial-up, and give up the expanded cable for a while and go back to basic. Keep and use your health club membership. You get the picture.

Taking a Leave of Absence—Pros and Cons

It's tempting to work for a few years and then take a several month leave of absence, or not start to work right out of school and travel for a month or two. Here are some things to consider—from someone (me) who took a leave of absence and loved it.

You are going to need resources to cover both your expenses while on your leave, and your first few weeks after your return to work since you will go a few weeks before that first paycheck gets deposited. Keep in mind your employer may fill your job while you're gone so you might end up on a "leave of quit." Then you need even more money until you find a new job.

Here are some of the pros for taking a leave of absence:

- You can experience new people, places, and things.
- You can explore other career and life options.
- You will probably become more self-confident and easygoing.
- It's often easier to manage a leave when you're young and relatively unencumbered (with a house, family, and so forth).

Here are some of the cons about taking a leave of absence:

- No income.
- Loss of seniority at work.
- Possibly no job to come back to.
- Gaps on your résumé.

Filling the Gaps on Your Résumé

If you take a leave of absence, or are unemployed for a period of time, filling out applications and having an broken job history on your résumé are going to be a problem. However, just as not having top grades can be managed, so can gaps in your work history.

Some employers value employees who are risk-takers—willing to take a leave of absence and experience new things. Academia and medicine often include "sabbaticals" as part of the job, so they may welcome your adventurism.

Don't try to "stretch" other experience to reduce the gaps—acknowledge the gaps. If you were researching a possible book, for example, say so—put that in the "gap" if it's true.

Going "Temp"

Maybe you can't find the job you want, or any regular job for that matter. There are lots of temporary placement agencies that can help you with part-time or short-term work. This serves several purposes:

- Avoids gaps in your work history
- Keeps the income flowing
- Gets you lots of experience you might otherwise never have had

Freelancing

Some people don't want to work for a big company or have decided to become an independent contractor. At this point in your working life, this may not be the approach for you. If you think it is, talk to people in your chosen field who are current or past freelancers and join the relevant professional organizations and Chambers of Commerce. You'll need some accounting and legal assistance since you have to pay your own taxes and make sure you are protected from lawsuits.

Finding Help

Here are some Websites that can help you in the job search and job loss process. In addition to the job websites at the beginning of this article, here are some other places to check out:

- www.state.XX.us
- www.sba.gov
- www.irs.gov
- www.hhs.gov

Practical Exercise

What is your game plan for finding a job when and if you lose your present one? If you are still a student, seek out someone who has been through the process and pick his or her brain. The approach used in the case study for finding a job is an excellent starting point. What would your game plan be if you are laid off? Factor in the job search process, collecting unemployment, and maybe working part-time.

My Game Plan

_____

_____

_____

_____

_____

_____

_____

_____

_____

_____

_____

_____

_____

_____.

9

Managing Your Money: The Basics

Your money goes many places. Earlier we looked at ways to manage credit and other forms of debt such as loans and payments (expenses). Now we'll go through the other side of money—choosing and managing the ways you handle your money. That means the money going into checking and savings accounts, money market accounts, investments, pension plans, and so forth.

Successfully managing your money is a major element in achieving financial and personal success. Kai Ge Y., a teenager in Denver, defines success this way:

I define financial success by the zeros in my bank account. I define it as not having to work and being able to take care of your own family. I believe it is also determined by what a person is comfortable with. Personal success to me is being happy with what I have. Money can't make me happy forever.

CHAPTER 23

Savings Accounts

For most of you, a savings account was probably the first type of "managed money" you ever had. Maybe you had a job or an allowance and you put part of the money into a savings account at a nearby bank. Simple and convenient. As you mature, your income rises and the options for managing your money grow dramatically.

Savings accounts are pretty easy—you put money in, and you can't take out more money than you actually have. You get a few percentage points in interest on an annual basis, and that's about it.

You can have money "swept" into your savings account from your checking account, and you might have an arrangement that takes money from your savings account to pay bills or cover shortfalls in your checking account. You may even be able to have your paycheck deposited into your savings account. You might also have an ATM card that accesses your savings account balance.

But that's about it. Savings accounts are pretty limited, since if you want money you have to either go to the bank and get it, or go to an ATM if your account allows that. The interest paid is pretty miniscule, so savings accounts aren't great long-term investment choices.

So what are your other options? The next chapters will explain some of the ways to handle and keep your money.

Practical Exercise

What are the reasons you have a bank account?

Checking Accounts

Checking accounts are usually a person's first foray into the world of managing money rather than letting it accumulate in a savings account. Checking accounts are also notorious for getting neophytes—new users—in lots of trouble.

A savings account is self-limiting. When there is no money left, that's it. You can't withdraw money you don't have.

Not so with a checking account. Although you are not supposed to write checks to spend money that you don't have, people try to do this all the time. Not a good idea.

Checking accounts may pay a very low interest rate, but the purpose of a checking account is not to make money or earn interest. The purpose of a checking account is simple—to have a place to put the money that comes in and have ready access to money from anywhere to pay bills.

Unlike a savings account, you can get to your money from almost anywhere—all you have to do is write a check or use your ATM card.

Using Checks Wisely

Do you have a checking account? A well-managed checking account is a valuable tool for two things—paying bills and building a credit history.

The most important thing to keep in mind when setting up and using a checking account is this:

Never write a check unless you know you have enough money *in your account right now* to "cover" (pay for) the amount of the check. The fact that you still have checks *does not mean you still have money*!

Check Writing Tips

Here are some tips for writing checks:

- Always fill out the check completely. Don't leave blank spaces. If there is space left over after you write the amount or the "payee's" name, draw a line to the end of the space.
- Always fill out your check *in ink*.
- Always write down the amount of each check *when you fill out the check, not later*, in your check register. If you are using an electronic system such as QuickBooks, make sure to fill out every field.
- If you use an ATM or check card, *always write down the amount of the purchase or withdrawal*. It is too easy to think, "Oh, I'll remember how much I spent and write it down later."
- If you aren't sure of your balance, you can use any ATM to do a "balance inquiry."
- With the advent of "Check 21," your checks are processed electronically and the full amount will come out of your account *immediately*. Never count on "the float"—the old days of being able to write a check before depositing money or at the same time you deposit money (or your paycheck) are *gone*!

- When you deposit money or checks into your account, make sure you get a receipt from the bank or ATM. Save these receipts *and verify that the bank credits the correct amount.* Banks do make mistakes. Your deposit receipt is the only proof you have that you put money in your account. See "Balancing Your Checkbook" later in this section.
- If your account includes a monthly service charge or fee, make sure you deduct the fee. If you only keep a small balance in your account and forget to deduct these fees, you could easily "bounce" a check.
- Don't write checks that are payable to "Cash." Always make your checks payable to a person or business, or to yourself.
- Checks you write to yourself, or checks other people or businesses write to you, must be *endorsed* on the back. That means you need to sign your name on the back of the check (in the space provided), *exactly as it appears on the "Pay to the Order of"* line, and write your checking account number under your signature. *Never endorse a check until you are inside the bank or in the drive-up teller window line.* If you are depositing the check, you should also write "for deposit only" under your checking account number on the back.

Setting Up and Managing a Checking Account

Here are some tips for setting up and managing your checking account(s):

- Make sure you understand the limitations and costs associated with your checking account.
  - ◦ Many accounts have monthly and/or "per check" or "per item" fees. If your account costs $5.00 per month, and you have to pay $0.10 per item, that means you will be charged $0.10 for each check you write and each check you deposit. If you write 10 checks each month and deposit two checks each month, you are going to be charged $5.00 plus $0.10 • 10 (or $1.00) plus $0.10 • 2 (or $0.20) for a total of $6.20.
  - ◦ Many banks charge noncustomers a fee for using the bank's ATMs. In addition, your bank may also charge a fee for using another bank's ATM. If you make three ATM transactions each month at a bank where you *don't have an account,* you could easily be charged $1.50 to $2.00 by your bank and the other bank for each withdrawal. That is $1.50 • 3 (for your bank) and $1.50 • 3 (for the other bank), for a deduction of $4.50 + $4.50, or $9.00 from your checking account.
- Banks usually charge you to print your checks. You can save money using a check-printing service, but if the service makes a mistake your checks will not be any good—they won't work. You need to deduct this amount from the balance in your checking account.
- Banks may also charge a fee for your ATM card. This can easily be $10 per year. Again, you have to deduct this from your account.
- When you get your checks, always make sure the information printed on them is correct. Check the account number and your name and address.
- Most checks are only good for 90 days to six months. Deposit or cash checks as soon as you get them.

Checking Account Safety Tips

- Never have your telephone number, driver's license number, or Social Security number printed on your check. Never give out your Social Security number when writing a check; if your driver's license number or telephone number is needed, it can be written on the check when you fill out the check.

- Treat your checks like cash. If you wouldn't leave your wallet somewhere, don't leave your checks there, either! Places you should never leave your checks (or your wallet):
  - In your car
  - In your desk at school or work
  - In a locker at the gym, at work, at school, at the pool . . .
  - At a friend's house
  - Hanging in a purse on the back of a chair
  - Stuffed in a backpack unless the pack is with you
  - On the beach or at the pool
  - On the sidelines at sports practices or games
  - Out of your sight when you are away from your room or home
- Never fill in the amount to be paid unless you also fill in the person or business to which the check is to be paid.
- Never write a check for "cash."
- Never endorse a check until you are ready to deposit it in the bank or cash it.
- Notify the bank immediately, by telephone and in writing or by e-mail, if your checkbook (or any checks) are lost or stolen or missing.
- Notify the bank immediately, in writing or by e-mail, if your address, name, or telephone number changes.
- If you make a mistake on a check, do not use whiteout or try to correct the mistake. Write a new check and shred the incorrect one.
- Never throw your checks or statements away. You may need them for taxes or other reasons. Once you no longer need your canceled (used) checks, *shred them. Do not throw checks of any kind in the trash.*

> **If your checks, credit cards, wallet, Social Security card, passport, or similar things are ever stolen or lost, report the details to the nearest police station right away. Call your bank, credit card company, and so forth. Notify the three main credit bureaus to put a fraud watch on your account. Go to the Post Office to get the forms to notify the U.S. government agencies about the loss of a Social Security card or passport.**

Here is a sample check and a sample check record or ledger (Table 24.1). Each place you need to make an entry or check information has been coded with a number.

Table 24.1. Sample Check

[1] Your Full Name Street Address City, State, Zip	[2] Check # [3] Date _____
[4] Pay to _____	
[5] Amount _____	[6] $_____
[7] Memo _____	[8] Signed _____
Routing #/Account #	

Sample Check Legend

1. This denotes the place where your name and address are printed. Always make sure this information is correct as soon as you get a new box of checks. If you need to put your telephone number and/or driver's license on a check, write the information above and/or below your address.

2. This denotes the check number. Each check has a higher number than the one that came before it. When you get a new order of checks, the first number should be one number higher than the number on the last check in the old order.

   Tip: Ask the bank to start your first order of checks with 1001 instead of 001. This makes it seem you have had the account for some time. Some merchants won't even accept your check if the number is "too low"—say, lower than 500.

3. Always write today's date in this block. Do not write some future date because you need to pay a bill and don't have enough money in your account. The person or business receiving the check is going to deposit it right away—the date you put won't make a difference. As a result, your check may bounce. This is not a good thing.

4. This is the "payee" line—the "pay to the order of" line. Here is where you specify who can cash the check.

   If the check is for you, in order to get cash, write *your name, not cash,* in this space (and endorse it on the back when you are actually ready to cash the check).

   Tip: If you have two checking accounts and are moving money from one account to the other by writing yourself a check, you follow the same steps as you would if you were cashing the check or depositing a check from someone else.

   It is important to draw a line from the end of the "payee" name to the end of your check so no one can change the name. It is also important to start the "payee" name at the far left edge of the check for the same reason.

   Example: If you are writing a check to Joe's Pizza, make sure you write it like this:

   Joe's Pizza ————————————————————————————————

   not

   Joe's Pizza

   It is very easy to change the second version to:

   Mike and Joe's Pizza or Allen G. Smith

   In this case, a different pizza place could cash the check, and a person named Allen G. Smith could also cash this check.

5. This is the first of two places where you write how much the check is for. On this line you spell out the full amount *in words.* Remember that numbers between twenty-one and ninety-nine are hyphenated (except for 20, 30, 40, 30, etc.). You don't write out the "cents"—instead, write them as numbers and place the number over 100.

   Example: If you are writing a check for $53.47, you write the amount, in words, as:

   Fifty-three and 47/100 ————————————————

   It is important to draw a line from the end of the "cents" to the end of the check so no one can change the amount or write something else there. It is also important to start the amount at the far left edge of the check so no one can insert a one, or two, or nine and make the amount $153.47, or $253.47, or $953.47!

   Tip: It is very important to make sure only the intended person or business can cash your check and that they can only cash the check for the amount you intended.

There are stories about people writing a check to the Internal Revenue Service to pay their taxes, and making the check payable to:

I R S

Imagine their shock when someone, not the IRS, intercepted the check and changed the payee to the following:

Mrs. I R Smith

Instead of paying taxes, they "gave" someone named Mrs. I R Smith the money they meant to go to the IRS to pay taxes.

To make matters even worse, imagine they left some room on the "Amount" line. Instead of:

One hundred ninety-five and 31/100___$ 195.31

The check was altered to read:

Fifty-One hundred ninety-five and 31/100___$5195.31

The check might bounce, and the person who wrote it would have two problems: The IRS would not be paid, and someone else would get a lot of money that did not belong to him or her.

6. This is where you write the amount of the check in numbers. This amount must match the amount you wrote in words.

    Tip: This is an excellent time to move to your check record or ledger and record all the information: Check number, date, amount, payee, and account number or reason for writing the check.

7. This is where you put important information you and/or the person or business cashing the check will need. Most bills tell you to put your account number here. If you are buying someone a gift, or making a transfer of money to another account, write the reason here. This helps when you balance your checkbook later, and is used for taxes if you itemize.

8. Sign your check the same way you signed the forms when you opened your checking account. If you don't, it is possible the bank won't accept the check when the payee tries to deposit or cash it. Don't dash off a signature that is not recognizable, unless that's how you signed at the bank originally!

Keeping a Check Record or Ledger

A check record or ledger is a simple version of a debit/credit sheet. The checks and cash you deposit are "credits" and the checks you write, ATM withdrawals you make, amounts you use with your check card, and fees the bank charges you are "debits." As long as your credits are greater than your debits, you won't bounce checks. The only way to be sure this is the case is to write down all the deposits and charges and keep a running total.

The process is really quite simple, and with a very basic calculator, your ledger or record, a pen, and a few minutes of time, you should never bounce a check.

Most banks either send back your actual checks or copies of your checks. I highly recommend using a bank that does one of these two things. All banks also give you a summary sheet of all your checks, charges, fees, deposits, and ATM withdrawals every month. This is your monthly statement.

Balancing and Managing Your Checkbook

Balancing and managing your checkbook is a two-part process.

The first part involves writing down all the charges you incur (ATM fees, bounced check fees, monthly fees, and so forth, and all the deposits you make), and keeping a running total.

The second part involves sitting down with your monthly statement and ticking off each check, charge, fee, and deposit shown on the statement against the record in your ledger or record. When you are done, the total from your running total should match the balance on your statement, but this is rarely the case!

Why? Three reasons.

First, it is easy to make math errors.

Second, the monthly statement may not reflect all of this month's checks and charges, and may reflect checks from last month that were slow to be sent to your bank, or charges you forgot to write down.

Finally, banks *do* make occasional errors, so a deposit may be missing or wrong, a check amount may have been entered wrong, or one of your checks may have been altered.

Keeping a Running Total

This is the most important ongoing step you can take to make sure you don't bounce a check.

BOUNCING CHECKS

Bouncing (or floating or kiting) checks is a very bad practice. It is also *very* expensive! Most banks charge $20–$30 for *every* check you bounce unless you can prove the bank made a mistake. To make matters worse, your bank may charge you a fee if someone else writes you a check that bounces. Finally, every time you bounce a check you are potentially damaging your credit history. Banks can, and do, report people who bounce checks. If you can't manage your own money (the money you earn and put in your own checking account), do you really expect a bank or other entity to trust you with a credit card, car loan, or mortgage?

How do you keep this running total? The bank or place that printed your checks makes it easy. And your personal banker (the person who helped you set up your account in the first place) will help you understand the process *if you ask for help*.

If you use a system such as Quicken or QuickBooks the process is simple, as long as you enter the data. The software does all the work for you. However, data generated by a software program is only as good as the data entered. If you enter garbage, you will get compacted trash back. It's called GIGO—Garbage In, Garbage Out.

Table 24.2 shows a simplified version of the chart in a check record or ledger. We'll use our old friends Alex and Phoenix to show how a bit of sloppiness can lead to big problems.

This is Alex's checkbook (Table 24.2). Phoenix's checkbook would look more like this (Table 24.3), don't you think?

Compare this to Alex's checkbook. Phoenix forgot to write the check charges and other fees down, and delayed depositing the check from the folks (but still bought the ticket) so checks started bouncing and more fees started accruing. Phoenix is in the hole.

Each bounced check, starting with the airline ticket for the trip home for the holidays, is going to bounce and cost $20–$30 in charges. This will continue until the check from the folks is actually cleared and credited to Phoenix's account.

Always write down every action in your account—ATM withdrawals, deposits, checks, electronically deposited or deducted checks, fees, and so on. Make sure to deposit checks you receive immediately. That means less time for the person or business that wrote the check to write other checks and cause the one you have to bounce.

Table 24.2. Sample Check Ledger or Record for Alex in College

Check #/Date	Payee/Reason	Starting Balance	Check Amount, Fee, ATM Amount, or Deposit	Ending Balance
Opened account 10/01/06		$500		
1001 10/02/06	Joe's Pizza/large pizza	$500	$12.35	$487.65
1002 10/02/06	Mrs. Smith/rent—Nov. 06	$487.65	$395.00	$92.65
New checks		$92.65	$20.00	$72.65
Monthly fees 11/06		$72.65	$6.20	$66.45
Deposit 11/15/06	Paycheck from Anne's Deli	$66.45	$195.57	$262.02
1003	VOID			
1004 11/16/06	Campus Store/Books	$262.02	$55.67	$206.35
1005 11/17/06	Myself/Cash	$206.35	$20.00	$186.35
11/20/06	Non-bank ATM withdrawal	$186.35	$30.00	$156.35
11/20/06	Fee-non-bank ATM cash	$155.35	$2.00	$153.35
Deposit 11/22/06	Check from parents	$153.35	$300	$453.35
1006 11/29/06	Airline for Dec. flight home	$453.35	$250.35	$203.00

This is a simple ledger, but you can see how failing to write down a few ATM and other charges could quickly lead to bounced checks. The smart money manager also made sure to wait a few days before writing checks against deposited checks, and always deducted checks he or she wrote right away.

Balancing Your Checkbook

Keeping a running total of the checks, deposits, charges, and other expenses associated with your checking account is a very necessary activity. However, sometimes both you and the bank make mistakes. (In fact, there are a few errors in the ledgers above; can you find them?) This is where your records, the deposit slips, your bank statements, and a few minutes of your time come into play.

Checks do not usually clear your checking account in the same order you wrote them. Why?

Table 24.3. Sample Check Ledger or Record for Phoenix in College

Check #/Date	Payee/Reason	Starting Balance	Check Amount, Fee, ATM Amount, or Deposit	Ending Balance
Opened account 10/01/06		$500		
1001 10/02/06	Pizza	$500	$12.35	$487.65
1002 10/02/06	Rent	$487.65	$395.00	$92.65
New checks	Didn't write charge down	$92.65	????	$92.65
Monthly fees 11/06	Didn't write charge down	$92.65	????	$92.65
Deposit 11/15/06	Paycheck from Anne's Deli	$92.65	$195.57	$288.22
1003	VOID			
1004 11/16/06	Campus Store/Books	$288.02	$55.67	$232.35
1005 11/17/06	Myself/Cash	$206.35	$20.00	$186.35
11/20/06	Non-bank ATM withdrawal	$186.35	Didn't write this down	$186.35
11/20/06	Fee-non-bank ATM cash	$186.35	Didn't write this down	$186.35
1006 11/22/06	**Airline for Dec flight home**	**$186.35**	**$250.35**	**$−64.00**
Deposit 11/28/06	Check from parents	$−64.00	$300	????

If you cash a check at the bank or at an ATM, the money comes out of your account right away. If you use your ATM card like a credit card, the money comes out immediately. However, if you write a check to a person or business, the check may clear right away or take days or weeks, depending on when it is deposited.

When you get your monthly bank statement, sit down with your deposit slips, checkbook ledger, and the ledger inside your statement.

Tick off each check number on the bank statement against your check ledger. Make sure the amounts match.

Tick off each ATM or other withdrawal against your receipts.

Tick off each deposit against your copies of the deposit slips.

Make sure you have deducted all the other fees from your account (monthly fees, check fees, ATM fees, bounced check fees, and so forth).

Then subtract the checks you have written since the end of the statement and add the deposits you have made since that time, and this is your new balance. If the amount does not match what you expected the amount to be, double-check your math in your checkbook ledger. If you can't find the error, call your bank.

If you find an error in the bank statement compared to your deposits or other receipts, call the bank right away.

Case Study

Alicia got her first checking account three months ago. She thinks all she has to do is check her balance every few days online and not worry about the deposits and checks and ATM withdrawals. Do you think this is a good idea? Why or why not? Do you think "Check 21" could pose a problem with Alicia's deposits? What might happen if a deposit doesn't get recorded properly at the bank or a check Alicia wrote is cashed for more than the amount she wrote it for?

Practical Exercises

1. List five things you can do to keep your checks and check-writing safe.

   _____.

   _____.

   _____.

   _____.

   _____.

2. How do you plan to ensure you don't bounce checks?

   _____

   _____

   _____

   _____.

3. Why do you think bouncing a check hurts your credit rating and credit score?

   _____

   _____

   _____

   _____.

Managing Your ATM/Debit/Bank Card

This little card is a very important piece of plastic. Treat it like you would any other credit card or cash. It is almost always tied to your checking account, although some ATM/debit cards are tied to savings accounts.

You get a PIN (personal identification number) code with your ATM card or similar cards. If you don't like the number, go into the bank and change it. *Do not write this number down anywhere.*

As soon as you get your ATM or other credit cards, make sure to either sign the back or write "See ID for signature" in the signature block. Be very careful to *not* mark out the three-digit code on the back.

There are seven digits on the back of any credit-type card, in the strip where you sign. The first four digits are the same as the last four digits on the front of your card (and these are the numbers you may need to verify the card used for a purchase if asked). The last three digits are there to protect you (to some degree) against unauthorized use of your card over the telephone or online. The person using the card has to provide these three digits to "prove" they have the actual card.

Your ATM or debit card functions much like a credit card, except that when there is no money in your checking account (or other account associated with the card) it will not work. You must therefore treat this card like any other credit card.

When you use your ATM card (or any credit card) make sure you get it back! Be careful using it in places where it leaves your sight (such as a restaurant) to avoid being "skimmed."

SKIMMING

Skimming is an increasing problem, especially at restaurants and overseas (when you are traveling). The concept is simple—the server or other person takes your card to another area, swipes it to create your charge slip, then swipes it again through a simple magnetic strip reader. This makes a record of all the data encoded in the strip and allows the person to create a duplicate of your card. They also write down the three-digit code on the back. Then they can make a facsimile of your card, or use it online or over the telephone, and charge away.

The worst part about being "skimmed" is the thief waits a few days or weeks before using your card information, so you never know where the thievery happened. Notify your bank (and/or credit card company) *immediately* if this happens. Your liability should be limited, but that doesn't help if someone has emptied out your bank account and you have to wait to get the money back.

Three more cautions when using your ATM or debit card.

1. When you are using the ATM machine, place your body between the PIN code pad and the rest of the world. Even better, get a friend to stand behind you to block the view. People have been known to "surf" for PIN codes by watching (sometimes at a great distance) people enter PIN codes at ATMs. Then they trap your card in the machine, or pick up a copy of your receipt, and make an identical card.

2. People crowd you and then grab some of the money that spits into the bin. Then they run before you can react. Make sure there is no one within arm's length before you begin your transaction, and stay aware of your surroundings. Don't set your purse or backpack down, either; those go missing, too.

3. If an ATM takes your card, but it doesn't go all the way inside, try to pull it back out. If you can see your card but when you pull it, it seems to be stuck, you may be a victim of another kind of thievery. In this case, the would-be thief has put something very sticky in the card slot to snag your card. After you leave to report the problem, the thief goes back with pliers and pulls the card out. In the meantime, he or she "surfed" your PIN code and now has both your card and your PIN. If your card goes into an ATM and won't come back out, call your bank immediately—collect if necessary. This is especially important if the card gets swallowed while you are overseas.

Remember, you *must* write down ATM or check card transactions since they come right out of your checking account. If you forget, you are going to start bouncing checks and wrecking your credit rating and history.

Here's how one teen explains how credit cards work and why a good credit rating is important.

> Credit cards are swiped and when approved paid for by the bank that carried the card. Then at the end of each month or whatever your pay[ment] period is a statement is sent that you need to pay either the minimum balance or the full balance. A good credit rating is important for buying a house or now maybe even jobs.—Kai Ge Y.

> **Always have a record of your bank and credit card telephone numbers so you can call right away if there is a problem. Don't wait—the rules are not the same for checking accounts and ATM cards as for regular credit cards, so you could lose far more money. Then your credit can be affected and it is very hard to fix this problem with the credit bureaus.**

Practical Exercises

1. Why do you think it is a bad idea to write your ATM card PIN (or any other PIN or password) down? What steps could you take to protect your many PINs and passwords (and "make them all the same" is not a good answer).

_____

_____

_____

_____.

2. How do you keep track of your ATM withdrawals and any service fees?

_____

_____

_____.

3. What would you do if someone is standing close enough to see what you are entering at the ATM?

_____

_____

_____.

CHAPTER 26

Managing Overdraft Protection

This is a form of loan that banks offer to their best customers—those who have already proven they can handle and manage credit and do not bounce checks. The purpose of this type of loan (or line of credit) is to ensure the good customers *don't* bounce checks. Ironic, isn't it?

The practice is simple. Any checks the customer writes that exceed the amount of money in the checking account will still be paid, up to the limit of the overdraft protection. This avoids bouncing checks and paying fees for each bounced check. There are fees with the overdraft account, but as long as the customer pays everything back as agreed, nothing happens to his or her credit rating. If anything, the rating gets better—go figure!

Overdraft protection is not free. If you use it, the charges are often similar to the fees for "returned" or "bounced" checks. Expect to pay about $25–$40 every time you use this "service." In addition, you are charged interest on the overdraft since it is effectively a loan from the bank to you.

Interest on overdraft protection can be quite high. Still, while the costs are high, using overdraft protection keeps your credit history from being hurt.

CHAPTER 27

Alternatives to Checks

What if you don't want or can't handle a checking account? How do you pay bills and manage your money?

There are other ways to pay bills. These ways might not be as convenient as a checking account, but checking accounts are not for everyone.

Money Orders—Many people never have a checking account. All their money goes into a savings account and they use the money to get money orders to pay their bills.

Cashier's or Bank Checks—Many people prefer this option to a checking account. All their money goes into a savings account and they use the money to get cashier's checks to pay their bills.

Debit or ATM Cards Tied to a Savings Account—Some banks will allow these cards to be tied to the balance in a savings account. This allows some bills to be paid without using checks, cashier's checks, or money orders.

Electronic or Online Banking—This is the new wave. Bills can be paid electronically from any account you choose.

10

Getting and Paying for an Education

Education isn't cheap, even if it's free. If you're in high school, it seems like the time to go to college will never come; then all of a sudden the time is here, your planning and applications are done, and you're on your way.

Sometimes your choices have to be made even before you start choosing a college.

How did (or will) your children pay for any higher education? If they get loans, who will be repaying the money? Did they know how to find scholarships and grants? Did they actually apply for any of these funds?

One parent responded:

Just read a quote in the *AARP Magazine*, "You can take out a loan for college, but you can't take out a loan for retirement." We once felt we were able to pay the entire college bill, but the changing economy has changed our strategy. We feel we can pay room and board while they take out loans for tuition, which they will pay back. We'll have a four year overlap of two teens in college. This may change to their taking 100% loans at a low interest. We'll pay the interest during the college years and would be open to helping them after college. Scholarship information is *scarce* in high schools. There is no set method for gaining information.

According to Libby M., a young working adult who is thinking about paying for graduate school:

Although I had a college fund set up by my grandparents I would need to take out loans for grad school. I would much rather search for grants/scholarships than take out a loan because the thought of debt scares me! If I do decide to go back to school I may have to apply for these [loan] funds.

And Kai Ge Y., a teenager, had this to add:

I intend to have scholarships to pay for college but if needed I will apply for a loan and slowly pay it off for myself. I know how to find scholarships. I have applied for some of these funds.

CHAPTER 28

Choosing a High School

You may have or seek an opportunity to attend less traditional or specialized high schools, but may never have considered this as an option. Sometimes you know exactly what you want to do later in life, or you have a particular interest, and you want to go to a school that focuses on that interest.

What sort of alternative high schools are available?

Traditional high schools with special interest programs: If your town or area has more than one high school, each one may have a different specialty. For example, one school may emphasize science and mathematics while another one focuses on foreign languages or performing arts. Other schools may be focused on a "fundamentals"-based education or take a creative, "open-school" approach. It is worth calling (or having your parents call) the different schools to see if one is better for you than another.

Vocational-technical high schools: Sometimes you already know you want to be a chef or mechanic or landscape designer, and the best way to spend your high school years is at a school that provides a more specialized, hands-on education. You still get the basics of a high school education and meet all your state's requirements for a high school diploma, but you also learn a skill or trade. This type of school is much like the European system of apprenticeship. The main difference is that European apprentices generally leave school at 16 and spend several years in a factory or machine shop or restaurant kitchen. Under the American system you get the training and the high school diploma, so if later you want to go to a college you have taken the high school courses you need.

Private and religious high schools: These schools provide a high school education that meets your state's requirements, but are outside the public school system. Many private schools have special areas of academic emphasis; others are simply alternatives to public schools.

International Baccalaureate (IB) high schools: The standards and requirements for a high school-equivalent diploma in much of the world are different (and more difficult) than in the United States. The IB certification or diploma is often needed if you want to attend a college or university in another country (even Canada). Many international students in the United States attend high schools with the IB option to ensure they meet the requirements to attend their home country's universities. The programs are quite challenging—lots of variety and homework!—but the reward can be a better shot at top colleges here and abroad as well as more scholarship opportunities.

Military high schools: There are a number of military high schools across the country. Some are affiliated with military colleges, but many are not. Some are boarding schools and some are not.

Boarding schools: These are another form of private school. Some of these schools mix "day" and "boarding" students; others are boarding only.

Practical Exercise

If you are about to enter high school, or maybe your younger sibling is still in junior high school, go through each option in this chapter and write a short summary about the pros and cons as they relate to your (or your sibling's) choice of high school.

CHAPTER 29

To "Gap" or Not to Gap

Taking a year off between high school and college is becoming increasingly popular around the world. The Europeans have been doing it for decades—they call it the "gap year." Canadians, Australians, and New Zealanders also favor this character-enhancing opportunity.

Many young adults like the gap-year concept because it gives them a break from studying between high school and college and gives them the chance to travel, work, explore, and meet other young people from all over the world. Colleges and parents like the idea because a year on your own changes your perception about many things and is a great maturity enhancer (Table 29.1).

Table 29.1. Gap Year: The Pros and Cons

Pros	Cons
A year makes a big difference in outlook and maturity	Delays college entry by at least one year
Working can help pay for college	Delays college graduation by at least one year
Travel is very enriching and eye-opening	College costs will be higher due to inflation
Many colleges value this experience	Some colleges will not hold a spot open for a year
There is a chance to meet people very different from those in high school	Can't just stop after a few weeks and go on to school—have to wait for the next term

The gap year is definitely not for everyone. However, if you aren't sure you want to go to college, or don't know where you want to go, or need to earn more to pay for school, or want to travel for a year, this is certainly an option worth exploring.

CHAPTER 30

What Do Colleges Look For?

Before you can get into a college (or other post–high school program) you need to decide where you want to go, where you are likely to be accepted, where you'll "fit," and how you're going to pay the bill.

Colleges give tremendous weight to what you do, or don't do, in high school, especially your grades and activities during your junior year and the first semester of your senior year.

Why Does High School Matter?

It's so tempting to do the bare minimum to get by in high school. After all, graduation is so far away, and there's always time to make up for poor grades when you're a junior or senior, right? And who cares about extracurricular activities or your part-time job?

Colleges and universities care—a lot. Grades, activities, and work are some of the differentiators that help them decide whom they want to accept. Why would a college or university want a young adult who spent most (or all) of his high school years barely passing, sitting in front of a TV or playing video games, or counting on her parents to pay for everything? College is about life, and that life starts in high school. College admissions people know that what you do in high school is a pretty good indicator of what you'll do in college.

Grades Count

Competition for space in the top colleges and universities is becoming stiffer, and the more popular branches of your state schools aren't much less competitive. In fact, some state schools are harder to get into than many private colleges, especially if you are not a state resident. So now colleges look back to all four years of high school, not just the last two years.

Activities Count

Why would colleges care what you do outside of the hours you spend in class? Because they want students who know that life is about more than just going to class and getting good grades. Grades are very important, but there are lots of smart people out there who never fit into college or post-college society because *all* they know

> If you are the Playstation champion of your high school, colleges are not likely to be impressed. If you design a new game for the Playstation, that carries a lot of weight. If you earn lots of As and Bs but never go out for a sport or work on the yearbook, you may miss out on an offer from the college of your dreams. Colleges want "well-rounded" students. If you want to get a full scholarship, you need to be very diversified *and* have good grades. The military academies, as an example, provide a four-year full scholarship and several hundred dollars a month, but you need top grades, at least one varsity sport, and several other activities or you won't even be considered.

how to do is study and get good grades. Colleges and universities want to turn out graduates who can succeed in the work world, and work is not about grades. The things you learn are essential, but it is the activities outside school that help you apply your knowledge.

So what activities do colleges look for? Volunteering, activism, sports, clubs, student government, coaching—almost anything that requires your active participation. Passive activities like video gaming, Internet surfing, TV watching, music downloading, and watching thousands of movies don't make the list, unfortunately!

Part-Time Work Counts

Colleges and universities are often very interested in applicants who have worked part-time, especially over summer and other vacations. Working shows you can manage your time and understand the need to earn money. Of course, it's very important to make sure your grades and other activities don't suffer because of your job.

College is a very sheltered environment (just like high school) because what you do there—study and go to classes—is not what you will do when you go out into the real world and start working full-time. That's why college admissions people like to see that you already know about the work world.

Looking for Scholarships and Other Money?

The College Planning section has lots of information on this hot topic. As you go through your high school years, it's worth reading this section so you can do some planning and maximize the money you can get for college. The more money you get, the greater your choice of colleges. The more money you get that doesn't have to be repaid, the more you'll have to spend when you graduate.

The Ideal Mix

Is there an "ideal" mix of grades, activities, and work? What do colleges *really* look for? What do scholarships committees really want from you?

Unfortunately, there is no magic formula that ensures you'll get into the college or university of your choice or get the money you need to pay for college. However, there are some things you can do to increase your chances of admission.

- Good grades are absolutely essential, but you already know that. But grades are not everything. If your grades are a bit lower than someone else's, but you have a diversified list of activities and interests, that is very important. Colleges want a diverse student body, not a group of brainiacs.
- Activities such as sports, clubs, the yearbook or newspaper, student government, and so forth, make you very attractive to college admission decision makers. Doing things while maintaining good grades shows you can manage and budget your time. This also shows you are interested in and aware of the world around you. Schools want diversity. You are also more likely to get more out of the college experience if your interests extend beyond your books.
- A part-time job during high school is just as valuable as other activities. Holding a job while keeping good grades shows you can manage your time. You are also learning important life skills that make you far more

likely to do well in college and the real world. If you are planning to work (work-study, co-op, part-time) at college, showing you can juggle work and school is something the colleges look for.

- Volunteering is also a good thing to have on your application. Community involvement almost always interests college admissions staff.
- Standardized test scores count, too. If you are taking the PSAT or similar tests, take them seriously. Ditto the SAT and ACT. Colleges can (and do) request *all* your test scores, so if you blow off the test ("I can always take it again next term") it can hurt your application. Attitude counts!

The Importance of Giving Back

Right now you have so much, and you are on the threshold of so much more. Isn't it time to think about what you can do for others? Isn't it great to know your services are in such demand? Even better, you can do something for others while doing something for yourself, and getting invaluable life experience at the same time.

How? You can volunteer.

If you've been looking for a job, you've probably already encountered the "no skills, no job" response. If you don't have skills and experience it's very hard to get any job, and almost impossible to get a job that is more than unskilled. But you have to have a job to get skills and experience, so what are you to do?

Volunteer.

Colleges love to see "volunteered as a (fill-in the blank)" on your application. It shows them you are able to think about more than just "what's in it for me" and it shows you are organized and have obtained valuable real-world experience and skills.

Employers like to see the same type of experience. Many employers feel it is their duty to give back to the community so they sponsor events such as a Habitat for Humanity house, or a Race for the Cure event. To fit in at a company, you need to fit the corporate culture. If the corporate culture includes volunteering, you are way above the competition if your résumé includes volunteer activities.

Where can you go to become a volunteer?

- Ask at your school.
- Ask at your place of worship.
- Ask your parents.
- Check with local hospitals and geriatric facilities.
- Check with day care facilities.
- Look in the community section of your local newspaper.
- Do an online search for local opportunities.
- Check out places such as Habitat for Humanity, the Girl/Boy Scouts, Boys/Girls Clubs, Big Brothers/Big Sisters, Junior Achievement, homeless shelters, and so forth.
- Be a tutor at a local school or after-school program.
- Check with your town/city/county—you might find trail building or other outdoor programs that need volunteers.

Many schools now require a certain number of hours of volunteer work as a graduation requirement.

Why Do People Volunteer?

The reasons for volunteering are many and varied. If you are in high school or college, some of the reasons are to get into a "better" college, get more money for school, get a better job after graduation, and so forth. Here are some other reasons:

- Because it's a graduation requirement
- Because it looks good on applications/résumés
- Because it is important to you
- Because you have a chance to combine your interests and talents
- Because you can gain skills and have a level of responsibility you can't get anywhere else
- Because it makes you feel good, or makes you appreciate what you have

Is It for You?

Volunteering isn't right for everyone. It takes valuable time, and not all experiences are rewarding or even useful. Choose your causes wisely, though, and you'll have the chance to learn, give, grow, and become more the person you would like to be.

A Parting Thought . . .

Here's another thing to keep in mind. Many offers of admission are provisional—even early-decision and other "guaranteed" programs. If your grades slip during your senior year, or you stop your extracurricular activities during the last half of your senior year, or you get arrested, the college reserves the right to withdraw your offer of admission or cancel your spot.

Case Study

Renée, a 16-year-old junior, is hoping to go to Northwestern, Stanford, or her home state college, University of North Carolina at Chapel Hill. She gets good grades (GPA = 3.33). She letters in three sports each year (field hockey, basketball, and swimming), is a senator in the student government, coordinates the layout for the yearbook, volunteers three times a week at a seniors' home, and works 16 hours a week (mostly Friday, Saturday, and Sunday) at the local delicatessen. Renée likes to spend at least two hours each day exchanging IMs with her friends, and still does two or three hours of homework each evening. She is chronically tired and grouchy.

Renée's grades are not quite up to the standards of any of her chosen schools. Her test scores are a bit off, too. She can take the ACT and SAT one more time before she has to send in her applications. She really needs scholarship and grant money if she's going to go to an out-of-state school, and that requires at least a 3.5 GPA and better test scores.

What could Renée do to help her case at each school?

First, although activities and work experience are important, grades are not to be ignored.

Second, because Renée is pretty sharp and organized, she is certainly the sort of student most schools would love to have. But she is overextended and that shows poor judgment, something the admissions committee might hold against her.

Renée is probably better off dropping one or two sports, cutting out the yearbook or student government, reducing her work and volunteer hours, and studying to raise her grades and test scores.

In fact, to show how mature she is, Renée could include in her application materials an essay that demonstrates how she reflected on her activities, grades, school choices, and scholarship needs and made some reasoned-out, difficult choices.

Then she needs to get her grades up to par and keep them there through her entire senior year (or risk losing her hard-earned acceptances).

Practical Exercise

List the factors you believe to be most important to college admissions officials. Write three or four sentences about why you believe the officials value these activities or factors. And how you are working to ensure you meet the requirements.

Factor #1

_____

_____

_____

_____

_____.

Factor #2

_____

_____

_____

_____

_____.

Factor #3

_____

_____

_____

_____

_____.

Factor #4

_____

_____

_____

_____

_____.

Factor #5

_____

_____

_____

_____

_____.

CHAPTER 31

Choosing the "Right" College or University

The Basics

Choosing Your College

First you need to decide what type of college:

- A traditional four-year college or university
- Less traditional colleges, such as those that include a five-year program with a "co-op" option
- Military colleges such as West Point or one of the other service academies
- International/overseas colleges
- Two-year junior college
- Community college
- Specialty schools such as an art institute, technology school, or trade school

Narrow Your Choices

Then you have to narrow your choices to colleges that "fit" your needs by considering:

- Costs
- Location
- Size
- Degrees and programs offered
- Graduation rates
- Admission criteria (grades, test scores, activities)
- Availability of financial aid, grants, work-study, co-op programs
- Types of activities, sports, and so forth
- Diversity of student body
- Other criteria that matter to you

Find the Money

Then you need to decide how you're going to get the money you'll need for tuition, books, fees, room, board, and other expenses. Some of the possibilities:

- Work for a few years to save the money you need
- Work part-time and go to school part- or full-time

- Join the military to get college benefits
- Work for an employer who will pay for your college courses
- Hope your parents can pay for you
- Apply for scholarships and grants
- Apply for student loans

The Details—Finding the "Right" College for You

There are thousands of colleges and universities to choose from, so how do you find the three or four that are the best fit for you?

The Reasons

People choose a college for any number of reasons. If you make a choice based on a careful evaluation of yourself, your needs, and your family's finances, you are far more likely to enjoy your college years than if you don't think through the process.

Before we look at the "right" reasons to choose a college, let's look at some "reasons" that may lead to regrets later.

The Wrong Reasons

All my friends are going there. This may seem like a good reason right now—after all, who wants to leave the friends they've hung out with for the past four years? However, people change, and college only speeds up this process. There are so many students and no guarantees you'll even see your friends once you get to campus. You may all have different courses and schedules, different roommates, get involved in different things, and drift apart. At that point you may find you don't like the college or the courses that interest you aren't available, or you hate the climate, or the school's too big (too small) and you are suddenly miserable.

My parents/sister/brother went there. Sometimes there is a "family tradition" that you may feel obligated to follow. Unfortunately, the traditional school may all wrong for you, while it was perfect for your parents or siblings. Maybe you grew up in Boston, but your mother went to Vanderbilt (in Nashville) so you think you should go there (or she wants you to go there). You can't understand the Southern accent, and you want to study dramatic arts. The school doesn't offer drama and almost everyone has a Southern accent. Your chances of liking the school aren't very high.

The school has a great football (basketball, hockey, golf …) team. Unless you are going to school to play a sport or maybe manage a team, this is a reason you'll probably regret.

I want to get as far away from home/family as possible. If you've never been far from home and family, or you rely heavily on your family and friends, this can be a very bad way to choose a school. Even the most self-sufficient student gets homesick, and it's hard to study when you're miserable or lonely.

I want to go to an Ivy League college no matter how much money I have to borrow. Graduating college with a heavy load of debt is not always a good idea. You have to repay college loans (bankruptcy probably won't get rid of that obligation) and those payments are going to eat into your salary. The most expensive education is not necessarily the best education, nor is it a guarantee of a good job or admission to medical or other graduate schools.

I want to go to law/medical/MBA school after graduation and college X has a great program. After four years at a school, you may want to go to graduate school somewhere different, or you may not want to go to graduate school at all (for the moment). College students tend to go through several majors and future career choices, so picking a college today based on what you may or may not want to do four years from now is probably not a good idea.

The "Right" Reasons

There is no one right reason for choosing a college. Many times the school you pick is a compromise that considers costs, grades, location, diversity, programs, courses, and much more. Choosing schools you have some chance of getting into is always a good starting place.

The Planning Calendar

Although the details will vary depending on whether your senior school year starts in August or September, here is a "final countdown":

- *The Summer before Your Senior Year:* Research colleges and funding options as outlined in steps in the beginning of this section.
- *All Year:* Keep your grades and activities going. No goofing off once the acceptance letters start rolling in!
- *August–September:* Plan a trip with your family to visit the top three or four colleges on your list. Maybe this is a road trip, or several weekend flying trips. Sign up for the September–October SAT and/or ACT test. Sign up for the National Merit or other scholarship tests.
- *September–October:* Take the ACT and/or SAT. Make sure you research the requirements for all the colleges you are interested in. Some colleges want the SAT, some the ACT, and some will take either one. A few colleges don't require either test. Take the National Merit Scholar test, Regents' tests, and similar tests.
- *Fall:* Complete and submit your applications.
- *December:* Prepare your Free Application for Federal Student Aid (FAFSA). You need to get a personal identification number (PIN), too. Complete any state aid applications. Research private scholarships online.
- *January:* Submit the FAFSA and other scholarship applications.
- *March–April:* Take advanced placement exams.
- *March–May:* The acceptance letters and financial aid/scholarship offers should arrive in this time period, so you'll need to compare them.
- *May–June:* Apply for student loans. Compare the terms carefully (see the Student Loan section of this book).
- *Summer after Graduation:* Get a part- or full-time summer job. Save at least half of your earnings for college.

> The college application process is involved and tedious. It is also expensive—several hundred dollars for many colleges. These are the main reasons your counselor probably recommends you limit your college choices to three or four schools. Of course, one of those schools could be one you think is a stretch (a long shot) in terms of your grades and other qualifications— never sell yourself short. One school should probably be a "safe" school, and the other one or two somewhere in the middle.

Practical Exercises

1. What are/were your reasons for choosing a college or other post–high school program (including the military)? List and explain at least 10 criteria, divided into "must haves" and "must not haves." See Table 31.1.

Table 31.1. Must Haves

Must Have	Must Not Have

2. What are (were) your reasons for choosing a college or university or other post-high school program? List and explain at least six reasons.

Reason #1

_____

_____

_____

_____

_____

_____.

Reason #2

_____

_____

_____

_____

_____

_____.

Reason #3

_____

_____

_____

_____

_____

_____.

Reason #4

_____

_____

_____

_____

_____

_____.

Reason #5

_____

_____

_____

_____

_____

_____.

Reason #6

_____

_____

_____

_____

_____

_____.

11

Maximizing Your Ability to Get Financial Aid: At Any Age

With the advent of tax deductions for a portion of college tuition (at least in some cases), Section 529 plans that have no time or age limits, and with more people returning to college at various points in their lives, financial aid can be a concern at any age.

Financial aid is not limited to the young or the poor any more.

CHAPTER 32

Where's the Money? For College, That Is!

The laws are constantly changing for the topics in this chapter, so always check with the schools, your academic advisors, and tax professionals for the latest information.

There are countless sources of money to help pay for college. Maybe your parents are going to pay for everything, or you've saved the money, or your employer is going to pay for your degree. If not, there are lots of other options. You can search online, talk to the colleges you are considering, talk to your school counselors, check out loans through the federal and state governments and also through banks, look for scholarships, and on and on and on. In this chapter you'll find lots of details and ideas, and worksheets to help you calculate how much money you're going to need.

One of the best college financial planning tools I've found is the booklet put out by the State of Colorado (and your state probably has a similar booklet): *The College Financial Workbook—You're Going Places.* To get a copy, visit www.collegeinvest.org, or call 1.800.COLLEGE.

Making the decision to go to college is only the beginning. You need a well-thought-out plan—a road map—to make sure you get to the right place and can afford to stay.

Going to college is an expensive proposition. We've already looked at a number of sources for academic and needs-based scholarships, grants, and so forth, so now let's take a look at the ways money can be accumulated and how the financial aid experts weigh each source.

There are lots of ways to accumulate money for college—even if you are past "normal" college age. Some of these methods can seriously impact (positively or negatively) your ability to get financial assistance for school. The key—who has control over the money. If you control your own money, 35% of it is considered available for higher education costs each year. If your parents control the money that will pay for your education, 5.6% is considered available each year. If someone else controls the account (such as your grandparents), it is likely that none of it will be considered available for higher education costs even though you will use it for that purpose.

If you are one of the very fortunate few whose parents are either multimillionaires or put tons of money away for your education from the day you were born, skip this section. If you were a child star or started a successful Internet company, maybe you have enough money to pay for college already. In that case you should just skip ahead to the sections on taxes and investments—they will be far more interesting to you.

On the other hand, if you are contemplating college, even if you're already in your 20s, there are some interesting savings approaches you and your entire family should know about.

> **Planning should start when you are in the first two years of high school—you need to decide to get the best grades you can and be active and involved in clubs, sports, and your community. Colleges care about all four years of your high school career. Waiting until you're a 17- or 18-year-old senior is tempting, but seriously limits your college and money options.**

Here are the main ways to accumulate (additional) money to pay for college (and in some cases, high school):

• Roth IRA
• Coverdell Education Savings Account (formerly the "Kiddie" or education IRA)
• Section 529 Prepaid Tuition Plan
• Section 529 College Savings Plan
• Uniform Gift to Minors Account/Uniform Trust for Minors Account (UGMA/UTMA)
• Traditional investment accounts
• Government savings bonds

Most of these options actually keep control out of the hands of the "beneficiary"—you, the future student. Most also allow the money to be used until you are 30 or even indefinitely.

Here's a summary of the control, tax, and contribution highlights of each accumulation option, along with the age at which the money must be used or control transferred.

Roth IRA

The Roth IRA is not really an educational savings program, but there are situations where the proceeds can be used for certain educational and other expenses without incurring taxes or penalties. People like to use Roth IRAs to save for retirement since the money that is put in grows tax-free. Since the contributed amounts are made with after-tax income (the money you have after taxes are deducted), the entire account value is usually free of any taxes.

There is no time limit for using this money, but annual contribution amounts ($4,000 for most people in 2005–2007) are great for the long haul, but don't amount to a lot in the short term. Since the money in a Roth IRA is earmarked for retirement, it does not count toward the money considered to be available to pay for your education.

There are better ways to get money for college.

Coverdell Education Savings Account (ESA)

When the ESA, as it is called now, first came out in the 1990s, it was designed to look much like a Roth IRA. The contributions, however, were very limited: $500 per student per year. The growth was tax-free, so if your parents or other relative started an account for you when you were born, and put in $500 each year, and earned about 8%, the account value could approach $20,000 when you were 18. And this money would be tax-free as long as it was used for qualifying higher education expenses. The only caveats:

• The money has to be used for higher education (or there are taxes and penalties)
• The money has to be used by age 30 (or there are taxes and penalties)
• If the original beneficiary (the future student) doesn't go to college, a new beneficiary can be named to avoid taxes and penalties

Since you don't control the money, it has a very small impact on your eligibility for financial aid.

Now, $20,000 would make a nice dent in the cost of State U, but that's about it. So a few years ago the rules were changed. Now people (including yourself) can put up to $2,000 per year into an ESA. That means there is a potential to have about $80,000 when you are 18—and that is some serious tuition money. Even better, there is a new plan called a Section 529 plan—and you can have both this 529 plan and an ESA. Harvard, here I come!

Seriously, there are some great benefits to the next two options—the two types of Section 529 plans.

Section 529 Plans

These next two accumulation options are called Section 529 plans because they are covered in Section 529 of the Internal Revenue Service (IRS) Code—that big book that covers all the rules about taxes. There are two types of plans authorized in this section:

- State prepaid tuition plans
- State college savings plans

The theory behind each plan is the same, but the schools where they can be used and guarantees provided are very different.

The State 529 Plans

Currently all states and the District of Columbia offer a prepaid tuition plan or a college savings plan or both.

Seventeen states offer both. These states are:

- Alabama
- Colorado
- Florida
- Illinois
- Maryland
- Massachusetts
- Michigan
- Mississippi
- Nevada
- New Mexico
- Pennsylvania
- South Carolina
- Tennessee
- Texas
- Virginia
- West Virginia
- Wisconsin

Two states offer just prepaid tuition plans. These states are:

- Kentucky
- Washington

Thirty-one states and the District of Columbia offer just college savings plans. These states are:

- Alaska
- Arkansas
- California
- Connecticut
- Delaware
- District of Columbia
- Georgia
- Hawaii
- Idaho
- Indiana

- Iowa
- Kansas
- Louisiana
- Maine
- Minnesota
- Missouri
- Montana
- Nebraska
- New Hampshire
- New Jersey
- New York
- North Carolina
- North Dakota
- Ohio
- Oklahoma
- Oregon
- Rhode Island
- South Dakota
- Utah
- Vermont
- Wyoming

Note that some of the states with savings plans, such as Alaska, Arizona, California, Connecticut, Georgia, Michigan, Minnesota, Missouri, Montana, New York, and Ohio, include elements of prepaid tuition plans in their college savings plans by offering a guaranteed investment option. In addition, states are constantly modifying their rules and programs, so the best source of current information is your state's website (www.state.XX.us).

Prepaid Tuition Plans

Each state and the District of Columbia have established at least one prepaid tuition plan. The tax rules and contribution requirements are different for each state, but at the federal level the money that is contributed grows tax-free.

Since the prepaid tuition plan is run by a state, the normal approach is to guarantee that a given contribution will cover a guaranteed portion of future tuition at one or more branches of the sponsoring state's land grant or other universities. Here's an example of how this guarantee works:

Let's say the tuition at State U-Parker is $8,000 in 2005. If someone sets up a Section 529 prepaid tuition plan and contributes $8,000 this year, the state will guarantee that money will grow at the same rate as tuition rises, no matter how many years it is before the plan's beneficiary (that's you) has before they go to college.

As long as you are accepted by, and attend, the schools that participate in your state's prepaid tuition plan, your tuition should be prepaid in proportion to the amount contributed by your account's donor. Note that the rules in each state are different, so this example is only a guideline. If the person or persons who contribute to the Section 529 prepaid tuition plan [the donor(s)] contribute 50% of the current annual tuition, then 50% of your tuition should be covered in the future.

But what if you don't want to go to that branch of State U? The donors should be able to get their money back from the plan, less certain charges and penalties. They could transfer the money to a Section 529 college savings plan and probably avoid taxes and penalties and still use the money for your education.

Here are some frequently asked questions about Section 529 prepaid tuition plans.

1. What are the limits on contributions?
2. What is the age limit for using the money in the plan?
3. What happens if you don't go to an eligible school?
4. How does a Section 529 Prepaid Tuition plan affect getting financial aid?
5. What are the tax benefits?
6. What are the plan guarantees?

How Much Money Can Be Contributed to Each Plan?

The contribution limits vary widely between states and plans.

In general, the total contribution limits for any type of Section 529 plan range between $235,000 and $305,000. The maximum any one donor can contribute (without owing gift taxes) to a plan is $11,000 per year, but there is a provision that allows a gift of $55,000 per donor if five-year averaging is used. This is probably more than you need to know right now, but you never know when the information will come in handy!

The Coverdell ESA is (currently) limited to $2,000 per student—no matter how many people contribute. So, if your grandparents put in $2,000 for you, your parents cannot contribute in the same year.

What about Taxes?

Taxes are always an interesting consideration. Up to now you probably haven't thought much about taxes, but that is about to change. Here's a chart to show you the tax considerations for the educational savings plans we just looked at (Table 32.1).

Table 32.1. Taxes and Educational Savings Plans

Savings Plan	Taxes on Invested $	Taxes on Withdrawn $	Taxes on $ not Used for School
Coverdell ESA	Taxes are paid on $ before contribution is made	No taxes at federal level; may be no taxes at state level	Penalties and interest charged; must use before age 30
529 Prepaid Tuition Plan	Taxes are paid on $ before contribution is made	No taxes at federal level; may be no taxes at state level	Penalties and interest charged; no age limit to use; may not be able to change beneficiary
529 College Savings Plan	Taxes are paid on $ before contribution is made	No taxes at federal level; may be no taxes at state level	Penalties and interest charged; no age limit to use; can change beneficiary
Roth IRA	Taxes are paid on $ before contribution is made	No taxes at federal level; may be no taxes at state level	Penalties and interest charged; no age limit to use

Uniform Gift to Minors Account/Uniform Trust for Minors Account (UGMA/UTMA)

Your parents may have set up an UGMA or UTMA for you when you were in elementary or junior high school. If so, this money is available for your tuition, but once you reach your state's age of majority control over the money passes to you. This usually happens when you are 18 or 19, but each state is a bit different.

Getting control of this money is both a good and a bad thing. You do not have to use the money for college; you can use it for anything you wish. Of course, once you've spent the money on a used Honda Civic, you have a car and no money for tuition.

There are certain limits to the amounts that can be contributed to UGMA/UTMAs to get the most favorable tax rates. There is no tax-free savings in these accounts. As long as the earnings are low, they are taxed at your very low tax bracket. One you turn 14 the entire increase in value (earnings and growth) is taxed to you.

In all likelihood your parents will roll the money in any UGMA/UTMAs into a 529 plan—a much better deal for them, and a way to ensure you can't take the money and go to Europe instead of college. What a bummer!

Perhaps the worst aspect of these accounts is what they do to your eligibility for financial aid. The assumption is that about 35% of the money will be used for your tuition and expenses each year, so your possible financial aid is reduced, dollar-for-dollar, by the money in your UGMA/UTMA—even if you used the money to buy a car or take a trip!

Traditional Investments

One of the ways many parents accumulate money to help pay the cost of your education is in more traditional investment options—CDs, investment accounts, mutual funds, brokerage accounts, and so forth. This is their money, not yours, and they don't have to give it to if they don't want to.

Some people consider borrowing from their retirement plan savings [the 401(k) or similar plan at work]. This is rarely a good idea, and you probably shouldn't count on your parents doing this. After all, it's their hard-earned retirement money! If you are working and have a similar retirement plan, you could tap it for school, but again, not a very good idea.

If you have been working and saving money, that is both a good and a bad thing. You have money to use for school and other expenses, but 35% or so of that money is counted as being available for your school costs—much like the money in UGMA/UTMAs.

Another major source of potential college money is the equity in a home. People use this money for tuition—the problem arises when your income is not high enough to pay the borrowed funds back. Then you either have to sell or lose the home.

From a tax perspective, the money in these accounts has some interesting considerations.

Personal Savings/Investments. This money (whether accumulated by your parents or you) is saved out of taxable income, and the interest, dividends, and growth are taxed at varying rates. The end result is money that is largely free of taxes—the dues have already been paid as you go along.

Retirement Savings/Investment. Not all retirement funds can be tapped to help pay for college.

We already looked at Roth IRAs, and any other IRA withdrawals or surrenders will be taxed and penalized. Not a good source of funds for college!

Money in many company-sponsored retirement plans may be available to use for college expenses. Assuming the plan allows this money to be used, the money is considered to be a loan (a loan to the person who put the money there) and must be repaid with interest. In addition, if the person who borrowed the money leaves the company, the full amount borrowed must be repaid (in a very short window) or there will be taxes and penalties assessed.

Home Equity. The media are filled with ads from mortgage companies, banks, credit unions, and other entities encouraging people to use the equity in their home as a source of funds. Every spring there seems to be a big push to get people to take out home equity lines of credit or loans to use for college tuition.

In my opinion, this is rarely a good idea—if anything goes wrong, there is a risk of losing the family home. From a tax perspective, there is no tax (currently) due. The interest may actually be tax-deductible, and this can be appealing to some people.

Government Savings Bonds. Certain government savings bonds (mostly those issued from about 1989 onward) *may* be transferable to a 529 plan with no taxes due.

Employer-Paid Tuition

If you are already working (even part-time), your employer may offer the best possible tuition payment plan—one where the company pays for you to go to college or grad school. This is a valuable benefit, and is offered by many companies; even small employers may pay part of your tuition. There are three really great advantages to employer-paid tuition:

- No taxes on the money.
- You are still eligible for financial aid if you need it.
- You can still use money in 529 plans (to any age) and Coverdell ESAs (until you turn 30).

Some employers require you to pay the tuition and then provide receipts to get reimbursed. If there is money in an ESA or 529 plan for your use you get to pay with money that grew tax-free and get reimbursed for your costs, so this is still an excellent arrangement.

Three very important caveats:

- You'll have to maintain a rather high grade point average (GPA)—probably at least a 3.0.
- You probably have to complete your degree in a certain time frame—generally no more than five years, and often in four years.
- You have to take a program of study that your employer approves—one that he or she sees value in.

Reducing Your College Expenses

Some things you can't control—tuition is what it is, and room and board rates aren't very flexible, either. But some aspects of your college expenses can be quite manageable.

Some of the areas where you can reduce your costs are:

- Buy used books, but make sure they are the correct edition and are not damaged or missing pages (including the answer pages at the back!).
- Sell your books when the term is over—books are rarely used more than a few terms, so waiting is not a good idea and saving them is silly—you will probably never open them again.
- Contact your friends by e-mail rather than calling long distance. If you can get Voice-over-Internet Protocol (VoIP) service, you can have "free" calling.
- If you take a cell phone, make sure it is the same carrier as your family's phone. If you and your friends have the same carrier, there shouldn't be any charges for "mobile to mobile" calling. Try to make other calls in the "free" minutes—evenings, weekends, holidays.
- Get a part-time job that fits your schedule and builds your résumé. Keep the hours to 12 or so a week—no point flunking out because of overwork!
- Get a roommate—on or off campus.
- Get a less-expensive meal plan if you skip a lot of meals.
- Get a refrigerator and microwave for your room and use them.

- Go to all the events you can with your student ID—most on-campus events are of good quality and free with your ID.
- Use credit cards sparingly—for true emergencies and necessities only.
- Don't have a car—most of what you will need is within walking distance, and you're sure to have at least one friend with a car for those trips to the mall, skiing, the lake, or whatever. A car is an expensive proposition—insurance, gas, parking, maintenance, payments, and so on. Campuses are lousy places to park, and tickets are frequent and expensive.

Understanding and Getting Financial Aid

More people than you might think actually qualify for financial aid. Just because both of your parents work and you want to go to an Ivy League school doesn't disqualify you for financial aid.

The Princeton Review's website (www.princetonreview.com/college/finance/) has some valuable calculators and links to help you through the complicated and time-consuming process of applying for financial aid. Your state probably has a similar website.

- *Tuition Cost Calculator*—to find out about how much it will cost to get a degree at your chosen school.
- *Estimated Family Contribution Calculator*—to find out about how much your family is going to have to pay toward your college costs.
- *FASFA and CSS PROFILE Form Strategies*—there are things you must do, questions you'll have, and ways to fill out these forms to maximize your financial aid.
- *Aid Comparison Calculator*—this helps you compare different financial aid packages.

You can also go directly to the Free Application for Federal Student Aid (FAFSA) website and download the forms and get help filling them out (www.fafsa.ed.gov). Note that you need a PIN to file your forms electronically. Go to http://pin.ed.gov to get your PIN, and do so no later than December of the year *before* the year you want to apply for financial aid.

Filling Out the FAFSA

Before you get started, get organized. This will make the process much easier. The following list summarizes the materials you'll need to fill out the form.

- Student's driver's license and Social Security card.
- W-2 forms and other earnings records (1099s, etc.) for both the student and the parents for the past year.
- Last year's income tax returns for both the student and the parents.
- Records of other income such as welfare, Social Security, aid program funds, veteran's benefits, and so forth.
- Current bank statements (a year's worth).
- Current business and investment mortgage information.
- Business and farm records (a year's worth).
- Records of investments, stocks, and bonds.
- Records of educational savings programs—529 plans, Coverdell ESAs, UGMA/UTMA accounts—set up for the benefit of the student.

Once you've completed and sent in the FAFSA, you'll receive a Student Aid Report (SAR). Make sure the information is complete and accurate. Very small errors in SAR information can have a big impact on how much, if any, financial aid you are eligible for.

One of the most important pieces of information on the SAR is your EFC—Expected Family Contribution. This is not necessarily a cash contribution requirement—it can come from loans, payment plans, and other resources. Anything above that amount is what you can generally cover with some form of financial aid.

Note that you need to list any colleges to which you might apply on your FAFSA—this ensures they get the EFC information so they can put together scholarship and financial aid packages. Once you have these offers, make sure to compare them side-by-side.

Your award letter(s) may or may not include awards for Stafford or PLUS loans (loans for your parents while you are a dependent and a student).

Types of Financial Aid Awarded under FAFSA

There are a number of financial aid options your financial package might contain. Each school awards financial aid in some combination of these options. "Free" money is almost always better than loans, and work-study is a toss-up compared to loans.

Here are the main types of financial aid you are likely to see in your award offer:

- Scholarships
- Work-Study
- Grants:
  - Federal Pell Grants
  - Federal Supplemental Educational Opportunity Grants
  - Other
- Federal Loans:
  - Stafford
  - PLUS
  - Perkins

You may also get aid offers direct from one or more schools, separate from your FAFSA results. These packages can include grants and scholarships. You may also apply directly for signature loans through Sallie Mae.

Here's a summary of the pros and cons of each type of financial aid:

Scholarships: This is essentially "free" money. But even free money is not without strings. You almost certainly have to attend a certain number of hours each term and maintain a certain grade point average.

Work-Study: This a program that allows you to work in a campus-based job with hours limited and tailored to your class schedule.

Grants: These are similar to scholarships but may be onetime only, or have to be reapplied for each year. Scholarships are from many sources but grants are normally from federal sources. They are similar to loans but do not have to be repaid. If the grant is from the school, it may include a requirement to teach, or tutor, or work for the school in some other way.

Loans: These are not free, but payment is delayed until some time after you graduate, or immediately upon failing to graduate. If you are a student who can't mix work and school, you may be better off with loans instead of work-study or grants, and if you are afraid your grades won't be good enough to meet the scholarship requirements, loans may be better for you. Interest rates are very reasonable.

More about Loans and Grants

There are several types of loans you should know about. The Stafford and PLUS loans are awarded through the FAFSA, but there is another option, the Signature Student loan.

Stafford loans are low-interest *student* loans available to families of all income levels. Rates are quite low—and can't go above 8.25%. You don't make your first repayment until six months after you graduate or leave college, so you have time to get a job, get settled, and then start paying your loan. To see the latest interest rate go to a website such as www.collegeinvest.org or www.salliemae.com.

PLUS loans are for your parents. The rates are low, although probably not as low as a Stafford Loan.

Perkins loans are low-interest (5%) loans for both undergraduate and graduate students with financial need. Your school is your lender. The loan is made with government funds, and your school contributes a share. You must repay this loan to your school.

Signature loans are the most popular form of student loan after the Stafford loan, according to the Sallie Mae website. The Signature Student loan is a privately insured, credit-based loan available through Sallie Mae's lending partners. One lender can finance the entire cost of your education, by combining a federal Stafford loan with a private signature student loan.

Pell Grants are based on federal money and the FAFSA results, but (unlike loans) do not have to be repaid. Generally, Pell Grants are awarded only to undergraduate students who have not earned a bachelor's or professional degree.

Federal Supplemental Educational Opportunity Grants (FSEOG) are available to students with exceptional financial need—those with the lowest EFC scores—and priority is given to students receiving Pell Grants. Again, these grants do not have to be repaid.

Another useful website to help you sort through all these grants and loans is www.studentaid.ed.gov. This site will give you the amounts, eligibility, interest rates, repayment terms, and other considerations for these grants and loans. Amounts and terms change regularly, so make sure to check this site for the latest information.

How Does Each Option Affect Your Ability to Get Financial Aid?

This may be the most important, and most often overlooked, consideration. Some college savings options have a major impact, reducing the amount of financial aid you can get dollar-for-dollar. Some options weigh far more heavily into the financial aid equation than do others. Table 33.1 will help you sort out the impact of each savings option.

Kris Z., a Denver-area teenager, plans to pay for college by combining several sources of funds:

I will pay for college through a combination of assistance from my family and my own savings. If I have to get loans I would repay them. Scholarships and grants are given not only for outstanding academics and athletics, but also for those in financial need. I will probably not apply for financial aid upon entering college.

Table 33.1. College Savings and Financial Aid: The Impact

Savings Option	Parents' Asset	Student's Asset	Impact on Aid
Coverdell ESA	No	Yes	35% considered available for costs—reduces amount of aid significantly
529 Prepaid Tuition Plan	No	Yes	100% considered available for costs—may totally eliminate financial aid
529 College Savings Plan	Yes	No	5.6% considered available for costs—minimal impact on aid availability
Roth IRA	Yes	No	Not factored in since this is a retirement asset
UGMA/UTMA	No	Yes	35% considered available for costs—reduces amount of aid significantly
Nonretirement Savings: Parents	Yes	No	5.6% considered available for costs—minimal impact on aid availability
Nonretirement Savings: Student	No	Yes	35% considered available for costs—reduces amount of aid significantly
Retirement Savings	Yes	No	Not factored in since this is a retirement asset
Home Equity Line/Loan	Yes	No	Not factored in

Traditional Sources of Funding

There are many ways to pay for higher education. Some of them may hold no appeal for you; some may be out of your reach; some may not work because of your family income or your grades, or the college you want to attend. Here are the most common traditional and alternative sources of college funding.

- Family resources and savings plans
- Your personal savings
- Student loans
- Alternative sources of funding
  - Grants
  - Work-study
  - Military and other government programs
  - Scholarships
  - Co-operative education programs

Here are some highlights for each funding method.

Family Resources and Savings Plans

Some families can afford to pay the entire cost of a college education for each child and not think twice about the cost. If you know one of these families, ask to be adopted.

The reality is most families will find a way to help their kids pay for college, but some or most of the money needs to come from other sources.

Some families set up various college savings for their children. If your family did this, great. If not, there are still ways that family members can contribute to your education in a tax-favored way, but those educational savings plans have lots of considerations so you need to talk to an accountant or tax advisor.

Some parents or grandparents set up UGMAs or UTMAs (Uniform Gift or Transfer/Trust to/for Minors Accounts) and put college savings in these accounts. Once this type of account is set up, it can't be canceled—it is essentially your account to do with as you please when you turn 18, or 19, or whatever your state's law says. At the same time, this money counts against you when you are applying for scholarships and loans. Bummer.

Your Personal Savings and Earnings

For many young adults this is one of the main sources of college funds. Hopefully you've been saving part of the money you've earned at various jobs, put part of each gift check and graduation check into this account, and are working part-time to continue to accumulate this money.

I'm sure it sounds hopelessly old-fashioned, but you'll get more out of your education if part (or all) of it comes out of your own pocket. And employers will value your discipline and skills.

WORKING PART-TIME

Working part-time during the school year has its pros and cons. On the one hand, you can earn money to buy life's little luxuries and accumulate money for the next semester's tuition and other costs. On the other hand, working during the school term is almost certainly going to affect your grades in a negative way.

The solution? Employers value real-world experience. If your part-time job affected your grades, make sure your job application cover letter includes a statement about working "X" hours per week, learning job skills, and paying "XX%" of your college tuition yourself. It really does make up for a lot.

Student Loans

This is the way many people finance a college education. The interest rate is very favorable and payments don't usually start until you have been working for a period of time after graduation. There are even programs (check out the Peace Corps, AmeriCorps, and other programs) that can earn you a break on your student loan repayments.

The primary source of the student loans I have been referring to is Sallie Mae—the Student Loan Marketing Association (www.salliemae.com). Beware though—failure to make scheduled payments can cost you dearly. Nonpayment hurts your credit rating and shows up on your credit reports. This makes getting many jobs difficult or impossible. It also makes it very hard to get a security clearance or good loan interest rates or the best credit cards.

Scholarships

College or other postsecondary education is expensive. No ifs, ands, or buts. Still, if you know where to look, there is a lot of money out there.

You may not be the world's best student or have the best grades, but that doesn't mean you can't get scholarships. Scholarships are "money for scholars" not just "money for grades." The money is for you as a scholar—meaning you as someone who is attending a school to learn. Scholarships can be "grades based," but many are based on your activities, interests, athletics, volunteer work, religion, ethnic background, and so forth.

There are several types of money you can use to pay for college. There are loans, money from your parents, money you earn, grants, fellowships, and "free" money. Of all of these, scholarships, otherwise known as "free" money, are my favorite. You don't have to pay the money back, you don't have to give up studying or socializing time to get it, and you aren't answerable to your parents for how the money is used. As long as you meet the terms and conditions of the scholarship provider, generally academic or grade based, you get the money, no additional strings attached.

In a "MoneySmart" column (*USA Weekend Magazine*, December 10–12, 2004), a young kindergarten teacher, Jamille Rogers, was featured. Why? Because she managed to accumulate $40,000 in scholarships, in amounts of $100 to $3,500, and pay the entire cost of a four-year education at the University of Central Arkansas. It can be done.

You can use the Web to search for "free" money. Here are some sites that either search for you, or offer links to other useful sites:

- www.collegeboard.com. This is the official website of the College Board. You can use this site to perform free searches for all kinds of scholarships.
- www.fastweb.com. There are a variety of scholarship listings on this useful site. There are more than 600,000 scholarship listings. Many are quite specific, some are unusual, and a few border on truly bizarre.
- www.srnexpress.com. This is the site of the Scholarship Research Network Express. Check it out.
- www.collegeanswer.com. This is the scholarship portion of the Sallie Mae (student loan) website. There is also useful information about other aspects of paying for college.

How do you qualify for these nonacademic (as well as academic) scholarships?

> **The first rule of shopping for scholarships: Avoid "scholarship shopping" or "scholarship matching" services. Although there may be a few legitimate ones out there, most require a fee (often several hundred dollars) and rarely deliver the money. A good general rule—if you have to pay to buy a list or get links to websites, forget it.**

Academic Scholarships

If you have really good grades and get outstanding scores on the ACTs or SATs, you may find colleges contacting you with offers of academic or other scholarships. In some states there are state-sponsored scholarships for top students. If you are a star athlete, you may be contacted about athletic scholarships. Finally, there are fully paid scholarships at the various military service academies and full scholarships through the Reserve Officers Training Corps (ROTC).

To get these academic scholarships you still need to be proactive. Many schools have a wide variety of opportunities, but you have to ask. Service academy and ROTC scholarships must be applied for, and you have to meet some rigorous but doable conditions.

College-Funded Academic Scholarships. Ultimately the colleges you are applying to are one of the best sources of financial aid. Become good friends with the financial aid officers at each college you are applying to. You should contact these officers long before you actually apply to a school; find out what scholarships are available and what you need to do to qualify for each one.

Some scholarships are tied purely to academics—the applicants with the best grades get the big bucks, regardless of financial need. Some scholarships are need based, and some are based on a mix of grades and need and activities.

GETTING MONEY AFTER THE FACT

It never hurts to visit the financial aid office after the fact—once you have decided to attend a school, pay a visit, make a call, send an e-mail, or write a letter, and ask about scholarships. You can even ask after the term starts—sometimes scholarships are awarded and the person decides to go to another school, or drops out, or fails to meet all the scholarship criteria. If you don't ask, you'll never know.

Always check on the availability of scholarships and other financial aid several times every year. Money sources change, as do the criteria for awarding money. Once you have a scholarship(s), make sure you know and meet the conditions for keeping it.

National-Level Academic Scholarships. There are many scholarships that are awarded on an academic basis, at the national level. The College Board site is a good place to look for these. Many of the standardized tests (such as the National Merit Scholarship program) grant scholarships based solely on test results or on a combination of grades and test results. Check with your school guidance counselor to see what's available, in addition to your Web searches.

State-Level Academic Scholarships. Many states have scholarships for students who meet certain academic standards and go to school in-state. Some of the scholarships (or grants, in a few cases) are specific to a college. For example, there are schools in Virginia that award scholarships or grants on a fairly liberal basis to students who will make an early decision on attending. New York State has its Regents' Scholarships, and many other states have similar programs.

> **The entities that grant academic-based scholarships are extremely unforgiving—if you fail to meet or exceed the conditions for renewing your scholarship(s), they will almost certainly be taken away from you. There aren't many second chances when it comes to keeping "free" money. The competition is stiff and there are dozens of other students lined up behind you hoping you'll fail to keep your scholarship.**

Alternative Sources of Higher Education Funding

If you spend some time surfing the college websites and financial aid sites, and maybe visiting chat rooms used by college students, you can find lots of less conventional ways to help pay for college. Some colleges are excellent sources of information as well.

Military/ROTC

ROTC Scholarships

If you are willing to commit to four to six years with a branch of the United States military—Air Force, Army, Navy, Marines, or Coast Guard—and meet some pretty exclusive requirements, the military has some all-expense-paid scholarship programs. You even get tax-free money every month of the school year, plus when you are attending a mandatory summer camp. In exchange you are expected to serve in the active military for a number of years, and in the Reserves for a few more years.

There is an extensive application process and physical to be completed. Your high school guidance counselor should have all the paperwork, or be able to direct you to the right place.

CONSIDERING THE MILITARY?

The military is not for everyone. If you fail to complete all the requirements, you can expect to have to pay back the military by serving as an enlisted member for a number of years. It is a "free" ride with lots of strings attached. Before you decide to take this ride, talk to people at a college ROTC unit (both the students and the military staff) and make sure this is the right choice for you.

What do you need to do and have to apply for an ROTC scholarship?

- You need to have a pretty high grade point average (GPA)—generally at least a 3.5 out of 4.0.
- You also need to have "lettered" in at least one sport (or participated at the equivalent level outside of high school).
- You need a stellar record of outside and extracurricular activities, especially activities where you had a leadership role. Volunteering is always valuable.
- You have to have a completely clean personal record—no arrests for any reason—and be a U.S. citizen.
- You need to get a recommendation from your senator or congressperson, or meet a few other special criteria.

Service Academy Programs

If you have always wanted to serve your country, this may be the choice for you. You get even more "free" money than with an ROTC scholarship, but the commitment and stresses are even higher.

How do you get this "free" ride? First, you need to have a sponsor—your congressional representative or one of your senators. In addition, there are other people who get to endorse one or more applicants, and children of certain veterans may also get an automatic endorsement.

The military has ROTC scholarships that can be applied for after you start college, too. There are three- and two-year programs— check with your college's ROTC unit at the beginning of your first or second year of college. By the way—that's how I paid for my last two years at a private university, and that was my first job.

The requirements are just as rigorous as for the ROTC scholarships, but the service commitment is longer— generally at least five years, and much longer if you get certain flying or nuclear submarine training programs after graduation.

Attending a service academy is both a way of life and an incredible commitment. When you graduate, you have a college degree, no debts, a commission in the military, and a heavy commitment. Not to be entered into lightly. As with the ROTC program, you can expect to become an enlisted service member if you fail to complete the four-year program. Dropping out is not really an option.

Nonacademic Scholarships

This is where the "real" money is. Thousands of associations, chambers of commerce, professional groups, service groups, and other businesses and organizations have scholarship funds. Colleges have funds for qualified athletes. There are programs for children of alumni (parents who graduated from a particular college or university) or children of people who belonged to certain sororities/fraternities or other groups. Christian/Catholic, Jewish, Muslim, and other religious groups may offer scholarships. Your high school may fund a scholarship or two. The military offers ways to save for college, and helps you with matching funds. The possibilities are almost endless.

Nontraditional Scholarship Sources

Some "nontraditional" scholarship search ideas:

- If you belong to an ethnic group (especially if you are adopted), try their associations—for example, the Polish American, Korean American, African American, or other groups in your area.
- Contact local chambers of commerce and ask if they have any leads for possible scholarships.
- Get active with a group such as Junior Achievement, Future Farmers of America, or other business/service clubs. They often have scholarships or are affiliated with or sponsored by groups that have scholarships.

Find out what business and professional groups your parents are involved with. Many of these entities have scholarship funds. Some places to consider—American Association of University Women, Lions, Rotary, and so forth.

Grants

There are many sources of grants for college funding. Grants are similar in some ways to scholarships—you don't have to pay them back and probably have to maintain a certain grade point average to keep them.

Work-Study

Many schools offer scholarship students a combination of programs to ensure there is enough money to cover tuition, books, fees, and room and board (if you don't live at home or with a relative). These programs may be federal or school sponsored.

One of the main ways scholarship students get spending money is through a program called "work-study." As long as you are taking at least a certain number of credit hours (generally 12 at a minimum and 15 as a maximum on the semester system), you get a part-time campus job. This job is tailored to your schedule, and usually pays a bit better than minimum wage.

If you are receiving grants, you may be limited in the amount of income you can earn, and work-study takes this into consideration.

Cooperative Education

Cooperative education (or co-op as it is often called) is a great way to combine a college education and get solid work experience. One of the best programs in the country is at Northeastern in Boston—almost all the students are co-op students.

The co-op program ensures you will work full-time or close to it several terms, so it takes an extra year to graduate. When you are finished, though, you have worked for more than a year (since you go to school on a year-round basis) and have real-world skills that employers love. You also have a lot of money toward your college and living expenses.

Practical Exercise

What are some of the means to fund education? Which do you think might make sense for you and your siblings?

CHAPTER 34

Stand Out in the Crowd

You need to articulate what makes you different. Start making a list of the things you do, above and beyond getting good grades, that makes you special. This is especially important if your grades are less than stellar!

You can fill-in Table 34.1 with some ideas.

Table 34.1. What Makes Me Special

Activities	Academic	Extracurricular	Leadership	Work

Academic Achievement

- Dean's list or honor role (number of terms)
- Prizes (poetry, writing, math, and so forth)
- SAT/ACT and other test scores
- Special mentions or letters of commendation

Extracurricular Activities

- Athletics
- Newspaper/yearbook
- Volunteer work
- Student government
- High school play
- Band
- Clubs (outdoor, chess, mathematics, computer, etc.)
- Ballet, gymnastics

Leadership Roles

- Director of school play
- Head of church outreach group
- President (or other officer) of student government
- Board member
- Volunteer coordinator
- Tutor/mentor
- Boy/Girl Scout troop leader

Work

- Part-time (tutor, babysitting, paper route)
- Full-time (summer jobs, "gap" year)
- Volunteer

There are so many things you have done, or will be doing, and without a list or chart, you're going to miss the one thing the scholarship committee wants to see. Keep a living, growing list.

Practical Exercise

What's your game plan to stand out from your peers?
   Write some of your ideas down and include a few notes about how you will implement each one.

_____

_____

_____

_____

_____

_____

_____

_____

_____.

12

Living within Your Means

Ah, the freedom of being a college student, or a new high school or college graduate. You can stay up as late as you want, visit any websites you want, eat what and when you want, and keep your room as neat or messy as you want.

But you still have to manage to live on the money you have available. The only other source of money you'll have is credit cards, and that's where the trouble can begin.

How do you avoid problems? By planning and creating a budget, of course. Ugh! Well, let's get on with it, anyway. It doesn't get easier if you put it off.

Do you discuss family income and budget concerns with your children? Do you think your children know how to make and follow a budget?

We discuss at length now that college is approaching. I trust that my teens can make and follow a budget because we don't rescue them from budget issues. They are excellent savers, pretty good spenders, and have limited impulses.—Devyn V.

Does your family have and follow a written budget?

One person handles the budget. It's not written but it is consistent month to month. [Our] budget includes savings and investments. . . . Impulse [purchases] over $100 are generally discussed. [Our teens] discuss all purchases . . . they are both bargain shoppers.—Devyn N., parent

CHAPTER 35

The Budget Process

Whether you are a student or working in a full-time job or unemployed, you need to—perish the thought—create and follow a *budget*. Unlike many governments, your budget actually has to balance; you have to live within your means.

So what goes into a budget, and what's in it for you?

Have you ever "run out of money before running out of month"? With a budget, it's easier to have your money and your month end at close to the same time. With a bit of planning and juggling, you might even run out of month *before* you run out of money!

What is a budget? The road map that allows you to buy a car, get an apartment, set up utilities, plan for what things cost, save for the future, and not run out of money each pay period.

Building a Realistic Budget

Budgets fail because they are either incomplete or unrealistic. If you leave expenses off your budget, you are doomed to fail—but if you cut expenses too closely, you are also setting yourself up for a fall.

Let's look at the elements of a budget.

You probably have one source of income—your job (or jobs). You have lots of expenses, debts, wants, needs, goals, and dreams. An ideal but realistic budget tries to balance all these elements. Sound hard? Let's give a shot, shall we?

A budget has two columns: Income and Expenses. Some of the items you are going to see in the sample budget's "Expenses" column may seem strange at first, but the items are actually the key to achieving your dreams and meeting your wants (as opposed to your needs).

What are expenses? Lots of things. Some things you have to pay to live, some things make your life easier, and some things make your life more fun.

Expenses

Expenses come in several types:

- Regular and necessary
- Irregular but necessary

> You've probably heard the expression "pay yourself first." This is really a critical expense. If you don't pay yourself, you won't have money for emergencies, money to retire, money to cover times of unemployment, and so on. "Paying yourself first" means allocating money to your retirement and nonretirement investments and emergency funds just like any other bill you need to pay—not waiting to see what's left over in your checking account at the end of the month. There's probably almost never anything left!

- Regular but not necessary
- Irregular but not necessary

Let's look at each type and see what falls into each category.

Regular and Necessary—These are the payments you have to make to keep a roof over your head, food on the table, and the debt collector away. They are also the expenses that go toward ensuring you can deal with emergencies, build a retirement account, and accumulate money for a home down payment and other reasons. These are monthly bills and expenses. They are "needs" rather than "wants."

Irregular but Necessary—These are payments you have to make for the same reasons as regular payments, but they are made less frequently than monthly. They are for "needs" rather than "wants."

Regular but Not Necessary—These are things you spend money on every month (or during the course of a month) that are "wants" rather than "needs." The fact that these expenses are not for "needs" does not make them "bad" expenditures, but it does make them worthy of a closer look.

Irregular but Not Necessary—These are the bigger "wants" that come up now and then. The fact that these expenses are not for "needs" does not make them "bad" expenditures, but it does make them worthy of a closer look.

Income

This one is easy for most of you—this is what's in your paycheck each pay period, after all the taxes and other things are taken out.

Blending Needs and Wants to Create a Budget

How do you bring the expenses together to make sure your income covers everything? Create a budget. Sit down, list all your expenses and expenditures, and see if your income can cover everything it needs to.

Writing things down is a pain, but it is necessary. When you go on a diet and don't seem to lose any weight, it is often because you don't realize how much the little nibbles add up. It's the same with money—it drips out of your wallet and checking account—it doesn't just fly away.

Before you actually start to build a budget here's an exercise to try:

For the next month, try writing down every bit of cash you spend. You'll have a record of your other expenses by going to your check record and credit card statements. Only then can you look for ways to improve your cash flow and cut your expenses. Then go back through your check register and your credit card statements for the past six months or year and see what your irregular expenses were.

Once you've done that, fill out Tables 35.1 and 35.2. To make these useful tools you need to be really honest with yourself.

Then there are the things that you don't always pay for every month—such as car insurance or new clothes.

Bringing Your Expenses Together

Now for the hard part:

Add the monthly amount for your *regular expenses* (and don't forget to pay yourself first and build that emergency fund) and the average monthly amount in the irregular expenses, and see what you need to cover your needs and your wants.

Table 35.1. My Monthly Expenses

Expense	Need or Want?
Rent or Mortgage	
Electric Bill	
Gas Bill	
Water/Sewer Bill	
Phone/Internet Bill(s)	
Cable/Satellite Bill	
Cell Phone Bill	
Monthly Grocery Bill	
Personal Care (haircuts, massages, etc.)	
Car Payment	
Fuel	
Parking	
Credit Card #1 Payment	
Credit Card #2 Payment	
Credit Card #3 Payment	
Student Loan Payment	
Emergency Fund Payment	
Investment Account Payment	
Health Club Membership	
Miscellaneous Expenses	
Meals Out	
Coffee and Snacks	
Books, Magazines, etc.	
PAYING MYSELF	
BUILDING MY EMERGENCY FUND	
Total Monthly Expenses	

Table 35.2. My Irregular Expenses

Expense	Need or Want?
Clothes, shoes, etc.	
Auto Insurance	
Homeowner's or Renter's Insurance	
Life Insurance	
Disability Insurance	
Car Maintenance	
Car Taxes and Registration	
Trips (Packages, Airfare, Hotels, Food, Entertainment, Souvenirs, etc.)	
Total Irregular Expenses ÷ 12 (to get monthly average)	

Write the total of two types of expenses here:

    A._____

If this amount is equal to or less than the amount that you take home each month (after taxes, insurance, and retirement savings are taken out), you are in excellent shape. If this number is more than your take-home pay, something needs to go—perhaps the $150 on Starbucks coffee and danish, some of the miscellaneous expenses, or some meals at restaurants.

If the previous amount is more than what you take home, try this: Subtract out the amounts that are for "wants" rather than "needs" and write the new, lower amount here:

    B._____

If the result in "B" is less than your take-home pay, you are in good shape because you can eliminate some of the "wants" and make ends meet. If the result in "B" is still greater than your take-home pay, you need to proceed to the really hard part of budgeting.

The Really Hard Part of Budgeting

If you aren't sure where your money goes, but you run out of money before you run out of month, here are two drastic steps to take until you get control over your finances:

- Put *all* your credit cards away for the next three months. This includes your ATM or other debit cards.
- Write down every cent you spend—even for the newspaper.

You will be truly amazed at how much less money you spend when you don't have ready access to your credit, ATM, and debit cards. You will also be shocked at how much money goes to "little" things that punch a hole right through your paycheck.

Once you have a handle on your spending, have your taxes being taken out at just the right level, are paying yourself first and contributing to emergency and retirement funds, it's time to move on. In the next section you'll learn about the (honestly) fun stuff—investments.

Practical Exercises

1. Why should you pay yourself first? How do you intend to pay yourself first?

    _____

    _____

    _____

    _____

    _____

    _____.

2. What are some of your needs? What are some of your wants? How do you decide what is a need, and what is a want?

    My Needs   *My Wants*

    _____   _____

    _____   _____

    _____   _____

    _____   _____

    _____   _____

    _____   _____

I decide something is a "need" by:

_____

_____

_____

_____.

I decide something is a "want" by:

_____

_____

_____

_____.

13

Saving and Investing

There are thousands of books about investing—in the markets, in mutual funds, in gold, in real estate, and on and on and on. Now that you have money accumulating and need to get more than the rate your savings account or a money market account will pay, let's look at some of your options.

In order to keep things simple, we'll focus on a few types of investments: mutual funds, CDs, and dividend reinvestment programs (DRIPs). There are enough variations in these three areas to keep most financial advisors busy and happy.

You can always call a mutual fund company and ask for materials so you can read the details yourself—we'll only scratch the surface here. You might also talk to several financial advisors—maybe your parents' advisor, your insurance advisor, and your friend who is working as an investment advisor at a big company. Make sure to read, but take everything with a large grain of salt, and that goes for all the investment-related magazines and articles you can find.

Start small, contribute regularly, understand that investments don't always go up, and stay in for the long haul. From Young American's Financial Center clients:
What *are the three most important things you learned about saving and investing money?*

1. It will help in the long run. 2. It requires time and careful placement, whether it be in a CD or a normal account with interest. 3. You want to place your money where you can get the most interest."—Derek N., 15

1. Saving allows your money to go farther. 2. Pay yourself. 3. Get the highest interest rate. My mother and Young Americans Bank [taught me about] saving some each month."—Vanessa N., 17.

CHAPTER 36

Building Your Savings and Starting an Investing Program

Investing and Saving 101

Tomorrow will be here before you know it. It is so tempting to pull a "Phoenix" and say you'll start saving and investing next month or next week or next year. It might even happen. For those of you who would rather start with smaller investments today and let tomorrow take care of itself, this section will explain the advantages of saving now, the basics of investing and markets, and much more.

Plan for the Unexpected

Why? Consider this example.

In the section on taxes, Phoenix chose to forgo health and disability insurance because it was more fun to have the extra $150 every month. Alex took the insurance and gave up the $150. The twins decided to go jet-skiing in the Florida Keys, and both wiped out and broke a leg and dislocated a shoulder. They also suffered some cuts, and one of the cuts got badly infected. Both were unable to go back to work for three months.

The upshot? Alex paid a $250 co-pay to the hospital, although the actual bill was about $5,700. The accident also required five $20 co-payments for office visits to take care of the infection and follow-up care, for a total cost of about $350. While off work, Alex also received about 60% of normal pay—tax-free, thanks to the $50 monthly contribution for disability insurance. So Alex wasn't out too much money—$350 in medical co-payments and a few hundred dollars in lost pay.

What about Phoenix? Well, the office visits actually cost about $150 each, and there were five of them. The x-rays and other services during those visits added another $500 to the bill. So the cost is already $1,250, and the hospital costs added another $5,700, so the running total Phoenix has to pay is $6,950. And to make matters worse, there will be no paycheck for three months. At $3,000 per month that's a loss of $9,000. Of course, there are no taxes to be paid during that time, but who cares?

This is only part of planning for the unexpected. Obviously, Alex made the right choice by contributing to health insurance and disability insurance premiums through work.

There is another part of planning for the unexpected and that is building a reserve fund against the day you are unemployed or have to pay out-of-pocket medical costs, or have to fly back East for a funeral, or similar expensive, unforeseeable, but likely events.

Build an Emergency Cash Reserve

Before you start putting a bundle into retirement or nonretirement savings (paying yourself), you need to make sure you can survive for a few months with little or no money coming in. The section on getting and losing a job showed at least part of the reason why this is so important.

How do you build this reserve, and how much do you need?

When you're first starting out on your own, you have many unmet or delayed needs and wants. Of course, everything you buy takes money, and if you can't pay up front and in full, that money takes the form of a loan or a charge to a credit card.

Once you have a job things look rosy, but with the massive, abrupt layoffs that abound, you could easily be without a job tomorrow, through no fault of your own. Then what? How do you pay the car loan, the rent or mortgage, the minimums on your credit card, and buy food and gas and pay utilities?

Just thinking about how to handle bills with no job is probably giving you a headache. But that's where the emergency fund comes in.

As long as your first "real" job lasts for a few years, you can (and really should) build a savings or money market account with enough money to keep you going for at least three months. If you have no other source of income, three months is a bare minimum; if you have income such as a part-time job and/or unemployment, this three-month figure will stretch for six months or more.

How Do You Build Your Cash Reserve/Fund?

Slowly, faithfully, and steadily.

It sounds rough, but for your first few years at your first major job you need to put 5–10% of each check into a savings account or money market account and *leave the money completely alone.* As long as you are working, that money is off limits.

If you do this, you'll quickly get used to not having the money, and you'll love the sight of your monthly account statement. Wouldn't it be nice to know you could take care of yourself and your monetary needs for six months? Then you aren't trapped in a job you hate; you can quit and take some time to travel or volunteer, switch to a part-time job and go back to school for another degree, or take time to look for a new job.

> **Nothing ever seems to go as planned, so plan for the unexpected.**

If your take-home pay is $1,000 or so, twice a month, your emergency fund contribution should be about $100 to $300 each month until you have accumulated about $6,000—three months of take-home pay.

That means you need to save for 60 months (60 • 100) at the low end, 30 months (30 • 200) at the middle level, and 20 months (20 • 300) at the high end. Of course, as your income and expenses rise, or you have to use your emergency fund, you need to replace and increase the balance.

It almost goes without saying you have to plan for the things you can't really plan for.

Ask your colleagues at work, your professors and friends at school, your parents, and your older siblings what the most unexpected and costly things are that ever happened to them. You'll be amazed at the answers.

Write down some of the things you can think of, some of the answers your informal survey participants gave you, and decide how you would deal with and pay for them:

- Minor fender-bender—costing less than your insurance deductible
- Broken tooth—no dental insurance
- Burn mark on the counter in your rental apartment
- You need a new hot water heater in your new house

- _____

- _____
- _____
- _____
- _____
- _____
- _____

Most people will simply say "charge it." While this is a viable short-term solution, it is also an expensive one. You could up the amount you put into your emergency reserve/fund, or set up another fund for "life's little emergencies."

Pay Yourself First

This is the mantra of many financial advisors and other professional advisors. And you're not going to get off easy here, either—I hold and push the same belief!

Example: As a young lieutenant, I was "forced" into a savings plan and my first credit card. It seems the Army believed no lieutenant should be without either one. I spent the first week of my Army stint going through lines and signing paperwork. There were lines to get uniforms, lines to get a room, lines to join the officer's club, and lines at the bank. Once I got into the line at the bank, I was told to fill out a bunch of forms. One got me a checking account and an order of checks. Another form got me a MasterCard with a $600 limit.

A third line opened up a savings account. Of course I hadn't received my first paycheck yet, so I had no money to put into the account. The final line solved that problem: I met the concept of "pay yourself first." I viewed it as "forced savings" but that turned out to be the best financial move I ever made.

Each unmarried lieutenant was supposed to pay $100 (by allotment) into a savings account every month (married officers only had to do $50). This was the amount the Army "suggested" and the bank "encouraged" by putting another form in front of me to sign.

So instead of the $666 I grossed (before taxes) each month, $100 was gone to savings. And the banker I spoke with was right—having been a poor college student a few months earlier, I didn't miss the money. Over time I increased the amounts, and never regretted it.

The Role of Your Checking Account

Make your checking account work for you instead of against you. Make your checking account a partner in the "pay yourself first" and emergency savings parts of your financial life. That means using your checking account's features to automatically transfer money to your emergency fund account and your investment account(s).

You should have your paycheck automatically deposited in your checking account. In fact, many employers insist you do this. The major advantages?

- No rushing to the bank to cover or deposit checks
- Knowing when your money will be in the bank
- Reducing the chances you'll bounce a check

You can also have regular monthly payments taken directly from your checking account, reducing the chances you will be late for a payment. If you do this, make sure the payment dates follow your automatic check deposit dates so there is enough money in your account.

The Role of Credit

Careful use of credit cards can help you to continue to "pay yourself first" and build an emergency reserve account. How? By managing your use of credit.

Avoid using more than 25–50% of your credit limit. This helps you manage your credit card payments and keep them to a level that does not disrupt your savings plans. If your credit card debt is getting out of control, you will need to make that your first payment (after adding to your emergency reserves). Paying credit card interest is like throwing money down the drain, especially if the credit card balance is due to consumables (CDs, meals, clothes, etc.).

How Do You "Pay Yourself First"?

Start with small amounts. You could put these amounts into a savings or money market account, then move the money to mutual funds every few months. You could go directly into mutual funds through auto-debits to your checking account. The important thing is to contribute regularly. Save/invest part of every windfall (birthday and graduation money, raises, former loan payment amounts, inheritances, etc.).

Practical Exercises

1. How will you build your emergency reserve, and how much do you believe you need?

   _____

   _____

   _____

   _____.

2. What are some "tricks" you might use to speed up building your emergency reserve?

   _____

   _____

   _____

   _____.

3. How much of your credit limit on each card do you think is a reasonable amount to use? If you have a choice between only paying the minimum on your credit cards to fund your emergency reserve, or not funding

your emergency reserve so you can pay more than the minimum on your credit cards, which would you do? What factors would help you make your decision (hint—the cost of borrowing could be a major factor)?

_____

_____

_____

_____

_____

_____

_____

_____

_____

_____.

CHAPTER 37

Saving and Investing: Advanced

If you've got some money left over after building your emergency reserve, you are ready to start paying yourself. The fun part is learning about and then choosing the ways you save and invest your money. So here we go . . .

Getting Started

No matter what type of investments you eventually choose, you need to do three things:

- Invest small, regular amounts every month.
- Invest at least 25% of every raise and bonus and windfall you ever get.
- Diversify your investments—don't put everything into your buddy's new Internet company or bank CDs.

Types of Savings and Investment Options

There are quite a few types of savings and investment options. Here are the main ones and their key subcategories. In later chapters you'll learn a lot more about specific types of investments. Some are ways to invest, some are actual programs.

The main categories of savings and investment programs are:

- Savings accounts, checking accounts, money market accounts
- Certificates of deposit (CD)
- Mutual funds—stock based, bond based, hybrid, and other types
- Dividend reinvestment programs (DRIPs) to buy small amounts of stock
- Personal retirement plans (Roth IRAs, traditional IRAs). Company plans are covered later.
- Section 529 plans (already covered in the Planning for College section)
- Individual stocks
- Government and corporate bonds, municipal (tax-free bonds), high-yield (junk) bonds, savings bonds

We already looked at the Section 529 plans and checking accounts. Corporate retirement plans will be addressed later, in the benefits and insurance sections. This chapter will emphasize the following investment options:

- Mutual funds
- DRIP programs

> **Dollar-cost averaging—the key to success:** The theory and practice are simple. Every month (or every pay period), transfer the same amount of money to your investments. Many mutual funds allow you to start with $25 per fund per month, as long as the money is taken automatically out of your checking account each month, but suffice to say it is an easy, effective, nearly painless way to contribute to a variety of (diversified) investments.

Mutual Funds

For most young adults, mutual funds are the first, and often only, type of investments they make. Your company retirement plans are going to offer options that are, or look like, mutual funds. Most larger insurance companies, stock brokerages, investment advisors, and banks will suggest mutual funds as a great starting point. Why?

Mutual funds allow you to own an interest in a wide variety of stocks and/or bonds. You don't have to worry about picking the investments, just the overall classification (growth, international, bond, and so forth—more on this soon). You don't have to wait until you have enough money to buy 100 shares of a stock or a $5,000–$10,000 face-amount bond.

There are many types of mutual funds, and you should make your choices based on several things:

- How much risk you are willing to take. Some investments have a far greater chance of both loss and gains than do others.
- How long you plan to be in (hold) the investments. If you want the money for emergencies, some funds are too risky—they go up and down too much. If you want the money for a house payment in five years, you can take a bit more risk. If the money is for retirement, you may be willing to take a lot more risk since you have years to recover from losses and accumulate more money.
- How old you are. If you are still in your teens or 20s you can afford to lose money if the flip side is a greater potential for high returns. Someone in his or her 40s or 50s is less willing to take this type of risk.

How Do Mutual Funds Work?

When you invest in a mutual fund, you are buying an interest in a diversified portfolio of stocks, bonds, CDs, precious metals, or some combination of these. You can't point to a few shares of stock in the fund's portfolio and say, "Those are *my* stocks." Instead, you, and thousands or millions of other investors, hold an "undivided interest" in the entire portfolio, in direct relation to the number of shares you own.

Fund Basics

Before you start investing, take a bit of time (maybe a lot of time) to explore some websites such as www.investopedia.com, www.morningstar.com, and the sites of various mutual funds you have heard of. There is a ton of information on these sites.

Next, take a "risk assessment" quiz. The mutual fund company websites have them, financial and insurance advisors have them, and you can always do a Google search for "financial assessment" or "risk tolerance" or something similar. Most of these assessments will give you a score on a scale of 1 (no tolerance for risk) to 10 (willing to ski over the edge and look back later).

Then comes the part most people skip and may end up regretting. Call the mutual funds and ask for *prospectuses*, brochures, and other information for the funds that fit your risk tolerance number. Once you receive these documents, take time to read them and highlight areas where you have questions or concerns. Then call the fund company back and speak to a registered representative (a licensed investment specialist) and get the clarifications and answers you need.

Next you want to understand how mutual funds are priced and how they are sold.

Shares and Share Prices

Mutual funds generally own 20 to 40 different stocks and/or bond types, in line with the fund's stated investment objectives and category. Few funds will concentrate more than 4–5% of their value in any one stock or bond.

How are mutual fund share prices determined? The details are complicated, but the basics are pretty simple:

- Mutual fund MNO has 100,000 shares.
- The fund owns 1,000 shares each of 30 different stocks. The price of ten of the stocks' shares is $10; the next ten stocks' shares are $20; the final ten stocks' shares are $30.
- That means the value of the shares in MNO mutual fund is:
  - $10 ☐ 10 stocks ☐ 1,000 shares = $100,000
  - $20 ☐ 10 stocks ☐ 1,000 shares = $200,000
  - $30 ☐ 10 stocks ☐ 1,000 shares = $300,000
- The total value of MNO mutual fund: $100,000 + $200,000 + $300,000 = $600,000
- Since there are 100,000 shares and the fund is worth $600,000, each share is worth $6.00.
- This value is the *Net Asset Value* (NAV)—the value of one share after all sales and other charges are deducted.

In the example about calculating share prices, if the overall value of MNO mutual fund rose by 10% and no new shares were added (keeping the total at 100,000), the NAV of each share would also rise by 10%. Some of the individual stocks may have gained in value, some stayed the same, and some lost value, but it is the overall rise or fall in value based on *all* the stocks that causes NAV to rise or fall.

This 10% rise in the value of a share of MNO mutual fund is a capital gain for you. It is the growth in the value of your investment (assuming you haven't added more money to the mutual fund). If the share price had fallen (if many of the stocks in MNO's portfolio had lost value), your share price would have fallen and you would have a capital loss.

Many mutual funds sell their shares directly to you at NAV. Some financial advisors also sell mutual fund shares (from a variety of companies) to you at NAV. Other advisors and mutual funds add a sales charge of some sort, so you have to pay more than the NAV to get the shares, but your shares are only worth the NAV amount. This second, higher price is called the *Public Offering Price* (POP).

Types of Mutual Fund Shares

There are many types of mutual fund shares, and several management approaches you need to understand.

All mutual funds (even so-called no-load funds) have some charges, expenses, and/or fees associated with them. The actual percentages are detailed in the prospectus. You will also find examples in the prospectus that show the effect of applicable fees and charges on an investment. Many of these charges are taken out before your investment is credited with capital gains and/or dividends. A professional financial advisor can explain these fees and charges and how they impact the growth (or loss) in your investment.

No-load mutual fund shares: These shares are the ones you buy at the NAV price. So NAV = POP. There are no sales charges, but there are other fees and expenses you never actually see.

Load mutual fund shares: Most "load" mutual fund shares are of one of three types:

- Front-end load or "A" shares: These are mutual fund shares sold at the POP rather than the NAV. Generally, the POP is a bit more than 5% higher than the NAV. So if the NAV is $5.70, the POP is about $6.00. The 30-cent difference (5% of the POP) is the commission paid to the company/person selling the investment. So if you bought $1,000 worth of these "A" shares, only $950 will actually go into the investment. This is a one-time charge.

If you buy large amounts of "A" shares, the sales charge declines. Usually you have to buy at least $50,000 worth to see a reduction in the sales charge.

- Back-end load or "B" shares: These are mutual fund shares sold at the NAV, but with a twist. As long as you hold the shares for a number of years (generally between five and ten years), there are no up-front sales charges. However, the annual fees and charges are much higher than with "A" shares so at the end of the holding period both "A" and "B" share investments are worth about the same amount of money. The prospectus gives a good explanation of "A" versus "B" when both options are available with a mutual fund's shares.
- Level-load or "C" shares: These mutual funds are sold at POP, but this POP is lower than for "A" shares. Instead of a 5% up-front sales charge, "C" shares have a 1% sales charge at time of purchase and an ongoing 1% management fee, in addition to other charges and fees. Many stockbrokers use a version of this share class when they offer "managed" money—they charge 1.0 to 1.5% per year of your invested money as a management fee. They may even use "no-load" funds for this service.

Investing is a fascinating field, but one that benefits from advice. And I don't mean the advice in financial magazines, on TV, or from your friends. Usually the only people who make money from tips are the brokers, the magazine publishers, and the TV speakers and advertisers. Get a good grounding in financial matters, especially investments, from a professional before you strike out on your own. You'll be glad you did.

Where and How to Buy Mutual Funds

You can buy mutual funds directly from the mutual fund company, from a broker or investment advisor, from many insurance agents, from financial planners, and from many banks, credit unions, or savings and loans.

You can also set up a program where a regular amount is taken from your bank account (usually your checking account) and transferred to one or more mutual funds every month. Most mutual fund companies have a minimum amount per transfer of $50 and a minimum amount per fund of $25. So you can transfer $50 and divide it into two funds. This is the way I recommend getting started.

If you choose this auto-transfer (electronic funds transfer or EFT) approach, there are two things you need to do: Have your pay check auto-deposited *and* remember to subtract the EFT amount from your checking account each month.

One of the most important financial moves you can make is to build an emergency fund—three months' worth of take-home pay. The EFT approach lets you transfer money out of easy reach (your checking account) and into something a bit farther away—a money market mutual fund. You can also start accumulating money for a house down payment in a stock-based or balanced mutual fund (more on those soon), and as your income grows start accumulating for the very long term via EFT.

This brings us to the explanations of the various types of mutual funds you are going to encounter. These explanations are very basic and top level, and no substitution for a thorough reading of a mutual fund's prospectus.

Mutual Fund Categories

Mutual funds are divided into five basic categories: Money market funds, bond (debt securities) funds, stock (equity securities) funds, balanced (stock and bond) funds, and asset allocation funds.

Equity-Based or Stock Mutual Funds

Stock mutual funds invest primarily in stocks, but they may also hold other investments such as preferred stock or cash. These stocks may be sold on the New York Stock Exchange, the NASDAQ, or other exchanges.

The objective of a stock fund is long-term capital appreciation (growth), not producing income (dividends). Bond funds, on the other hand, seek to generate dividends. At your age you are far more likely to invest in stock funds than bond funds. However, stock funds may generate some dividends since some stocks pay dividends and the fund may hold cash (in CDs, treasury bills, and/or money market funds) and these generate interest and/or dividends.

There are six primary types of stock (equity) funds. Each type has a somewhat different focus.

- Large Capitalization (large-cap): These stock mutual funds invest mainly in the stocks of "blue chip" companies—large, well-known industrials, utilities, technology, and financial services companies valued in the billions of dollars. Since the fund's investments are in well-established companies, the funds are generally considered to be less risky than so-called mid-cap and small-cap stocks and funds. On a scale of 1 (virtually no risk) to 10 (very risky), these funds might be considered to be between a 5 and a 7.
- Middle Capitalization (mid-cap): These stock mutual funds invest in companies that are worth hundreds of millions to a few billion dollars. Mid-cap stocks and funds are considered to be riskier than large-cap stocks and funds—perhaps 6 to 8 on the scale of 10—so there is generally a greater risk of loss of value and a greater growth potential than with large-cap investments.
- Small Capitalization (small-cap): These stock mutual funds invest in so-called emerging companies. Emerging companies are generally worth less than $100 million, and are expected to have significant potential for future growth and profit. Small-caps are generally considered the riskiest stocks—about 8 to 10 on the 10-point scale—with the expectation of higher returns. Small-cap funds are far more volatile than other types of stock mutual funds or other asset categories.
- International: These stock mutual funds invest in stocks traded on foreign exchanges but purchased in the United States. International funds are subject to additional risks such as currency fluctuation, political instability, and the potential for illiquid markets. The risk scale of these funds can vary greatly, from about a 5 to as high as a 10.
- Global: These stock funds are similar to international stock mutual funds except that they include U.S. and other North American stocks—international funds generally do not invest in the U.S. and may exclude part or all of North America. The risk scale of these funds can vary greatly, from about a 5 to as high as a 10.
- Sector: These stock mutual funds invest in specific industry sectors such as technology, financials, health, or energy. Since they are not diversified across many industries, these funds may involve a greater degree of risk than stock mutual funds with more variety. The risk scale of these funds can vary greatly, from about a 7 to as high as a 10.

Why Buy Stock (Equity) Mutual Funds?

Few investors (that's what you are now!) can afford to buy 100 shares of a stock, let alone 100 shares of a number of stocks. This makes it hard to invest and even harder to diversify your investments to reduce your risk. Historically, stocks have been the best-performing long-term (10+ year) investment. Nonetheless, even the bluest of blue chip stocks go up and down in value, so mutual funds also rise and fall in value.

Many investors buy stock mutual funds because, historically, stocks have outperformed other types of investments over the long term. However, the value of the stocks in the fund's portfolio may go up or down as the market rises or declines. Remember, past performance is no guarantee of future results.

Debt-Based or Bond Mutual Funds

Bond funds invest in four main types of bonds:

- Corporate (taxable) bonds. These are low-to-moderate risk—about a 3 to a 5 on a scale of 10.
- Municipal (tax-free) bonds. These are low-to-moderate risk—about a 3 to a 5 on a scale of 10.
- U.S. government (taxable) bonds, notes, and bills. These are low-risk—about 1 or 2 on a scale of 10.
- High-yield (junk) corporate and municipal bonds. These are high-risk—about 6 to 10 on a scale of 10.
- International (taxable) bonds. These are moderate to high risk—about 4 to 8 on a scale of 10.

Bond mutual funds are intended to provide investors with a steady stream of income instead of capital gains. At your age these funds, with the possible exception of high-yield and international bonds, are probably not very appealing.

Bond Fund Types

Government Bond Mutual Funds: These funds invest in bonds, notes, and bills issued by the U.S. Department of Treasury as well as various federal agency bonds (mortgage-backed and others).

Municipal Bond Mutual Funds: These funds invest in municipal bonds issued by state and local governments and their agencies to fund projects such as schools, streets, highways, hospitals, bridges, and airports. Municipal bonds can be insured or noninsured securities. Income generated from municipal bonds may be tax-free.

Corporate Bond Mutual Funds: These funds invest in bonds issued by corporations to help fund business activities.

High-Yield (Junk) Bond Mutual Funds: These funds are hybrids of corporate and/or municipal bond funds. They are risky because some of the bond-issuers are "in default," meaning they aren't making payments, or are in bankruptcy.

International Bond Mutual Funds: These funds are similar to their counterparts in the preceding four areas. There is additional risk because of currency, political, and other factors.

Money Market Mutual Funds

Money market funds invest in short-term securities such as Treasury bills and CDs. Most money market funds offer a higher rate of interest than bank savings accounts. Unlike bank savings accounts, money market funds are not normally insured.

Balanced Mutual Funds

These are hybrid mutual funds that invest in a variable mixture of stocks, bonds, and cash. They generate both dividends and capital gains (or losses). On a scale of 1 to 10, these funds are between a 4 and a 6.

Asset Allocation Mutual Funds

These are like a "fund of funds." If your risk tolerance profile indicates a 5, that doesn't mean you have to invest only in funds with a risk tolerance in the 4 to 6 range. Instead, you could choose an asset allocation approach where your money is allocated among all the preceding categories to keep your average risk tolerance number in your desired range. In an asset allocation fund, your assets are diversified into cash, bonds, and stocks, weighted according to the portfolio strategy. The fund manager periodically redistributes the assets to keep in line with your risk tolerance profile. Portfolio strategies generally differ according to risk tolerance. Some of the asset allocation portfolios you might see are:

- Aggressive Growth (risk tolerance of 8 to 10 and long-term investment goals)
- Growth (risk tolerance of 6 to 8 and long-term investment goals)
- Growth and Income (risk tolerance of 4 to 7 and mid- to long-term investment goals)
- Income (risk tolerance of 1 to 5 and near-term income needs)

DRIPs

Maybe you really want to start accumulating a few shares of stock—not just shares in mutual funds. If you can buy at least 100 shares, you might want to go to a stockbroker or call a discount or online brokerage and set up an account. Otherwise you might consider the DRIP (dividend reinvestment program) option. Many large and small companies allow individual investors to buy very small amounts of stock, as long as all the dividends are reinvested in the company. To find DRIP companies, call the investor relations department or do a Google search for "dividend reinvestment program."

Practical Exercises

1. What do you consider a "good" allocation of mutual funds by type (by percentage) for someone your age? Why?

   _____

   _____

   _____

   _____

   _____.

2. What do you consider to be your risk tolerance range (on a scale on 1 = very low to 10 = I live for risk taking)? Why?

   _____

   _____

   _____.

3. What will you do with a $100 pay increase? Assume you have $70 after taxes. Why?

   _____

   _____

   _____

   _____

   _____.

CHAPTER 38

Personal Retirement Plans

How Much Do You Think You'll Need to Retire?

I asked several teenagers and young adults to answer this difficult question, and here's what they had to say:

> Once I retire in about 42 years!! ugh!! I would guess that I would need over $100,000 a year with inflation, which means I will need to save a great deal if I'm retired for 30–40 years.—Libby M., working young adult

> I don't know how much money I will need because it depends on my lifestyle. I know inflation is slightly below the interest on a bank account. So leaving money in a savings [account] will not be the best idea for retirement. I don't know how much money I withdraw each year in the last 30–40 years.—Kai Ge Y., teenager

> $50,000 sounds like average income. I'll need to shoot higher.—Derek N., 15, Vanessa N., 17

Individual Retirement Accounts (IRA)

In addition to company-sponsored retirement plans (covered later), there are several individual retirement account (IRA) plans to choose from:

- Traditional deductible IRAs
- Traditional nondeductible IRAs
- Nondeductible Roth IRAs

> **Even if you are still living with your parents you can set up an IRA. In fact, as long as you are earning income and filing a tax return (the 1040 short form, probably) you can have any of the three types of IRA.**

If you are not covered by and/or eligible for a company retirement plan, you absolutely, positively should be contributing the maximum allowable amount (or as close to that as possible) to an IRA. Even if you are covered at work (whether you participate or not) you should try to fund an IRA. IRAs are limited by a number of factors including income and eligibility for a company-sponsored plan. As your income rises you may not be able to keep funding an IRA.

Just because you are young, you are not excluded from putting money into an IRA. All you need is a job. You can put the full amount you earn into an IRA, up to the maximum allowed contribution each year. One young adult I know started her IRA when she was a teenager:

> I've had an IRA for years that I put money in for my retirement.—Libby M., a young working adult in Denver

As the Time Value of Money chapter showed, the time to fund something is as early as possible so you get the maximum benefit from compounding.

Let's look at the three types of IRA and their benefits and limitations.

Nondeductible Traditional IRA

Unless you are in a very high tax bracket and already contributing the maximum allowable amount to a company-sponsored retirement plan, this option is probably not going to interest you.

This type of IRA is funded with after-tax dollars. The growth is tax-deferred, so when you take the money out there will be taxes due on the growth, but not your original invested amount. If you take the money before age 59½, there will also be a 10% penalty due.

You can put up to $4,000 (2005–2007) and $5,000 (2008 and beyond) or the full amount you earned, if it's less, into this IRA each year. After 2006 the contribution limit is indexed for inflation.

Deductible Traditional IRA

This used to be the IRA of choice before the advent of the Roth IRA. Your contributions are made before taxes, and the growth is tax-free. However, when you take the money out, the entire value is fully taxable as income. In addition, there is a 10% penalty on withdrawals before age 59½.

There are also some critical income and eligibility requirements if you qualify to contribute to an employer-sponsored plan.

If your employer does not offer a retirement plan or you are not eligible to participate yet, there are no income restrictions on your deductible IRA contributions. If you are eligible, even if you choose not to participate in your employer's plan, Table 38.1 shows the income limits for making the full deductible IRA contribution.

Table 38.1. Deductible IRA Contribution Limits

	2005 Income Limits	*2006 Income Limits*
Single	Full contribution allowed: Up to $32,000 Decreasing contribution: $32,001–$41,999	Full contribution allowed: Up to $32,000 Decreasing contribution: $32,001–$41,999
Married	Full contribution allowed: Up to $52,000 Decreasing contribution: $52,001– $61,999	Full contribution allowed: Up to $52,000 Decreasing contribution: $52,001–$61,999

You can put up to $4,000 (2005–2007) and $5,000 (2008 and beyond) or the full amount you earned, if it's less, into this IRA each year. After 2006 the contribution limit is indexed for inflation.

Once you are 70½, money has to start coming out, no more money can go in, and taxes have to be paid.

Nondeductible Roth IRA

You've probably heard about the Roth IRA. Why is it such a big deal? Because it is a very smart investment.

Most retirement plan savings are made with tax-deductible dollars. That means sooner or later taxes will have to be paid on the contributed money. In addition, the growth in most retirement accounts is also tax-deferred, so there is a double whammy—everything in your retirement account is fully taxable, at the same rate as income, just at the time you want to sit back and enjoy retirement.

Not so with the Roth IRA. You don't get to take a current tax deduction for the money you put in each year, but the entire value of the account is free of tax when you retire (at or after age $50\frac{1}{2}$). You never have to take money out, and can keep contributing as long as you have income (Table 38.2).

Table 38.2. Nondeductible Roth IRA Contribution Limits

	2005 Income Limits	*2006 Income Limits*
Single	Full contribution allowed: Up to $95,000 Decreasing contribution: $95,000–$109,999	Full contribution allowed: Up to $95,000 Decreasing contribution: $95,000–$109,999
Married	Full contribution allowed: Up to $150,000 Decreasing contribution: $150,001– $159,999	Full contribution allowed: Up to $150,000 Decreasing contribution: $150,001–$159,999

You can put up to $4,000 (2005–2007) and $5,000 (2008 and beyond) or the full amount you earned, if it's less, into this IRA each year. After 2006 the contribution limit is indexed for inflation. The only eligibility consideration is your income, not whether you are or could be in a pension or retirement plan at work.

Now you're ready to begin investing.

Practical Exercise

If you contribute to an IRA, are you going to choose a Roth IRA or a deductible, traditional IRA? Why? If you aren't going to contribute, why are you making that choice?

_____

_____

_____

_____

_____

_____

_____

_____.

14

Understanding, Obtaining, and Managing Personal Insurance

Insurance is one of those things most people would prefer to ignore—until they need the coverage and benefits, that is—and then it's too late.

Many of your insurance needs may be provided for by your employer, or made available through your place of work for you to purchase. However, some forms of insurance are strictly personal purchases and others are necessities when you are between jobs, working at a place that has no benefits, or are in business for yourself.

CHAPTER 39

Auto Insurance

If you own a car, your state *requires* you have at least liability insurance to legally register your car. If you have financed (taken out a loan for) the car, the lender almost certainly requires you to have "full" insurance coverage: liability, collision, and other than collision (comprehensive) coverages.

You should be able to get insurance through your family's auto policy while you are still in school, but it may be very expensive.

Once you are on your own it really pays to shop around for the best insurance rates. They can vary wildly based on your driving record, grades, age, zip code, and so forth. There are "insurance shopping services" that may help compare prices, and your state Division of Insurance office may have a flyer with estimated insurance costs for the companies that do business in your state.

Always check with the family insurance company when looking for your own insurance policies, and with the big companies (State Farm, Allstate, Farmers, etc.). Make sure to check your rates every year—there may be a better option.

> **It can be done—the best things to do are maintain at least a 3.0 out of 4.0 GPA, take a defensive driving course, and take professional lessons or in-class instruction. Then be very careful, follow all the laws, and avoid tickets and accidents.**

How Much Coverage Is Enough?

Your state requires certain amounts of insurance to enable you to pay the costs of an accident when you are at fault. These amounts (called limits) are often very low, and do not begin to cover the cost of a serious accident. Your insurance agent will probably recommend something like $250,000 per person and $500,000 per accident—go for it. The added cost is not that much and one accident that exceeds your policy limits can really ruin your life and your credit rating.

If you have (or want) to carry collision and comprehensive coverage, most of the cost is based on the cost to repair your car, and your driving record. The one factor you can really control is the deductible—the amount of any accident (you cause) that you are willing to pay yourself. The higher your deductible, the lower your insurance premium (cost). But your lender may not let you have a really high (say $1,000) deductible.

INSURANCE POLICY BELLS AND WHISTLES

There are lots of bells and whistles you can get with your auto insurance policy. The one you should *never* be without is Emergency Road Service/Rental Reimbursement. If your car breaks down (flat tire, empty gas tank, burst radiator hose, etc.), this coverage gets you towed to a garage. It's much faster than waiting for an automobile club and only costs $10 or so per year. This is also the benefit that covers the cost of a rental car while yours is being repaired.

When your premium notice (bill) arrives, pay close attention to the due date. *Don't* be late—ever. If you are late, the insurance company can drop you like a hot potato.

Be very careful about making claims, too. If someone "keys" your car and it will cost $750 to fix the damage, and you have a $250 comprehensive deductible, it may be tempting to claim the damage to get the $500. Don't go there. The next time you make a claim, your insurance company will probably pay—and then cancel your coverage.

What ever you do, don't succumb to the temptation to go "naked"—you *must* have insurance. One claim could easily bankrupt you, and you could lose your car, too.

Case Study

Murgatroid decided to go without auto insurance on his brand new Saab. He had insurance long enough to register the car and get a loan, then dropped all insurance. Two months later he wrecked the car—and the accident was entirely his fault. What do you think happened?

Answer: Many things could have happened. Here are some of the most likely:

- Murgatroid still has to pay for the car even though it is totaled and he has no way to get the car fixed.
- He will get a number of expensive traffic tickets.
- He will have a very difficult time getting another car loan or insurance in the future.

Practical Exercise

How might you make your auto insurance more affordable?

_____.

_____.

_____.

CHAPTER 40

Personal Property Insurance

You may not own a home, but you still need to protect your stuff. Sure, your stuff may not be worth much, but that isn't much consolation if someone steals it, or the upstairs bath floods your closet and your clothes all mildew—you have to *replace* these things, and that costs money.

While you are living at your parents' their insurance should cover your belongings. In the dorm, you may or may not still be covered—ask your family insurance agent.

Once you are on your own, you need insurance to cover your property.

COVERING YOUR STUFF INSIDE YOUR CAR

If your car looks like most people's cars, it is likely filled the stuff you need for your daily routine and weekend fun. The items you leave in your car are largely *not* covered by your auto insurance policy. Most things in your car (CDs, clothes, laptop, and so on) are normally covered by homeowner's or renter's insurance. Don't get caught short. It's bad enough to have all your luggage and your laptop and CDs stolen from your car while you're on vacation, but it's far worse to have to cover the loss yourself.

There are three ways to insure your personal belongings:

- Renter's insurance
- Homeowner's insurance
- Condo insurance

Renter's Insurance

This is the insurance that will cover your stuff in your dorm or apartment (or in your car). It doesn't cover the building itself, so the insurance is quite reasonable. You should only pay $100 to $300 per year (unless you've had a lot of claims or live in a very dangerous or expensive area).

Condo Insurance

This is a form of homeowner's insurance. It covers more than just your belongings, but less than your entire condo. Why? Because the condo association has insurance that covers the outside of the building. Your responsibility is for your stuff and the walls and appliances inside your condo. This insurance is a bit more expensive than renter's insurance, but not too much more so.

Homeowner's Insurance

This form of personal property insurance covers both your stuff and the building you live in. It probably will run from $500 to several thousand dollars per year, depending on where you live, the number of claims you've made, the value of your home and stuff, and so forth.

WHY HOMEOWNER'S/RENTER'S INSURANCE MATTERS

I have had renter's, condo, and homeowner's insurance for many years, and had never "needed" any of them. Over the years I have paid more than $15,000 for property and contents insurance. In late 2000 I was gone for a few weeks, and returned to find my house almost destroyed. A valve under the kitchen sink had simply burst, and water had run from the main level to the lower level for a week. The final repair bill was over $80,000. With full replacement cost I was able to replace everything, and the repairs included new drywall and paint for the entire house, new hardwood floors and carpet, and removal of several tons of trash. Plus the insurance company paid for 12 weeks in an extended stay hotel while the work was being done. Was it worth having the insurance? Well, duh!

All these types of insurance include liability coverage for the damage you do to other people's stuff (if your air conditioning unit leaks onto a neighbor's kitchen table, for example—your policy probably will pay for the repairs to your place and hers, as well as fix her table).

There are also two main options for paying the costs of your loss: actual cash value (ACV) and replacement cost. I highly recommend replacement cost. If you have an old sofa that has an ACV of $50 (what you could sell it for, if anyone would even want it!) and it is ruined in a fire, the insurance company will only give you $50 for the sofa. You still need a place to sit, and a new (or even decent used) sofa is going to cost $500. Where are you going to get the remaining $450? That's where the replacement cost option comes in to play. It pays the cost of your new sofa. The cost differential for the insurance premium? Probably less than 5–10%.

You can't do much to control the cost of the insurance other than shop different companies and take a higher deductible. Insurance companies have formulas they apply based on the value of your home, its size, and so forth.

Be very careful about making small claims, especially in a three- to five-year period. Having lots of claims may cause your insurance to be cancelled or raise the rates dramatically.

One way to reduce your auto and personal property insurance costs is to have both with the same insurance company (not just through the same insurance agent). Most companies give sizable discounts for having more than one policy with them. The second (or subsequent) policy could also be life insurance.

Practical Exercises

1. What are the three ways to cover personal property inside your car?

      _____.

      _____.

      _____.

2. Why do you think it is smart to have replacement coverage on your renter's insurance policy?

_____

_____

_____

_____ .

CHAPTER 41

Life Insurance

Life insurance—who needs it? Maybe you.

If you are married with children, or planning to have children, both spouses almost certainly need some life insurance. Even if only one spouse works, the loss of the nonworking spouse can be financially difficult or even disastrous.

If you are single, the question is a bit harder to answer. If you expect to get married soon, or are a single parent, or have others who depend on you, then you probably need to consider having some life insurance.

That brings us to the questions of what type of life insurance and how much to have.

The Main Types of Life Insurance and Their Uses

First and foremost, never buy life insurance as an investment. Life insurance should only be bought when its death benefit will serve a purpose—replacing income, paying for child care when a spouse dies, paying death taxes, and so on. If there is an investment benefit in addition, great.

Second, never borrow money to pay for your life insurance. Too many people have tapped home equity or the cash in another policy to buy life insurance, and regretted it later.

Another consideration—your smoking habits (including chewing tobacco and the occasional cigar). If you have used any form of tobacco in the past year, you are going to pay higher smoker rates. In the case of term life insurance, this can triple your cost versus that of a nonsmoker. In the case of permanent insurance, it still adds 10–15% to your premium cost.

Finally, make sure you understand the main types of life insurance and which best fits your needs.

Here are the main types of life insurance you need to know about. There are also hybrids, but I'll let your insurance specialist explain them to you.

> **You may get some amount of insurance through your place of work. Keep in mind that if you need insurance this is almost certainly not enough, and the only way you can keep the insurance when you leave is to pay a very high price to convert the insurance to a personal plan.**

- Term life insurance
- Universal life insurance
- Whole life insurance
- Variable life insurance
- Group life insurance

Let's look briefly at each type, and when it is most commonly used.

Term Life Insurance

This is "pure" insurance. You pay a premium every month (or quarter, or year, or on some other schedule) and you are guaranteed a certain amount of insurance will be paid if you die (barring fraud or certain other conditions). The money you pay buys insurance, pays the agent, and covers the insurance company's costs—that's about it.

At this point in your life, term life insurance is probably exactly what you need, but later on your needs may change, and there are ways to plan for this—choose the "right" form of term life insurance at the outset. In the meanwhile you can buy hundreds of thousands or even millions of dollars of life insurance for $50–$100 per month.

Term life insurance comes in many forms, but the options you should look for are:

- Convertibility
- A 20- to 30-year guaranteed level premium

Convertibility

This is very important. This provision allows you to convert, or change, part or all of your term life insurance death benefit amount into another type of life insurance that is more "permanent." The forms of "permanent" life insurance are universal, whole, and variable. More on those shortly.

Once you convert term life insurance, your premium (cost) will rise dramatically, but by setting the premium at the right level you will be able to keep the converted insurance for a very long time—to age 100 or longer.

Why convert? Because you now want to keep your insurance longer than the original premium guarantee would last, or because you have a serious illness that may last longer than the guaranteed premium period. Of course there are other reasons, but those are the main ones.

> **Don't miss a payment on term life insurance or you may have no insurance. There is no cushion as with other, more permanent forms of life insurance.**

Guaranteed Level Premiums

This is important because the cost of life insurance actually rises each year older you grow. Insurance companies now have plans that average the premium over 10, 20, 30, or even 40 years so you will know what to expect.

Universal Life Insurance

This is actually a form of term life insurance that includes a cash value component. That means if you miss a payment and there is enough cash in the policy, you won't lose your insurance.

By structuring your premium payments properly, you can ensure the policy will stay in force until it "endows"—generally around your age 100.

The cash value can be tempting—you can borrow and repay it tax-free, but remember—this type of policy costs far more than the same amount of term life insurance death benefit. You can easily pay 10 or 20 times more for a permanent life insurance policy than for a convertible term life insurance policy.

Whole Life Insurance

This is another form of permanent life insurance. In fact, when it was designed many years ago it was structured to last for a person's "whole life"—hence the name. As with universal life insurance, it includes a cash value component. That means if you miss a payment and there is enough cash in the policy, you won't lose your insurance.

Premium payments are structured to ensure the policy will stay in force until it "endows"—generally around your age 100 as long as you don't borrow too much money from the cash value.

The cash value can be tempting—you can borrow and repay it tax-free, but remember—this type of policy costs far more than the same amount of term life insurance death benefit. You can easily pay 10 or 20 times more for a permanent life insurance policy than for a convertible term life insurance policy.

Variable Life Insurance

This is another form of permanent life insurance. As with universal and whole life insurance, it includes a cash value component. That means if you miss a payment and there is enough cash in the policy, you won't lose your insurance.

The main difference between variable and other forms of permanent life insurance is the way the cash accumulation is handled. Universal and whole life insurance policies invest the cash that accumulates in bond-like investments that pay interest. That limits the amount of growth of your cash value, but it also ensures at least a small amount of (2–3%) growth. Variable life insurance lets you choose how to invest your cash accumulation, using various options, called separate (or investment) accounts that look much like the mutual fund categories you learned about a few chapters ago.

Since there is more risk investing in stock-based investments (but more growth potential, too) than in bond-based investments, it is a good idea to "overfund" this type of life insurance. That means paying more than you need to in order to ensure there is enough cash in the policy to keep it going during poor stock market performances.

This is the other type of life insurance that often appeals to young adults—if you have the money to fund it you can get potentially tax-free growth on a large sum of money, and you can borrow it later.

Group Life Insurance

This is the life insurance you get and/or buy at work. As long as you are working for the sponsoring employer, you can keep the insurance. When you leave, the insurance goes away, unless you want to buy permanent life insurance, paying smoker rates, based on your current age. Can you smell expensive?

How Much Life Insurance Is Enough?

This is a hard call to make. As very rough idea, 6 to 10 times your annual income is a starting place. Insurance companies generally have limits so you are not worth more dead than alive, so 12 to 15 times your income is about the maximum you'll be able to get.

What Does It Take to Get Life Insurance?

No matter how little insurance you want (except for group life insurance), you are probably going to have to take a physical, give blood, give samples for an HIV/AIDS test, and so forth. Larger amounts of insurance (say $250,000 and up) have even more requirements.

You have to fill out an application, sign releases so the insurance company can get medical and credit and driving records, and maybe provide tax returns.

The Bells and Whistles of Insurance

Insurance policies have so many features, options, and other creative aspects that it is really worth talking to a specialist to make sure you get what you want, need, and can afford. In fact, talk to several specialists before you make a buying decision.

Practical Exercise

When it comes your turn to buy life insurance, what kind do you think you should buy, and why?

_____

_____

_____

_____

_____

_____.

CHAPTER 42

Personal Disability (Sick Pay) Insurance

Do you know what your most valuable asset is? Your car? Boat? Home? Entertainment system?

The answer is: None of the preceding. Your most valuable asset is your ability to earn an income.

Think about it: If your average income over the next 40 years is $50,000 per year, that's $2,000,000. What if you are hurt or sick and can't earn that money for a year or two or longer? How will you live? How will you amass the money you need to retire?

There are lots of statistics about your chances of becoming disabled, but on average you have about a one in three chance of being unable to work for at least three months at some time in your life, and once you are out for three months, many disabilities stretch out for years.

Think it will never happen to you? Here are some disabilities that wreck careers, even though at first they seem trivial:

- You hurt the tendon in one of your fingers, and now the finger is permanently stiff. No big deal? It is if you are a dentist or surgeon or a writer!
- You blow out your knee and it takes a full year before you can comfortably stand for more than 20 minutes. No problem? What if you are a nurse or a surgeon or a house painter?
- Your night vision becomes so poor you can't drive from an hour before sunset to an hour after sunrise. So what? If you are in sales and need to meet with clients in the evening, how are you going to get to their place and get safely home?

There are some ways to replace your income, starting with worker's compensation. Unfortunately, none of the preceding situations is likely to be covered by worker's comp. The situations probably did not arise from work, so they are not considered work related, so they are excluded.

The other way to replace your income is with disability income (sick pay) insurance. Rates vary greatly depending on your profession (roofers' rates are through the roof and CPA rates are very low), your age, and how much you earn. Private insurance companies are your source for information—go through one of their agents—unless your company provides this insurance for you.

How much does it cost on your own? A general rule is about 3% of your income.

CHAPTER 43

Personal Medical Insurance

If you can't get group medical/health insurance, there are options to cover yourself. Accidents and illnesses happen with startling suddenness. Even a quick trip to an "Urgent Care" facility can cost several hundred dollars, and most illnesses and injuries require several visits and then follow-up care such as physical therapy.

Ask your family or personal insurance agent for your options, or contact your local Blue Cross/Blue Shield or Kaiser Permanente office to see what your options are. Paying premiums hurts, but when you consider a "simple" broken ankle can cost several thousand dollars, an appendectomy $20,000 or more, and a baby even more than the first two things, it just doesn't make sense to go without.

Keep in mind that you usually have to be a full-time student to keep coverage under your parents' health/medical insurance plan, and even that goes away sometime between 19 and 25.

Tip: One way to reduce the cost is to have a very high deductible. Chances are, the policy won't cover any of your expenses during the year and you'll have to pay for all of your medical expenses. But if that major accident or illness happens, you won't be looking at bankruptcy or ruin.

15

Putting the Pieces Together

If you've made it this far, you have learned lots of diverse financial information. Now it's time to try and bring the pieces together.

CHAPTER 44

Building a Personal Financial Plan

Okay, you are probably entering information overload, so let's stop, regroup, and put all the things you've been reading into a plan you can use.

Combining the Elements You've Learned So Far into a Financial Plan

What is a financial plan? There are many definitions, but let's use this one:

> A financial plan is a personally tailored document that identifies your resources, expenses, and goals and combines them into a road map to get you where you want to go. It is a living document that benefits greatly from frequent revisiting, reassessment, and retooling.

What goes into a financial plan?

- Your resources—sources of income, scholarships, allowances, grants, loans for school
- Your expenses from your budget worksheet
- Your goals and dreams
- Your plan of attack

Why do you need a financial plan?

For the same reason you need a budget or a business plan if you want to start a business: to identify your route and keep you on track.

Let's look at some simplified sample financial plans. We'll start with a good one (Alex) and a bad one (Phoenix). Then we'll look at a few other plans for other situations.

The plans you are going to see here are very top level. If you are working with a financial professional, you are going to need to gather all the "Standard Financial Plan Materials" in the table, and the end result will be a very nice document that includes graphs, charts, and an asset allocation plan.

Working on your own, you need to gather the documents and do a risk self-assessment. Then you are ready to talk to someone at a mutual fund company to help you allocate your savings and investments to meet your goals and risk tolerance.

> **If you are working with a financial or insurance or tax advisor that person may have a worksheet you can use to draft your financial plan. That's a great starting point. You can also search online to sites and find sample plans.**

Standard Financial Plan Materials—Summary

- Your budget
- List of expenses that could be reduced
- Pay stubs (six months or more)

- Checking account statements (six months or more)
- Other bank statements (six months or more)
- Investment account statements (six months or more)
- Credit card statements (six months or more)
- Loan statements (six months or more)
- Insurance statements (six months or more)
- Tax returns for the past three years
- A list of goals and objectives
- A list of planned major ($500 or more) purchases
- Questions and concerns

Alex's Plan

Each of the documents in the summary list pays a role in creating Alex's plan.

- The budget (1) will show Alex where the money goes. It also shows how much is being saved and spent. The list of expenses that could be cut (2) will show where additional money could be saved to add to the various savings programs and help meet goals.
- The various financial records (3–10) will show Alex where the money comes from and where it goes.
- The goals and objectives (11) will help Alex focus his or her available cash to meet short, mid-, and near-term goals such as paying off a car loan (mid term), buying a new home entertainment system (short term), buying a house (mid to long term), and/or retiring at 55 (long term).
- Item 12, major purchases, is important since planned purchases incur far less debt and financial problems than impulse purchases.
- Item 13—Think about questions and concerns. Eventually you'll probably meet with a financial advisor and these will be addressed.

Alex makes $36,000 a year, and takes home about $2,200 each month. Here is where the money goes each month:

$1,000—fixed, basic expenses such as rent, utilities, food
$150—irregular expenses such as insurance, vacations
$150—coffees and meals out, miscellaneous
$300—emergency reserve (current value is $3,000)
$400—credit card and car loan payments (car loan balance is $15,000; credit card balances total $2,000)

That leaves about $200 Alex could use to start an investment program, use to contribute to the company 401(k), or simply "blow." There is also a fair amount of "wasted" money in coffees and meals, so Alex might be able to carve out another $100 per month. And when the $6,000 goal for the emergency fund is reached (in another 10 months), Alex will be able to greatly increase the amounts invested, and spend a bit more on the fun things in life.

Alex has a few goals:

- Get the emergency reserve account up to $6,000. That's a short-term goal and should be reached in about 10 more months.

- Accumulate $1,000,000 in the company retirement plan by age 55—that's in 33 years.
- Accumulate $1,000,000 in personal investments in the same time.
- Have enough money for a house down payment in five years—about $20,000 at 10% down.

Other considerations

- Alex expects to get 4% raises on average and a promotion (or job change) with a 10% raise every three years. That will increase take-home pay by about 4% a year, plus the bigger raise every three years. Alex plans to save half of any additional take-home pay, and enjoy the rest. So next year another $44 can go into investments each month, another $46 the next year, and a whopping $165 or so in the third year.
- Alex plans to set up and fund a Roth IRA as long as the income levels allow.
- As soon as Alex has the money saved for the house down payment, Alex will start contributing the maximum to his company's 401(k) plan—and they will add another 3% of salary—free money.

> **You might consider entering your budget and financial data into an Excel spreadsheet. That makes tracking, managing changes, and adding data much easier.**

Without going through all the details, Alex will easily have all the money for all his or her goals—and then some.

Phoenix, on the other hand, may never crawl out of the debt hole, as you shall soon see!

Phoenix's Plan

Each of documents in the summary list pays a role in creating Phoenix's plan.

- The budget (1) will show Phoenix where the money goes. It also shows how much is being spent—Phoenix is not saving a dime. The list of expenses that could be cut (2) will show where money could be saved to create the various savings programs and help meet goals.
- The various financial records (3–10) will show Phoenix where the money comes from and where it goes.
- The goals and objectives (11) will help Phoenix focus his or her available cash to meet short-, mid-, and near-term goals such as paying off a car loan (mid term), buying a new home entertainment system (short term), buying a house (mid to long term), and/or retiring at 55 (long term).
- Item 12, major purchases, is important since planned purchases incur far less debt and financial problems than impulse purchases.
- Item 13—Think about questions and concerns. Eventually you'll probably meet with a financial advisor and these will be addressed.

Phoenix makes $36,000 a year, and takes home about $2,400 each month. Unlike Alex, Phoenix doesn't contribute to health insurance or take any other benefits offered by the employer—that gives Phoenix another $200 per month to spend. Here is where the money goes each month:

$1,000—fixed, basic expenses such as rent, utilities, food
$450—irregular expenses such as insurance, vacations

$350—coffees and meals out, miscellaneous
$0—emergency reserve
$600—credit card and car loan payments (car loan balance is $25,000; credit card balances total $15,000)

That leaves nothing available to build an emergency fund or start an investment program, or use to contribute to the company 401(k). Phoenix simply "blows" a lot of money and has a huge debt ($40,000, and only 23!) to deal with. There is a fair amount of "wasted" money in irregular expenses, coffees, miscellaneous, meals, and so on. Phoenix could start here to get the money needed to pay off debts and build an emergency reserve. Phoenix simply spends too much on the fun things in life and has the debt to show it.

Where Alex's financial plan focuses on the future, Phoenix's plan needs to focus on the here and now—getting a handle on credit cards, reducing expenses, and building an emergency reserve. Only then will investing become a possibility, and with Phoenix likely to lose his or her job, problems are looming.

The best financial plan at this point for Phoenix would be to do several things:

- Cut the meals, coffees, and miscellaneous expenses to $100 per month.
- Use $150 of the $250 saved to buy into the company health/medical insurance plan.
- Put the credit cards away until the debt is paid off.
- Reduce the irregular expenses (probably vacations!) from $450 to $150. That will free up enough money to work on the credit card debt and build an emergency reserve.
- Put the additional $100 from the meals and miscellaneous expense savings toward credit card debt. Put $100 of the savings from the irregular expenses (the vacation that otherwise would add to the credit card debt!) toward reducing the credit card balance.
- Put the remaining $200 from the irregular expenses savings into an emergency reserve fund.
- Shape up at work to keep the job, and work back into the boss's good graces to get raises that can go to investments and debt reduction.

Unfortunately Phoenix will probably not change anytime soon, and in a few years will have no job and will have declared bankruptcy. Bummer. Even worse, the BMW 330i will have long since been repossessed.

Plan #3: Accumulating Money for College or Graduate School

This is a relatively simple plan, but one of the hardest to stick with. You can't really start to save much until you can get a job, and that usually means being 16. Then you are limited in accumulating money because you have to go to school and keep your grades up so your working hours are limited. Plus you want to hang with your friends, and enjoy the few summers of freedom you have left. But you need money for college—so you're stuck between a rock and a hard place.

Planning for the next few years is hard enough, and you certainly don't want to hear that this planning is good for you and will help you throughout your life and make planning for far off retirement easy—so I won't tell you these things, even though they are true!

If you are able to work 16 hours a week during the school year (about 38 weeks) and 30 hours a week during the summer (for 12 weeks, leaving two weeks for a vacation), and earn $10 per hour, you are going to earn about $9,680 (for 968 hours of work). You'll end up paying about $1,680 in various taxes, so you'll actually take home about $8,000. If you save half of this money for the two years you have left in high school, you will have a bit more than

$8,000 (since you'll earn a bit of interest). If you continue to work summers and earn about $3,000 after taxes, you can make a major contribution toward your college expenses.

Colleges and employers value your work experience more than you can imagine. They also value the line on your résumé that reads, "Earned over XX% of my college expenses while maintaining a 3.XX GPA.

THE COOLEST THING ABOUT FINANCIAL (OR ANY OTHER TYPE OF) PLANNING

Getting started is hard—harder than you can ever imagine until you've been there. But once the plan is in place it keeps rolling forward, with minor inputs from you. Your inputs are pretty simple—more money from each raise, bonus, or other windfall, and occasional (perhaps annual) reviews of your goals, risk tolerance, and investment performance.

Most people spend longer planning a two-week vacation than they spend planning the rest of their lives.

16

Let's Merge

Whether you are living with a roommate or two, a partner or significant other, or a spouse, combining assets and/or sharing expenses is very difficult. Money differences probably cause more split-ups than any other problem or issue does.

When I spoke with a focus group of young adults to get their inputs for the topics you've been reading about, they really wanted to see four things:

- How to look for a job
- How taxes work
- How to understand investments
- How to combine two or more incomes

So here are some ideas to help you out, whether you have a roommate or two, a spouse, or a partner. Love may make the world go 'round, but money woes and arguments often make it grind to a halt!

CHAPTER 45

When Two Become One

Merging assets, incomes, debts, and goals is a real challenge when you move in together or get married. It's even an issue with roommates.

Merging two households—even when neither of you has much to merge—is never easy. You might not be getting married just yet, but living together is just as stressful when it comes to financial matters. Even living with a roommate (platonic or otherwise) is filled with potential money and other financial issues.

Here are some living arrangements that involve at least some degree of shared financial resources—intentional or otherwise:

- College roommates
- Flat-, house- or apartment-mates
- Cohabiting couples
- Married couples
- Young adults living with parents or other family members

Not many young adults have the luxury of living alone. Until you have the financial resources to pay your own way, you are probably going to have to deal with some sort of blended financial arrangements. Each person in a living arrangement has certain expectations, goals, and dreams—especially when it comes to earning, spending, and saving money.

Here's a little quiz for you to help determine your "money style." People with different money styles can live together quite comfortably, but it takes work. Even people with the same styles can be so different in other areas that they have lots of conflicts around money (Table 45.1).

One solution to merging money is to have three checking accounts—yours, mine, and ours—and specific expenses that come out of each account. The theory and practice are fairly simple. Each person is responsible for his or her own personal expenses, from his or her personal account. Then the shared expenses are allocated so each person contributes to the "ours" account and the common bills are paid from this account.

Credit cards and loans are another issue. It is far better to handle these on a "yours and mine" basis—otherwise, you could get stuck with two problems:

- Someone else's unpaid debts
- A wrecked credit history for things you never bought, owned, saw, or used

Before you get too far into this "merger" business, it might be worth exploring views and values with a trained third party (a counselor of some sort). Money is just too touchy to deal with between two or more people—at least for most people.

Table 45.1. Money Styles

	Spending	Saving	Big Ticket Items	Other People's Money
The Spender	Spends everything every month but avoids excessive debt; doesn't pay off credit cards every month.	Plans to start saving "next year" or "next time." Doesn't realize tomorrow never comes.	That's what credit cards are for, right? Plans, but still buys on impulse, too.	Usually picks up the tab; always wants to pay his or her share. Tips generously.
The Saver	Saves a planned amount every month—pays self first; pays off credit cards every month, with rare exceptions.	Saves a set amount every pay period, before doing anything else. Conservative investments only.	Plans carefully to ensure the purchase is needed and the money will be there when the bill is due.	Rarely treats. Never complains when someone else picks up the tab. Tips exactly 15%.
The Negotiator	Discusses every expense; makes deals for allowable credit card spending and balances.	Discusses when, where, how much to save. Often gets nothing done—too busy talking.	Discusses the purchase endlessly and rarely actually buys anything.	Discusses who will pay the bill. Rarely picks up the tab without gaining a future concession. Tips 17.5%.
The Budgeter	Puts everything into a column—not flexible; has a budget for credit cards, too.	Has a line item for savings and investment. Not too conservative, but not a risk-taker, either.	Everything has to be in the budget. Not highly flexible in the near-term; add big ticket items to next month's budget.	Rarely picks up the tab unless it was in the budget (e.g., Joan's birthday lunch). Tips exactly 15%.
The Investor	Invests a planned amount every month—pays self first; uses credit cards with reasonable care.	Doesn't believe in savings accounts—just stocks. Invests every month, and has several retirement accounts.	Tries to plan for large purchases. Reluctant to take money from investments even when the item is needed.	Picks up the tab if he/she sees something in it for himself or herself. Tips 20%.
The Miser	Saves everything—at the risk of not paying bills; doesn't have a credit card.	Maxes out retirement accounts and other savings, but in a very conservative way.	Doesn't buy anything new. Tries to avoid major purchases or expenses.	Never picks up the tab. Tries to avoid going out at all. Tips 10% or less.
The Splurger	Blows the budget or planned savings with regularity; maxes out credit cards.	Won't even think about saving or investing. Wants it all right now.	Buys whatever strikes his/her fancy. There's no time like the present!	Always picks up the tab. Always tips at least 20%. Tries to buy friends.

17

Employer-Provided or -Sponsored Benefit Plans

Believe it or not, many people actually choose to work for a company based on its benefits. They will forgo some salary to have great health insurance or a top-notch retirement plan or stock options.

WHAT ARE BENEFITS REALLY WORTH?

The prevailing figure for the value of employer-provided benefits is between 25% and 40% of your actual pay. Don't believe it? How about this: If your employer provides health insurance and pays most of the cost, that is a big savings for you. It is worth even more if you break an ankle diving or skiing or whatever, since for a few dollars you get fixed, but the actual cost may have been $5,000–10,000 or more. That's like a huge pay raise.

CHAPTER 46

Group Insurance Benefits

Insurance provided to groups is almost always less expensive than insurance you buy on your own. Why? Because a group includes lots of people who will never or only occasionally use the insurance benefits, so much of the premium can go to cover the few people who use lots of benefits. When an individual buys insurance, there is often the intent to use as many benefits as possible, so the premiums get used up quickly.

What are the main types of group insurance plans you'll encounter at work?

Health/Medical Insurance

The two top benefits most people expect from their employer are health insurance and a retirement plan.

Health/medical insurance is very expensive to get on your own, so it is one of the most valuable benefits you get from your employer. Costs for this insurance have been skyrocketing because health and medical care costs have shot up well above the rate of inflation. That means you are probably going to have to pay some of the cost of insurance.

Most employers you are likely to work for will offer some form of health/medical insurance. However, if you work for an employer with fewer than 100 employees, the likelihood of offering this type of insurance is much lower than at employers with thousands of employees. If you work less than 24–30 hours a week, you may not qualify for health/medical insurance under your employer's plan.

In order to manage costs, most employers now shift part of the premium expense to you. This means you may have to pay as much as one quarter to one half of your insurance costs, and half to all of your family members' insurance costs. When you consider that a routine physical can easily cost $1,000, a simple fracture $5,000, and a healthy pregnancy and delivery $15,000, the cost is actually a bargain.

COBRA/Continuation

Although most forms of group insurance go away when you are no longer part of the group (when you leave the employer, for example), there are provisions that allow you to keep your health/medical insurance as long as you are willing to pay the full price.

This plan, called COBRA (Consolidated Omnibus Retirement Act) for groups with 20 or more participants and Continuation (or something similar) for smaller groups,

Most company benefit plans—insurance and retirement—require you to make a choice in certain limited "windows" (time frames). If you miss or skip your window, you may have to wait three to six months or even a full year before you can choose the benefit again. You may also be limited as to when you can make changes or add/drop family members. Read your employee handbook and other materials carefully and ask HR staffers lots of questions.

lets you pay the employer the cost of your insurance (plus 2.5% for administrative expenses) and keep your insurance for 18–36 months, and sometimes longer.

If you can afford the premiums and/or need the insurance benefits, this is a fabulous benefit. However, most young adults can't afford the cost and let the insurance go. You only have about 30 days from the end of your employment to let your former employer know you are choosing COBRA/Continuation, so don't let your window of opportunity pass you by.

Disability Income Insurance

This is the insurance program that replaces part or all of your take-home pay if you are sick or injured and unable to work. If the illness or injury is work related, workers' compensation may cover some of your salary, but disability income (DI) insurance is usually more comprehensive, flexible, and generous.

There are two types of group DI insurance:

- Short term
- Long term

Short-Term DI Insurance

This is the form of DI insurance that pays for the first 13 to 26 weeks of a covered disability. Often your employer pays the cost of this insurance, so it doesn't come out of your pay. This is both a good and bad thing.

If your employer pays for your insurance and you ever receive DI payments, the payments are probably taxable, and they are only 60–70% of your regular gross (total) pay. That is going to leave you with less income than if you were working—a lot less income.

If you pay your own DI insurance premiums, any benefit you receive will be tax-free. At 60–70% of your gross (total) pay, you should take home about the same amount as when you were able to work.

Long-Term DI Insurance

Long-term DI insurance picks up where the short-term plan leaves off. That means it starts paying when you have been disabled for 13 to 26 weeks. You continue to receive benefits for as long as the insurance contract allows—often until you are eligible to retire—as long as you are off work because of a covered disability.

Normally you pay for this insurance (so you can choose not to—just like Phoenix), but it is so cheap that forgoing it doesn't make sense. Figure on about $25–$50 per month, and you'll get tax-free income for as long as a qualifying disability lasts.

Workers' Compensation

You don't pay for this. By law, your employer is almost certainly required to buy this insurance for all employees.

This insurance pays benefits for certain work-related illnesses and injuries, including medical treatment and maybe rehabilitation services.

Life Insurance

Many employers provide $50,000 of group term life insurance for each employee, often at no cost to you. You are also able to increase this amount at a very low cost.

If you have a family or other obligations, or you can't get or afford other life insurance, it may be very worthwhile to buy additional insurance at work.

Keep in mind this insurance is only available at such low rates while you are working for the employer.

CHAPTER 47

Retirement Plans and Stock Options

You always want to accumulate your own investments for emergency reserves, nonretirement savings, and IRA savings, but your employer may offer one or more qualified retirement plans and/or stock option programs to help supercharge your retirement savings. Some employers even give you matching—or *free*—money as an incentive to contribute to a retirement program.

Here are the main forms of company-sponsored (so-called qualified) retirement plans:

- SEP-IRAs
- SIMPLE IRAs
- 401(k)s
- 403(b)s
- Defined benefit plans
- Defined contribution plans
- Profit-sharing plans
- 457 Deferred Compensation plans

The plans you are most likely to encounter are 401(k) plans, profit-sharing plans, and SIMPLE IRAs, so I'll give you the most information about them, with highlights of the other plans.

401(k) Plans

These qualified retirement plans are named after the section of the IRS Code that authorized them. Many companies offer these retirement plans, often in combination with a profit-sharing plan (PSP).

The money you put into a 401(k) is taken out of your pay after Social Security and Medicare taxes are deducted, but before any other taxes are applied. That means your contributions are tax-deferred and will be taxed when you eventually take the money out at retirement.

Since your contributions are tax-deferred and the money is meant for retirement, taking money out before retirement is going to involve paying all the deferred taxes *and* a 10% penalty.

There is now a Roth 401(k) option that lets you put in *after tax* dollars. This money grows *tax free*, not merely *tax deferred*. This is truly the best of both worlds—what you have is 100 years yours at retirement—*no taxes due*. The same applies to 403(b) plans.

How Much Can You Contribute to a 401(k) Plan?

In 2005 you can contribute up to $14,000, and in 2006 this amount goes to $15,000.

Why Contribute to a 401(k) Plan?

The best reason to contribute is to get the tax deferral or tax-free growth with the Roth option. If you put $3,000 into a 401(k) (that's $250 per month), you will defer paying the taxes on that money. So your take-home pay doesn't drop by $250, it only goes down by about $150–200 depending on your tax bracket.

The next best reason to contribute to a 401(k) plan? To get "free" money from your employer. If your employer has a PSP, you may be entitled to matching funds of as much as 3% of your gross pay. There are strings attached, as you'll see in the PSP section, but they aren't too bad.

One more reason—it's easy. You set up the deduction and it just keep going and going and building and building. No effort on your part, and you don't even have to remember to subtract the money from your checking account—it comes out before your paycheck goes to the bank.

Normally you have to work for an employer for six months to a year before you are eligible to contribute to a 401(k) or similar plan, but not always.

Investing Your Money

Smaller companies tend to use "pre-canned" 401(k) plans—packages. Larger companies usually have a plan with an administrator and lots of investment options.

To understand the investment options available, go back and revisit the mutual fund information we covered earlier. You are probably going to have 10–20 mutual funds to choose from, so choose wisely. This is not the time to be too conservative and pick all bond mutual funds or too aggressive and pick all small-cap mutual funds. Keep in mind your risk tolerance and invest accordingly.

Borrowing Your Money

Many 401(k) plans allow you to borrow part of your account value for certain purposes such as an illness or the purchase of a first home. If you use this feature, do so with extreme care. Why? Because you have to pay your account back, and you have to do so with interest.

In addition, when you are paying your 401(k) loan back, you have to do so with money that is first subject to Social Security and Medicare taxes (again).

Finally, if you leave the company you must immediately pay the remaining balance of your loan or you will owe taxes and the 10% early withdrawal penalty on the amount outstanding.

Getting Your Money Out

At the end of this chapter there is a discussion on taking your money out of a company-sponsored retirement plan when you leave the company.

Profit-Sharing Plans (PSPs)

These are the plans where your employer gives you a share of the profits. The PSP may be tied to a 401(k) or 403(b) plan, or it may not.

There are conditions attached to getting and keeping this "free" money:

- You normally have to work for the employer for six months to as much as two years before you are eligible.
- There is a vesting schedule—you don't get full ownership of the money from your employer until you've been there for five to seven years or so.
- Your employer doesn't have to give any money, but when money is given it must be done on the same basis for all eligible employees.
- Most employers have additional criteria and max out their contributions at 3–6% of your compensation.

403(b) Plans

These plans are much like 401(k) plans as far as limits and PSPs go. They are offered by nonprofits, schools, hospitals, and similar employers.

The rules don't allow these plans to invest in mutual funds—they have to use tax-sheltered annuities (TSA) with investment options that look much like mutual funds but are not mutual funds.

SIMPLE IRAs

The SIMPLE IRA is a plan that is tailored to small businesses. Rather than a master account and plan administrator [as is the case with the 401(k) and 403(b) plans], there are simple plan documents and the plan functions as an IRA (individual retirement account). You control your money.

The SIMPLE IRA plans allow you to contribute up to $10,000 in 2005 and 2006. In addition, your employer will put between 1–3% of your salary into your accounts (although there are additional rules so the money may not be given to you every year).

You get to invest your money into the range of mutual funds available with the SIMPLE IRA plan your employer chooses.

Since there is no administrator or company oversight, you usually can't borrow from these plans.

SEP IRA Plans

These plans are also forms of IRAs, but the money is contributed entirely by your employer. If you meet the plan conditions (length of employment and some other things), you get the same percentage of your salary as all the other employees get. The allowable percentage is the lesser of 25% of your compensation or $45,000 (in 2006) adjusted each year for inflation.

Few employers offer these plans because they have to "give" too much to their employees. You will probably never see one of these plans unless you start your own business and only have partners, not employees!

Defined Benefit Plans

These are the some of the "old-style" retirement plans your grandparents expected from their employers. There aren't many around, and those that still exist are often in financial trouble.

These plans agree to pay a defined amount at the time you retire, and are normally funded by the employer. They are expensive to maintain and fund.

Defined Compensation Plans

Like the defined benefit plans, the few of these that still exist are often in financial trouble.

These plans agree to pay a defined percentage of compensation at the time you retire (based on some average of salary and the number of years you worked), and are normally funded by the employer. They are expensive to maintain and fund.

Section 457 Deferred Compensation Plans

Some companies and many state and city entities (such as police and fire departments) allow employees to defer part of their income into a plan that makes the money available when the person retires.

Stock Options and Other Incentives

If you go to work for a start-up company (or start one yourself) especially in the high-tech or Internet fields, you are likely to be offered some sort of stock option or other incentive plan in lieu of a typical salary. You may get a low salary, but if the business succeeds you will make a killing when you exercise your stock options and then sell the stock.

Some companies offer a mix of salary and commission (base plus commission or draw against commission) and that can greatly increase your earnings if you're good at sales. Some companies offer a large chunk of your pay as an incentive-based bonus.

Taking Your Retirement with You

To leave, or not to leave—your retirement money, that is—that's the $100,000 question. You've moved on to another employer, or retired, or are otherwise between jobs. But your retirement account is still at the place you left. Is a former employer's pension plan and administrator really the best place to manage your hard-earned retirement dollars?

Sometimes it makes sense to leave retirement money with a former employer, but many times it simply does not. Some money either can't be moved, or is very difficult to move. For example, money (or the promise of money) in a deferred compensation plan, defined benefit plan, or defined compensation plan is usually going to have to stay where it is. However, the money you have accumulated in other qualified retirement plans, such as a 401(k), 403(b), SIMPLE IRA, SEP-IRA, or profit-sharing plan, can almost always be moved.

Why would you consider moving your qualified retirement plan money? Where can you move the money? How do you go about moving the money?

First of all, if you no longer work somewhere, whatever the reason, ask yourself, "Why would I even consider *leaving* my money in a plan over which I have no control? What's in it for me?"

Once you have left the company, you will have greatly limited access to information about the company's retirement plan. You'll have to make sure you keep the plan administrator informed of your whereabouts so you get current information, and you'll be on your own when it comes to making investment decisions.

People tend to move money out of a former employer's qualified retirement plans for one or more reasons:

- Control
- Access
- Safety

- Diversification
- Anger
- Better options
- Access to a new employer's plan

Control is the major reason people move money out of a company plan. Anger is the probably the second most common reason, and access to better options is likely the third most frequent reason for moving money.

Where Can You Move Your Money?

You can move money to two places:

- Another qualified plan (at your new employer)
- Your personal IRA(s)

For many people, moving money to traditional or Roth IRA account(s) they personally control is the best possible choice.

If your former plan is a 403(b) TSA, you have a chance to take your money out of an annuity (with its attendant expenses and insurance costs) and move the money to a bond- and equity-based IRA.

Keep in mind you cannot borrow from your personal IRA accounts the way you could from a 401(k) or similar account. You can take money out for 60 days and replace it, then wait 365 days and do it again. In addition, you can take money out of your Roth IRA without penalties (for example, to buy a first home), but that is not a loan—you probably can't simply repay the Roth IRA withdrawal.

Getting Your Money Out

In many cases you can contact your former employer(s) and have your retirement plan money transferred directly to your traditional IRA. You may even be able to pay taxes and put some of the money into a Roth IRA. Then the money you take out in the future will be tax-free, or you can leave it in the Roth IRA indefinitely.

If you decide to move your company retirement account(s) to your IRA, there are some important considerations.

First, you want to transfer the money in such a way that you are not subject to a 20% automatic withholding tax.

Next, you need to follow your former employer's transfer/rollover rules to the letter, or it will take a long time to get your money. Many pension plan administrators have specific forms you have to use; some may even require signature guarantees (from your bank). In other cases you have a very tight window for getting your money out—perhaps the request must be made by the 15th of the month preceding the end of the quarter before the quarter when you want to get the money. And then you may have to wait another 90 days or more.

Finally, you need to work closely with the custodian of your company's retirement plan to make the transfer a smooth one. Mistakes can be costly in terms of penalties, taxes, lost opportunities, and more.

CHAPTER 48

Other Employer-Offered or -Sponsored Benefits

Many employers offer employees perks that are actually very valuable benefits. Think how much more you would have to earn to pay for these things yourself.

Tuition Payment or Reimbursement

Your employer may offer a fabulous benefit—fully or partially paid or reimbursed college or graduate school tuition. If you want to pursue a degree in an area that your employer sees as adding value to the company, tuition money may be yours for the asking.

Vacation and Paid Time Off

Most companies offer a number of paid holidays—generally about ten per year.

Most companies also allow two or three weeks of paid vacation time each year. You may be able to carry up to one year of vacation time forward, but if you have "banked" more than two years of vacation time, you may lose some of the days.

Some employers (especially schools and the government) may allow you a number of sick days, and let you bank those days you don't use.

Finally, many employers are going to a system of "floating" days off—holidays that you can take to extend a paid vacation or make a long weekend.

You may also get some "personal time" for doctor's appointments and the like, and community service time to work on volunteer projects or go to a court hearing.

Unpaid Time/Leave of Absence

Some companies allow you to take a period of time off as an unpaid leave of absence, or even a paid sabbatical. Others make you take a "leave of quit."

Cafeteria/Section 125 Plans

This area can get a bit confusing since the term "cafeteria plan" is used interchangeably with "Section 125 Plan."

Section 125 Plan Basics

A Section 125 plan refers to the section of the IRS Code that allows employers to establish a plan where you can put pretax dollars to take out for certain expenses such as

- Medical insurance premiums
- Deductibles
- Unreimbursed medical expenses (including dental and vision)
- Child care expenses

The money goes into your account each pay period and must be spent in full at the end of the year or your employer gets to keep it.

Cafeteria Plan Basics

A cafeteria plan really refers to a way of allocating benefit dollars (on the part of the employer) and choosing benefits (on your part). These benefits may include

- Dollars to pay for the balance of your share of the medical insurance premium.
- Dollars to use to "buy" extra vacation days, sick days, or similar benefits.
- Dollars to use for other insurance options.

18

Planning for Major Purchases
without Breaking the Bank

You are in the "major acquisitions" phase of your life. That is a great place to be if you can manage to coordinate your wants and needs so you don't dig yourself into a well of debt. Debt, in the form of credit cards and loans, can be both your biggest benefit and your worst nightmare. The choice is entirely yours.

CHAPTER 49

The "Wise" Use of Debt

At the beginning of this book you read over and over how important credit is and how careful you must be so you manage it rather than it managing (and controlling) you. Using credit (cards and loans) wisely is easy to learn. You either take it slowly until you have a feel for how much you can manage, or you get immediately over your head, and lose your cards, your car, and your good name. I wish there was a place in between, but there really isn't.

So how much debt is enough? How much is too much?

Enough Debt

If you can normally pay your credit cards in full each month, while still paying your other expenses and obligations, your debt level is okay.

If you can make your loan payments on time *every* month, your debt level is okay.

If you occasionally carry a balance but still make well over the minimum monthly payment, your debt level is probably okay, but be careful.

Too Much Debt

If you can only make minimum payments on your credit cards, your debt level is too high.

If you make occasional late payments on your loans (or other expenses such as rent and utilities), your debt level is too high.

If you are transferring credit card balances from one card to another to get a lower interest rate, your debt level is too high.

If you are at or near your credit limit on even one credit card, your debt level is too high.

If you are using one credit card to make the minimum payment on another, your debt level is too high.

If you routinely have to pay for basic items such as groceries and books with credit cards, your debt level is probably too high and your use of credit is probably unwise.

Facing Bankruptcy

If you miss or skip credit card payments altogether, you are flirting with bankruptcy.

If you miss or skip payments (loans, rent, etc.) altogether, you are flirting with bankruptcy.

If you are getting new credit cards because your old ones are at their limits, you are flirting with bankruptcy.

If you are avoiding answering the telephone because you think it is someone trying to collect money you owe, you are flirting with bankruptcy.

CHAPTER 50

Making the Big Purchases

As you move through young adulthood, you are going to need and want to make major purchases. You'll probably start with a used car, pay for college or other schooling, then buy a new car, then a house, and maybe a boat a few years later. With a bit of planning, these purchases can be easy to complete and the loans simple to qualify for.

Unless you have pots of money or inherit a bundle, you are almost certain to need to borrow money to make these purchases.

You'll also have certain "wants" that involve big expenses and may or may not be a good use of your credit cards and loans—the expensive vacation, the honeymoon, an engagement ring, and so forth.

Most big purchases require a down payment of 10–20% of the purchase. This shows the lender you are responsible and serious. You are able to focus and accumulate money, and still meet your other expenses and obligations. This is very important in the world of lending.

The easiest way to accumulate the down payments you need is to save in a regular, systematic way. If you have been saving $300 every month for the past five years you are going to have almost $20,000—a good down payment for your first condo or house. If you simply wake up one morning and say, "Gee, I'm really tired of this apartment, I think I'll go buy a house," you are going to have a bit of a problem—a $20,000 one to be precise.

Sorting Needs and Wants

When it comes to using credit cards and loans, there is a big difference between a need and a want. You may need a reliable, low-mileage car, but you want a new sports car. The first one is affordable; the second will destroy your budget and take all the money you've been accumulating toward a house down payment.

Funding the car is going to probably take a loan. The used car may need a $12,000 loan for four years and the sports car a $30,000 loan for six years. You can afford the payments on the used car loan without stopping your house down payment savings; to afford the sports car loan will take all your house down payment savings as a car down payment and the money you've been saving to pay the higher, longer loan payments.

You get two weeks off from work each year. You *need* to get away—maybe a camping and bicycling trip with three friends from school. You estimate the cost at $500 each. But what you *want* to do is go to Europe for two weeks and stay in three-star hotels and rent a car, at a cost of about $2,000.

You know you have enough money in your checking account (since you've been skipping your morning coffee for a few months and saving the money) to pay for the camping trip. Your buddies are eager to go. You can fund the European trip using your credit card—you just got a new one with a $3,000 credit limit and you're ready to take it for a test ride.

Life is filled with choices. Instant gratification and funding both needs and wants is probably more than your income, budget, and goals can stretch to accommodate. That doesn't mean you can't have fun; as the two preceding examples show, fun is in the eye of the beholder, and doesn't have to wreck your savings strategies or break your bank.

19

Starting a Business

Maybe you've decided the corporate world isn't for you, or you have a great lawn care service going, or you love to cook and want to make money doing what you enjoy. Then maybe you should consider starting a business.

CHAPTER 51

The Major Elements for a Successful Business

So you think you want to be in business for yourself . . .

Okay, here are some things you need to know to get yourself organized and build a business that succeeds. Let's start with the basics.

Have a Well-Thought-Out Plan

You need a business plan. This plan is your "road map to success." You probably wouldn't just get in your car and drive from Baltimore to West Covina, California, without making some plans—getting maps, checking road construction and detours, finding places to stay, getting enough cash for the trip, and so on. So why would you want to start a venture that could become your life's work without a road map?

Even if your business is a summer lawn service or day care, having a plan can really help you make more money. Being able to put a line in your résumé "Wrote and implemented a business plan for a *successful* summer landscaping business" means something to future employers. This is the sort of accomplishment that helps you stand out in a field of new graduates.

If you are going to work as a sales rep (insurance, computers, recruiting, etc.), a business plan will help increase your success—you'll be head and shoulders above the other reps in the office.

Writing Your Business Plan

Your plan for success needs to be in writing. I have included a sample outline for a plan, and you can see dozens of additional plans if you poke around the SBA's website at www.sba.gov. There's an entire section of sample business plans, plus tons of tips and ideas to help you succeed.

Your business plan lets you and possible investors (your friends, parents, bankers, loan co-signers) know what you plan to do and how you plan to do it.

By putting your plans down in writing, you help yourself identify the issues before they take you by surprise and trip you up. You are an entrepreneur and are taking a big risk starting your own business. More power to you.

So what goes into a business plan?

> **According to various SBA statistics, fewer than 80% of all businesses last more than five years. In fact, as many as 50% don't make it through the first two years. Sometimes things just go wrong, or the person chose the wrong business, but in an awful lot of cases the business idea just wasn't thought out properly and documented. Remember: Proper planning prevents poor performance!**

Your Business Plan

1. Tell the world about your business
   - General description
   - History of your idea or product or service
   - List of your products and/or services
   - Who will your customers be?
2. Management and Ownership
   - Your and your partners' biography(s) or résumé(s)
   - Explanation of how your background and skills fit your business
   - A chart showing the roles of each partner
3. Marketing and Sales
   - Analysis/information that shows there is a need for your products/services
   - Scope/size of your market—you need data here
   - Trends in your market
   - Who is your competition/what sets you apart from your competition
   - Pluses and minuses of your products/services
   - Pricing structure, and how you decided what your prices would be
   - Sales strategy—how, where, and when you will sell your products/services
4. Financial Information
   - Where will your start-up and operating money come from?
   - If you are looking for a loan, how much and how you reached that amount
   - What the loan is for—how the money will be used
   - How the loan will be repaid
   - Projected income and balance sheet
   - Financial records if your business has been around for a few years
   - Description of collateral—property that can be sold to pay your loan if you don't
   - Personal financial statements

Why Go through This Process?

Even if you aren't looking for a loan you need to know where you are and where you're going. Use this basic structure to get yourself focused, and you just might go a very long way.

Be Realistic

Few things ever go quite as planned. You think you've sold your first insurance policy or lawn care package, and then the client changes her mind. Clients don't always pay their bills. Their checks bounce. They take forever to pay.

On the other hand, if you are focused and reliable, your business can grow by leaps and bounds through referrals.

Your success is largely in your hands—go for it!

Get Free and Low-Cost Help

Your city or town probably has a great source of information and support for budding entrepreneurs of all ages—the local Small Business Development Center, or SBDC. These organizations are a part of the SBA, and are usually located with your Chamber of Commerce or a local community college. The SBDC has free counseling, lots of low-cost courses, and trained specialists to help you and your business.

Don't overlook the SBA itself. There is a group called SCORE—that's the Service Corps of Retired Executives—and their auxiliary group called ACE—the Active Corps of Executives. These executives are retired from any number of places (SCORE) or actively working as small business owners (ACE) and offer free assistance writing your business plan. They also have a number of low-cost courses to help you plan for taxes, benefits, problems, and more.

Finally, check out the local Junior Achievement group—they may be located in any number of places but your school should be able to get you their address and telephone number.

Pricing Your Products/Services

It's very important to price your offerings fairly and adequately. Many new business owners make three mistakes:

- They don't do thorough research on similar goods or services to get pricing data.
- They underprice their goods and services.
- They fail to value their biggest asset—their time.

Remember you have lots of working hours that won't generate any income. You spend unpaid time:

- Writing your business plan
- Marketing your goods and services
- Preparing invoices
- Trying to collect payments
- Talking to potential clients, vendors, employees, etc.
- Trying to find operating capital
- Doing errands—the bank, the office supply store, paying bills
- Maintaining your books
- And on and on and on

If you are able to actually work—for pay—20 hours a week, you are doing well.
On top of all the time you spend doing things that don't bring in money, you may have to:

- Pay employees
- Pay for several types of business and personal insurance
- Pay the cost of benefits
- Pay rent or other expenses

All of these things are part of the "cost of doing business" and must be factored into the prices of your goods and services, or you'll never make enough money and may even go out of business.

Here's a simple plan for pricing a service. Let's use one I am familiar with: Writing Services.

Pricing for a Writing Services Business

Desired monthly income after expenses/before taxes:	$6,000
Available working hours each month:	100
Costs of doing business:	
• Memberships	$ 200
• Car expenses	$ 600
• Insurance	$ 500
• Entertaining clients	$ 300
• Rent for meeting rooms	$ 100
• Office supplies, postage, etc.	$ 300
• Printing and copying	$ 300
• Utilities and telecommunications	$ 200
• Contributions to retirement plan	$ 500
Total costs of dong business:	$3,000

That means I have to earn $6,000 + $3,000 = $9,000 to cover my costs and make the income I want. Since I can't work 165 hours a month (part of my time is spent doing the things than make up my costs of doing business), I have to bring in $9,000 in just 100 hours of work. That means I have to charge $90 per hour—about twice what I would be paid at a technical writing company.

Managing Taxes and Insurance

If you are in business for yourself, you have to deal with all the taxes and insurance payments yourself, too. That means making sure you have all the required insurance and make the required tax payments on time.

I always recommend using a payroll and accounting service to handle these expenses. Then you won't be late or miss something important because there is someone to remind you. The costs are quite reasonable—maybe $50 to $100 per month. The fines and penalties for late payments and mistakes are horrendously high—hundreds or even thousands of dollars—even for a small business owner.

Here are just some of the taxes and insurance you may be dealing with:

- Federal income tax withholding and payments
- State/city income tax withholding and payments
- Social Security tax withholding and payments
- Self-employment tax withholding and payments
- Medicare tax withholding and payments
- Federal unemployment tax payments
- State unemployment tax payments
- Workers' compensation insurance payments
- Business insurance payments
- Other insurance payments

So the money you may pay a tax service is small potatoes, and your time is worth a lot more than what you'll pay the tax professionals.

Examples of Businesses You Might Consider

If you are ready to plunge ahead and go into business for yourself, maybe as a summer opportunity, here are some options to consider. They are fairly easy to start, with low start-up and operating costs, and in high demand in many areas.

Make sure you do your business plan and price your goods and services before you start looking for clients.

- Lawn-mowing service
- Babysitting service
- Computer repair and trouble-shooting service
- Chauffeur service
- Meal preparation and delivery service

Glossary

Acronyms

ACE	Active Corps of Executives
ACT	American College Test
ATM	Automated teller machine
CCCS	Consumer Credit Counseling Service
CD	Compact disk or certificate of deposit
COBRA	Consolidated Omnibus Retirement Act
CPA	Certified public accountant
DI	Disability income (insurance)
DMA	Direct Marketing Association
DNC	Do not call (list)
DRIP	Dividend reinvestment program
DSL	Digital subscriber line
DVD	Digital video device or disk
DVD-R	Digital video device or disk—recordable
EFC	Expected family contribution
EFT	Electronic funds transfer
EIN	Employer identification number
ESA	Education savings account
FAFSA	Free Application for Federal Student Aid
FSEOG	Federal Supplemental Educational Opportunity Grants
GPA	Grade point average
GPS	Global positioning system
HR	Human resources
IB	International baccalaureate
ID	Identification
IRA	Individual retirement account
IRS	Internal Revenue Service
ISP	Internet service provider
MBA	Master of Business Administration
NAV	Net asset value
PIN	Personal identification number
POP	Public offering price
PSP	Profit sharing plan

SAR	Student aid report
SAT	Scholastic Aptitude Test
SBA	Small Business Administration
SBDC	Small Business Development Center
SCORE	Service Corps of Retired Executives
SEP IRA	Simplified Employee Pension (SEP) Plan IRA
SIMPLE IRA	Another IRA plan available through some small employers
SSN	Social Security number
TSA	Tax-sheltered annuity
UGMA	Uniform Gift to Minors Account
UTMA	Uniform Trust for Minors Account
VCR	Video cassette recorder
VoIP	Voice over Internet Protocol

Definitions

Bounce	To write a check for which there is not enough money in your account
Employer-sponsored retirement plan	401(k), profit sharing, 403(b), SEP IRA, SIMPLE IRA, etc.
Equifax	A major credit bureau
Experian	A major credit bureau
Grace period	The time from when a statement comes until your payment must be received by the lender
Gross pay	The total amount you earn before taxes and other deductions are made
Net pay	This is the amount you actually take home after all deductions and taxes are taken out
Sallie Mae	The Student Loan Marketing Association
Skimming	The process of taking your credit card and running it through a small electronic device to steal, or skim, the card information from the magnetic strip
Surfing	The process of watching someone use an ATM to get that person's PIN code
Transunion	A major credit bureau

Useful Forms and Documents

IRS Forms

Tax Return Forms

Form 1040 Department of the Treasury—Internal Revenue Service
U.S. Individual Income Tax Return 2005 (99) IRS Use Only—Do not write or staple in this space.

For the year Jan. 1–Dec. 31, 2005, or other tax year beginning ____ , 2005, ending ____ , 20 ___ OMB No. 1545-0074

Label (See instructions on page 16.) Use the IRS label. Otherwise, please print or type.

LABEL HERE

Your first name and initial | Last name | Your social security number

If a joint return, spouse's first name and initial | Last name | Spouse's social security number

Home address (number and street). If you have a P.O. box, see page 16. | Apt. no.

City, town or post office, state, and ZIP code. If you have a foreign address, see page 16.

▲ You **must** enter your SSN(s) above. ▲

Checking a box below will not change your tax or refund.

Presidential Election Campaign ► Check here if you, or your spouse if filing jointly, want $3 to go to this fund (see page 16) ► ☐ You ☐ Spouse

Filing Status
Check only one box.

1 ☐ Single
2 ☐ Married filing jointly (even if only one had income)
3 ☐ Married filing separately. Enter spouse's SSN above and full name here. ►
4 ☐ Head of household (with qualifying person). (See page 17.) If the qualifying person is a child but not your dependent, enter this child's name here. ►
5 ☐ Qualifying widow(er) with dependent child (see page 17)

Exemptions

6a ☐ **Yourself.** If someone can claim you as a dependent, **do not** check box 6a
b ☐ **Spouse**
c **Dependents:**

(1) First name Last name	(2) Dependent's social security number	(3) Dependent's relationship to you	(4)✓ if qualifying child for child tax credit (see page 19)
			☐
			☐
			☐
			☐

If more than four dependents, see page 19.

Boxes checked on 6a and 6b ___
No. of children on 6c who:
• lived with you ___
• did not live with you due to divorce or separation (see page 20) ___
Dependents on 6c not entered above ___
Add numbers on lines above ► ☐

d Total number of exemptions claimed

Income

Attach Form(s) W-2 here. Also attach Forms W-2G and 1099-R if tax was withheld.

If you did not get a W-2, see page 22.

Enclose, but do not attach, any payment. Also, please use Form 1040-V.

7 Wages, salaries, tips, etc. Attach Form(s) W-2 | 7
8a Taxable interest. Attach Schedule B if required | 8a
b Tax-exempt interest. **Do not** include on line 8a | 8b
9a Ordinary dividends. Attach Schedule B if required | 9a
b Qualified dividends (see page 23) | 9b
10 Taxable refunds, credits, or offsets of state and local income taxes (see page 23) | 10
11 Alimony received | 11
12 Business income or (loss). Attach Schedule C or C-EZ | 12
13 Capital gain or (loss). Attach Schedule D if required. If not required, check here ► ☐ | 13
14 Other gains or (losses). Attach Form 4797 | 14
15a IRA distributions | 15a | b Taxable amount (see page 25) | 15b
16a Pensions and annuities | 16a | b Taxable amount (see page 25) | 16b
17 Rental real estate, royalties, partnerships, S corporations, trusts, etc. Attach Schedule E | 17
18 Farm income or (loss). Attach Schedule F | 18
19 Unemployment compensation | 19
20a Social security benefits | 20a | b Taxable amount (see page 27) | 20b
21 Other income. List type and amount (see page 29) | 21
22 Add the amounts in the far right column for lines 7 through 21. This is your **total income** ► | 22

Adjusted Gross Income

23 Educator expenses (see page 29) | 23
24 Certain business expenses of reservists, performing artists, and fee-basis government officials. Attach Form 2106 or 2106-EZ | 24
25 Health savings account deduction. Attach Form 8889 | 25
26 Moving expenses. Attach Form 3903 | 26
27 One-half of self-employment tax. Attach Schedule SE | 27
28 Self-employed SEP, SIMPLE, and qualified plans | 28
29 Self-employed health insurance deduction (see page 30) | 29
30 Penalty on early withdrawal of savings | 30
31a Alimony paid b Recipient's SSN ► | 31a
32 IRA deduction (see page 31) | 32
33 Student loan interest deduction (see page 33) | 33
34 Tuition and fees deduction (see page 34) | 34
35 Domestic production activities deduction. Attach Form 8903 | 35
36 Add lines 23 through 31a and 32 through 35 | 36
37 Subtract line 36 from line 22. This is your **adjusted gross income** ► | 37

For Disclosure, Privacy Act, and Paperwork Reduction Act Notice, see page 78. Cat. No. 11320B Form **1040** (2005)

Form 1040 (2005)   Page **2**

Tax and Credits	38	Amount from line 37 (adjusted gross income)	**38**	
	39a	Check { You were born before January 2, 1941, ☐ Blind. } Total boxes if: { Spouse was born before January 2, 1941, ☐ Blind. } checked ► 39a ☐		
Standard Deduction for—	b	If your spouse itemizes on a separate return or you were a dual-status alien, see page 35 and check here ►**39b** ☐		
	40	**Itemized deductions** (from Schedule A) **or** your **standard deduction** (see left margin) . .	**40**	
	41	Subtract line 40 from line 38	**41**	
• People who checked any box on line 39a or 39b **or** who can be claimed as a dependent, see page 36.	42	If line 38 is over $109,475, or you provided housing to a person displaced by Hurricane Katrina, see page 37. Otherwise, multiply $3,200 by the total number of exemptions claimed on line 6d	**42**	
	43	**Taxable income.** Subtract line 42 from line 41. If line 42 is more than line 41, enter -0- .	**43**	
	44	**Tax** (see page 37). Check if any tax is from: **a** ☐ Form(s) 8814 **b** ☐ Form 4972 . . .	**44**	
	45	**Alternative minimum tax** (see page 39). Attach Form 6251	**45**	
• All others:	46	Add lines 44 and 45 . . . . ►	**46**	
Single or Married filing separately, $5,000	47	Foreign tax credit. Attach Form 1116 if required . . .	**47**		
	48	Credit for child and dependent care expenses. Attach Form 2441	**48**		
	49	Credit for the elderly or the disabled. Attach Schedule R . .	**49**		
Married filing jointly or Qualifying widow(er), $10,000	50	Education credits. Attach Form 8863	**50**		
	51	Retirement savings contributions credit. Attach Form 8880 . .	**51**		
	52	Child tax credit (see page 41). Attach Form 8901 if required	**52**		
	53	Adoption credit. Attach Form 8839	**53**		
Head of household, $7,300	54	Credits from: **a** ☐ Form 8396 **b** ☐ Form 8859 . . .	**54**		
	55	Other credits. Check applicable box(es): **a** ☐ Form 3800 **b** ☐ Form 8801 **c** ☐ Form _____	**55**		
	56	Add lines 47 through 55. These are your **total credits**	**56**	
	57	Subtract line 56 from line 46. If line 56 is more than line 46, enter -0- . . . . . ►	**57**	
Other Taxes	58	Self-employment tax. Attach Schedule SE	**58**	
	59	Social security and Medicare tax on tip income not reported to employer. Attach Form 4137	**59**	
	60	Additional tax on IRAs, other qualified retirement plans, etc. Attach Form 5329 if required .	**60**	
	61	Advance earned income credit payments from Form(s) W-2	**61**	
	62	Household employment taxes. Attach Schedule H	**62**	
	63	Add lines 57 through 62. This is your **total tax** . . . . ►	**63**	
Payments	64	Federal income tax withheld from Forms W-2 and 1099 . .	**64**		
	65	2005 estimated tax payments and amount applied from 2004 return	**65**		
If you have a qualifying child, attach Schedule EIC.	66a	**Earned income credit (EIC)**	**66a**		
	b	Nontaxable combat pay election ► **66b**			
	67	Excess social security and tier 1 RRTA tax withheld (see page 59)	**67**		
	68	Additional child tax credit. Attach Form 8812	**68**		
	69	Amount paid with request for extension to file (see page 59)	**69**		
	70	Payments from: **a** ☐ Form 2439 **b** ☐ Form 4136 **c** ☐ Form 8885 .	**70**		
	71	Add lines 64, 65, 66a, and 67 through 70. These are your **total payments** . . . . ►	**71**	
Refund	72	If line 71 is more than line 63, subtract line 63 from line 71. This is the amount you **overpaid**	**72**	
Direct deposit? See page 59 and fill in 73b, 73c, and 73d.	73a	Amount of line 72 you want **refunded to you** . . . . ►	**73a**	
	► b	Routing number ⬚⬚⬚⬚⬚⬚⬚⬚⬚ ► **c** Type: ☐ Checking ☐ Savings		
	► d	Account number ⬚⬚⬚⬚⬚⬚⬚⬚⬚⬚⬚⬚⬚⬚⬚⬚⬚		
	74	Amount of line 72 you want **applied to your 2006 estimated tax** ►	**74**		
Amount You Owe	75	**Amount you owe.** Subtract line 71 from line 63. For details on how to pay, see page 60 ►	**75**	
	76	Estimated tax penalty (see page 60)	**76**		

Third Party Designee

Do you want to allow another person to discuss this return with the IRS (see page 61)? ☐ **Yes.** Complete the following. ☐ **No**

Designee's name ►	Phone no. ► ( )	Personal identification number (PIN) ► ⬚⬚⬚⬚⬚

Sign Here

Joint return? See page 17.

Keep a copy for your records.

Under penalties of perjury, I declare that I have examined this return and accompanying schedules and statements, and to the best of my knowledge and belief, they are true, correct, and complete. Declaration of preparer (other than taxpayer) is based on all information of which preparer has any knowledge.

Your signature	Date	Your occupation	Daytime phone number ( )
Spouse's signature. If a joint return, **both** must sign.	Date	Spouse's occupation	

Paid Preparer's Use Only

Preparer's signature ►	Date	Check if self-employed ☐	Preparer's SSN or PTIN
Firm's name (or yours if self-employed), address, and ZIP code ►		EIN	
		Phone no. ( )	

Form **1040** (2005)

✸ *Printed on recycled paper*

Department of the Treasury—Internal Revenue Service

Form 1040EZ

Income Tax Return for Single and Joint Filers With No Dependents (99) 2005

OMB No. 1545-0074

Label

(See page 11.)

Use the IRS label.

Otherwise, please print or type.

L A B E L H E R E

Your first name and initial	Last name

Your social security number

If a joint return, spouse's first name and initial	Last name

Spouse's social security number

Home address (number and street). If you have a P.O. box, see page 11.	Apt. no.

▲ You **must** enter your SSN(s) above. ▲

City, town or post office, state, and ZIP code. If you have a foreign address, see page 11.

Checking a box below will not change your tax or refund.

Presidential Election Campaign (page 12) ▶

Check here if you, or your spouse if a joint return, want $3 to go to this fund? . . . ▶ ☐ **You** ☐ **Spouse**

Income

Attach Form(s) W-2 here.

Enclose, but do not attach, any payment.

1 Wages, salaries, and tips. This should be shown in box 1 of your Form(s) W-2. Attach your Form(s) W-2. .... **1**

2 Taxable interest. If the total is over $1,500, you cannot use Form 1040EZ. **2**

3 Unemployment compensation and Alaska Permanent Fund dividends (see page 13). **3**

4 Add lines 1, 2, and 3. This is your **adjusted gross income.** **4**

5 If someone can claim you (or your spouse if a joint return) as a dependent, check the applicable box(es) below and enter the amount from the worksheet on back.
☐ **You**   ☐ **Spouse**
If someone cannot claim you (or your spouse if a joint return), enter $8,200 if **single**; $16,400 if **married filing jointly.** See back for explanation. **5**

6 Subtract line 5 from line 4. If line 5 is larger than line 4, enter -0-. This is your **taxable income.** ▶ **6**

Payments and tax

7 Federal income tax withheld from box 2 of your Form(s) W-2. **7**

8a Earned income credit (EIC). **8a**

b Nontaxable combat pay election. **8b**

9 Add lines 7 and 8a. These are your **total payments.** ▶ **9**

10 **Tax.** Use the amount on **line 6 above** to find your tax in the tax table on pages 24–32 of the booklet. Then, enter the tax from the table on this line. **10**

Refund

Have it directly deposited! See page 18 and fill in 11b, 11c, and 11d.

11a If line 9 is larger than line 10, subtract line 10 from line 9. This is your **refund.** ▶ **11a**

▶ b Routing number [   ] ▶ c Type: ☐ Checking ☐ Savings

▶ d Account number [   ]

Amount you owe

12 If line 10 is larger than line 9, subtract line 9 from line 10. This is the **amount you owe.** For details on how to pay, see page 19. ▶ **12**

Third party designee

Do you want to allow another person to discuss this return with the IRS (see page 19)? ☐ **Yes.** Complete the following. ☐ **No**

Designee's name ▶	Phone no. ▶ ( )	Personal identification number (PIN) ▶ [ ]

Sign here

Joint return? See page 11.

Keep a copy for your records.

Under penalties of perjury, I declare that I have examined this return, and to the best of my knowledge and belief, it is true, correct, and accurately lists all amounts and sources of income I received during the tax year. Declaration of preparer (other than the taxpayer) is based on all information of which the preparer has any knowledge.

Your signature	Date	Your occupation	Daytime phone number ( )
Spouse's signature. If a joint return, **both** must sign.	Date	Spouse's occupation	

Paid preparer's use only

Preparer's signature ▶	Date	Check if self-employed ☐	Preparer's SSN or PTIN
Firm's name (or yours if self-employed), address, and ZIP code ▶		EIN	
		Phone no. ( )	

For Disclosure, Privacy Act, and Paperwork Reduction Act Notice, see page 23.

Cat. No. 11329W

Form **1040EZ** (2005)

Form 1040EZ (2005)

Use this form if

- Your filing status is single or married filing jointly. If you are not sure about your filing status, see page 11.
- You (and your spouse if married filing jointly) were under age 65 and not blind at the end of 2005. If you were born on January 1, 1941, you are considered to be age 65 at the end of 2005.
- You do not claim any dependents. For information on dependents, use TeleTax topic 354 (see page 6).
- Your taxable income (line 6) is less than $100,000.
- You do not claim any adjustments to income. For information on adjustments to income, use TeleTax topics 451-458 (see page 6).
- The only tax credit you can claim is the earned income credit. For information on credits, use TeleTax topics 601-608 and 610 (see page 6).
- You had only wages, salaries, tips, taxable scholarship or fellowship grants, unemployment compensation, or Alaska Permanent Fund dividends, and your taxable interest was not over $1,500. But if you earned tips, including allocated tips, that are not included in box 5 and box 7 of your Form W-2, you may not be able to use Form 1040EZ (see page 12). If you are planning to use Form 1040EZ for a child who received Alaska Permanent Fund dividends, see page 13.
- You did not receive any advance earned income credit payments. If you cannot use this form, use TeleTax topic 352 (see page 6).

Filling in your return

For tips on how to avoid common mistakes, see page 20.

If you received a scholarship or fellowship grant or tax-exempt interest income, such as on municipal bonds, see the booklet before filling in the form. Also, see the booklet if you received a Form 1099-INT showing federal income tax withheld or if federal income tax was withheld from your unemployment compensation or Alaska Permanent Fund dividends.

Remember, you must report all wages, salaries, and tips even if you do not get a Form W-2 from your employer. You must also report all your taxable interest, including interest from banks, savings and loans, credit unions, etc., even if you do not get a Form 1099-INT.

Worksheet for dependents who checked one or both boxes on line 5

(keep a copy for your records)

Use this worksheet to figure the amount to enter on line 5 if someone can claim you (or your spouse if married filing jointly) as a dependent, even if that person chooses not to do so. To find out if someone can claim you as a dependent, use TeleTax topic 354 (see page 6).

A. Amount, if any, from line 1 on front . . . . A. _____

B. Is line A more than $550?
  ☐ **Yes.** Add $250 to line A. Enter the total. ⎫ . . . . B. _____
  ☐ **No.** Enter $800. ⎭

C. If **single,** enter $5,000; if **married filing jointly,** enter $10,000 . . C. _____

D. Enter the **smaller** of line B or line C here. This is your standard deduction . . . . D. _____

E. Exemption amount.
  - If single, enter -0-.
  - If married filing jointly and you checked—   ⎫
    —both boxes on line 5, enter -0-.   ⎬ E. _____
    —only one box on line 5, enter $3,200.   ⎭

F. Add lines D and E. Enter the total here and on line 5 on the front . F. _____

If you did not check any boxes on line 5, enter on line 5 the amount shown below that applies to you.
- Single, enter $8,200. This is the total of your standard deduction ($5,000) and your exemption ($3,200).
- Married filing jointly, enter $16,400. This is the total of your standard deduction ($10,000), your exemption ($3,200), and your spouse's exemption ($3,200).

Mailing return

Mail your return by **April 17, 2006.** Use the envelope that came with your booklet. If you do not have that envelope or if you moved during the year, see the back cover for the address to use.

Form **1040EZ** (2005)

Withholding Form

Form W-4 (2005)

Purpose. Complete Form W-4 so that your employer can withhold the correct federal income tax from your pay. Because your tax situation may change, you may want to refigure your withholding each year.

Exemption from withholding. If you are exempt, complete only lines 1, 2, 3, 4, and 7 and sign the form to validate it. Your exemption for 2005 expires February 16, 2006. See Pub. 505, Tax Withholding and Estimated Tax.

Note. You cannot claim exemption from withholding if (a) your income exceeds $800 and includes more than $250 of unearned income (for example, interest and dividends) and (b) another person can claim you as a dependent on their tax return.

Basic instructions. If you are not exempt, complete the **Personal Allowances Worksheet** below. The worksheets on page 2 adjust your withholding allowances based on itemized deductions, certain credits, adjustments to income, or two-earner/two-job situations. Complete all worksheets that apply. However, you may claim fewer (or zero) allowances.

Head of household. Generally, you may claim head of household filing status on your tax return only if you are unmarried and pay more than 50% of the costs of keeping up a home for yourself and your dependent(s) or other qualifying individuals. See line **E** below.

Tax credits. You can take projected tax credits into account in figuring your allowable number of withholding allowances. Credits for child or dependent care expenses and the child tax credit may be claimed using the **Personal Allowances Worksheet** below. See Pub. 919, How Do I Adjust My Tax Withholding? for information on converting your other credits into withholding allowances.

Nonwage income. If you have a large amount of nonwage income, such as interest or dividends, consider making estimated tax payments using Form 1040-ES, Estimated Tax for Individuals. Otherwise, you may owe additional tax.

Two earners/two jobs. If you have a working spouse or more than one job, figure the total number of allowances you are entitled to claim on all jobs using worksheets from only one Form W-4. Your withholding usually will be most accurate when all allowances are claimed on the Form W-4 for the highest paying job and zero allowances are claimed on the others.

Nonresident alien. If you are a nonresident alien, see the Instructions for Form 8233 before completing this Form W-4.

Check your withholding. After your Form W-4 takes effect, use Pub. 919 to see how the dollar amount you are having withheld compares to your projected total tax for 2005. See Pub. 919, especially if your earnings exceed $125,000 (Single) or $175,000 (Married).

Recent name change? If your name on line 1 differs from that shown on your social security card, call 1-800-772-1213 to initiate a name change and obtain a social security card showing your correct name.

Personal Allowances Worksheet (Keep for your records.)

A Enter "1" for **yourself** if no one else can claim you as a dependent . . . .   **A** _____

B Enter "1" if:
- You are single and have only one job; or
- You are married, have only one job, and your spouse does not work; or
- Your wages from a second job or your spouse's wages (or the total of both) are $1,000 or less.   } . . **B** _____

C Enter "1" for your **spouse**. But, you may choose to enter "-0-" if you are married and have either a working spouse or more than one job. (Entering "-0-" may help you avoid having too little tax withheld.) . . . .   **C** _____

D Enter number of **dependents** (other than your spouse or yourself) you will claim on your tax return . . . . . .   **D** _____

E Enter "1" if you will file as **head of household** on your tax return (see conditions under **Head of household** above) .   **E** _____

F Enter "1" if you have at least $1,500 of **child or dependent care expenses** for which you plan to claim a credit . .   **F** _____
   (**Note.** Do **not** include child support payments. See **Pub. 503,** Child and Dependent Care Expenses, for details.)

G **Child Tax Credit** (including additional child tax credit):
- If your total income will be less than $54,000 ($79,000 if married), enter "2" for each eligible child.
- If your total income will be between $54,000 and $84,000 ($79,000 and $119,000 if married), enter "1" for each eligible child plus "1" **additional** if you have four or more eligible children.   **G** _____

H Add lines A through G and enter total here. (**Note.** This may be different from the number of exemptions you claim on your tax return.) ▶ **H** _____

For accuracy, complete all worksheets that apply.
- If you plan to **itemize or claim adjustments to income** and want to reduce your withholding, see the **Deductions and Adjustments Worksheet** on page 2.
- If you have **more than one job** or are **married and you and your spouse both work** and the combined earnings from all jobs exceed $35,000 ($25,000 if married) see the **Two-Earner/Two-Job Worksheet** on page 2 to avoid having too little tax withheld.
- If **neither** of the above situations applies, **stop here** and enter the number from line H on line 5 of Form W-4 below.

- - - - - - - - - - - - - - - - - -   **Cut here and give Form W-4 to your employer. Keep the top part for your records.**   - - - - - - - - - - - - - - - - - -

Form **W-4**	**Employee's Withholding Allowance Certificate**	OMB No. 1545-0010
Department of the Treasury Internal Revenue Service	▶ **Whether you are entitled to claim a certain number of allowances or exemption from withholding is subject to review by the IRS. Your employer may be required to send a copy of this form to the IRS.**	2005

1 Type or print your first name and middle initial	Last name	**2** Your social security number

Home address (number and street or rural route)	**3** ☐ Single ☐ Married ☐ Married, but withhold at higher Single rate. **Note.** If married, but legally separated, or spouse is a nonresident alien, check the "Single" box.
City or town, state, and ZIP code	**4** If your last name differs from that shown on your social security card, check here. You must call 1-800-772-1213 for a new card. ▶ ☐

5 Total number of allowances you are claiming (from line **H** above **or** from the applicable worksheet on page 2)   **5** _____

6 Additional amount, if any, you want withheld from each paycheck . . . .   **6** $ _____

7 I claim exemption from withholding for 2005, and I certify that I meet **both** of the following conditions for exemption.
- Last year I had a right to a refund of **all** federal income tax withheld because I had **no** tax liability **and**
- This year I expect a refund of **all** federal income tax withheld because I expect to have **no** tax liability.

If you meet both conditions, write "Exempt" here . . . . ▶ **7** _____

Under penalties of perjury, I declare that I have examined this certificate and to the best of my knowledge and belief, it is true, correct, and complete.

Employee's signature
(Form is not valid unless you sign it.) ▶ _____   **Date** ▶ _____

8 Employer's name and address (Employer: Complete lines 8 and 10 only if sending to the IRS.)	**9** Office code (optional)	**10** Employer identification number (EIN)

For Privacy Act and Paperwork Reduction Act Notice, see page 2.   Cat. No. 10220Q   Form **W-4** (2005)

Form W-4 (2005)
Page **2**

Deductions and Adjustments Worksheet

Note. Use this worksheet *only* if you plan to itemize deductions, claim certain credits, or claim adjustments to income on your 2005 tax return.

1	Enter an estimate of your 2005 itemized deductions. These include qualifying home mortgage interest, charitable contributions, state and local taxes, medical expenses in excess of 7.5% of your income, and miscellaneous deductions. (For 2005, you may have to reduce your itemized deductions if your income is over $145,950 ($72,975 if married filing separately). See *Worksheet 3* in Pub. 919 for details.) . . .	1	$ _____

2   Enter:
$10,000 if married filing jointly or qualifying widow(er)
$ 7,300 if head of household
$ 5,000 if single or married filing separately   . . . .   **2** $ _____

3	**Subtract** line 2 from line 1. If line 2 is greater than line 1, enter "-0-"	3	$ _____
4	Enter an estimate of your 2005 adjustments to income, including alimony, deductible IRA contributions, and student loan interest	4	$ _____
5	**Add** lines 3 and 4 and enter the total. (Include any amount for credits from *Worksheet 7* in Pub. 919) .	5	$ _____
6	Enter an estimate of your 2005 nonwage income (such as dividends or interest)	6	$ _____
7	**Subtract** line 6 from line 5. Enter the result, but not less than "-0-"	7	$ _____
8	**Divide** the amount on line 7 by $3,200 and enter the result here. Drop any fraction	8	_____
9	Enter the number from the **Personal Allowances Worksheet**, line H, page 1	9	_____
10	**Add** lines 8 and 9 and enter the total here. If you plan to use the **Two-Earner/Two-Job Worksheet**, also enter this total on line 1 below. Otherwise, **stop here** and enter this total on Form W-4, line 5, page 1 .	10	_____

Two-Earner/Two-Job Worksheet (See *Two earners/two jobs* on page 1.)

Note. Use this worksheet *only* if the instructions under line H on page 1 direct you here.

1	Enter the number from line H, page 1 (or from line 10 above if you used the **Deductions and Adjustments Worksheet**)	1	_____
2	Find the number in **Table 1** below that applies to the **LOWEST** paying job and enter it here	2	_____
3	If line 1 is **more than or equal to** line 2, subtract line 2 from line 1. Enter the result here (if zero, enter "-0-") and on Form W-4, line 5, page 1. **Do not** use the rest of this worksheet	3	_____

Note. If line 1 is *less than* line 2, enter "-0-" on Form W-4, line 5, page 1. Complete lines 4–9 below to calculate the additional withholding amount necessary to avoid a year-end tax bill.

4	Enter the number from line 2 of this worksheet 4	_____	
5	Enter the number from line 1 of this worksheet 5	_____	
6	**Subtract** line 5 from line 4	6	_____
7	Find the amount in **Table 2** below that applies to the **HIGHEST** paying job and enter it here	7	$ _____
8	**Multiply** line 7 by line 6 and enter the result here. This is the additional annual withholding needed . .	8	$ _____
9	**Divide** line 8 by the number of pay periods remaining in 2005. For example, divide by 26 if you are paid every two weeks and you complete this form in December 2004. Enter the result here and on Form W-4, line 6, page 1. This is the additional amount to be withheld from each paycheck	9	$ _____

Table 1: Two-Earner/Two-Job Worksheet

Married Filing Jointly						**All Others**	
If wages from **HIGHEST** paying job are—	AND, wages from **LOWEST** paying job are—	Enter on line 2 above	If wages from **HIGHEST** paying job are—	AND, wages from **LOWEST** paying job are—	Enter on line 2 above	If wages from **LOWEST** paying job are—	Enter on line 2 above
$0 - $40,000	$0 - $4,000	0	$40,001 and over	30,001 - 36,000	6	$0 - $6,000	0
	4,001 - 8,000	1		36,001 - 45,000	7	6,001 - 12,000	1
	8,001 - 18,000	2		45,001 - 50,000	8	12,001 - 18,000	2
	18,001 and over	3		50,001 - 60,000	9	18,001 - 24,000	3
				60,001 - 65,000	10	24,001 - 31,000	4
$40,001 and over	$0 - $4,000	0		65,001 - 75,000	11	31,001 - 45,000	5
	4,001 - 8,000	1		75,001 - 90,000	12	45,001 - 60,000	6
	8,001 - 18,000	2		90,001 - 100,000	13	60,001 - 75,000	7
	18,001 - 22,000	3		100,001 - 115,000	14	75,001 - 80,000	8
	22,001 - 25,000	4		115,001 and over	15	80,001 - 100,000	9
	25,001 - 30,000	5				100,001 and over	10

Table 2: Two-Earner/Two-Job Worksheet

Married Filing Jointly		**All Others**	
If wages from **HIGHEST** paying job are—	Enter on line 7 above	If wages from **HIGHEST** paying job are—	Enter on line 7 above
$0 - $60,000	$480	$0 - $30,000	$480
60,001 - 110,000	800	30,001 - 70,000	800
110,001 - 160,000	900	70,001 - 140,000	900
160,001 - 280,000	1,060	140,001 - 320,000	1,060
280,001 and over	1,120	320,001 and over	1,120

 Printed on recycled paper

Right to Work Certification

Department of Homeland Security
U.S. Citizenship and Immigration Services

OMB No. 1615-0047; Expires 03/31/07

Employment Eligibility Verification

INSTRUCTIONS
PLEASE READ ALL INSTRUCTIONS CAREFULLY BEFORE COMPLETING THIS FORM.

Anti-Discrimination Notice. It is illegal to discriminate against any individual (other than an alien not authorized to work in the U.S.) in hiring, discharging, or recruiting or referring for a fee because of that individual's national origin or citizenship status. It is illegal to discriminate against work eligible individuals. Employers **CANNOT** specify which document(s) they will accept from an employee. The refusal to hire an individual because of a future expiration date may also constitute illegal discrimination.

Section 1- Employee.
All employees, citizens and noncitizens, hired after November 6, 1986, must complete Section 1 of this form at the time of hire, which is the actual beginning of employment. **The employer is responsible for ensuring that Section 1 is timely and properly completed.**

Preparer/Translator Certification. The Preparer/Translator Certification must be completed if Section 1 is prepared by a person other than the employee. A preparer/translator may be used only when the employee is unable to complete Section 1 on his/her own. However, the employee must still sign Section 1 personally.

Section 2 - Employer.
For the purpose of completing this form, the term "employer" includes those recruiters and referrers for a fee who are agricultural associations, agricultural employers or farm labor contractors.

Employers must complete Section 2 by examining evidence of identity and employment eligibility within three (3) business days of the date employment begins. If employees are authorized to work, but are unable to present the required document(s) within three business days, they must present a receipt for the application of the document(s) within three business days and the actual document(s) within ninety (90) days. However, if employers hire individuals for a duration of less than three business days, Section 2 must be completed at the time employment begins. **Employers must record: 1)** document title; **2)** issuing authority; **3)** document number, **4)** expiration date, if any; and **5)** the date employment begins. Employers must sign and date the certification. Employers must present original documents. Employers may, but are not required to, photocopy the document(s) presented. These photocopies may only be used for the verification process and must be retained with the I-9. **However, employers are still responsible for completing the I-9.**

Section 3 - Updating and Reverification.
Employers must complete Section 3 when updating and/or reverifying the I-9. Employers must reverify employment eligibility of their employees on or before the expiration date recorded in Section 1. Employers **CANNOT** specify which document(s) they will accept from an employee.

- If an employee's name has changed at the time this form is being updated/reverified, complete Block A.

- If an employee is rehired within three (3) years of the date this form was originally completed and the employee is still eligible to be employed on the same basis as previously indicated on this form (updating), complete Block B and the signature block.

- If an employee is rehired within three (3) years of the date this form was originally completed and the employee's work authorization has expired **or** if a current employee's work authorization is about to expire (reverification), complete Block B and:

— examine any document that reflects that the employee is authorized to work in the U.S. (see List A **or** C),

— record the document title, document number and expiration date (if any) in Block C, and

— complete the signature block.

Photocopying and Retaining Form I-9. A blank I-9 may be reproduced, provided both sides are copied. The Instructions must be available to all employees completing this form. Employers must retain completed I-9s for three (3) years after the date of hire or one (1) year after the date employment ends, whichever is later.

For more detailed information, you may refer to the Department of Homeland Security (DHS) Handbook for Employers, (Form M-274). You may obtain the handbook at your local U.S. Citizenship and Immigration Services (USCIS) office.

Privacy Act Notice. The authority for collecting this information is the Immigration Reform and Control Act of 1986, Pub. L. 99-603 (8 USC 1324a).

This information is for employers to verify the eligibility of individuals for employment to preclude the unlawful hiring, or recruiting or referring for a fee, of aliens who are not authorized to work in the United States.

This information will be used by employers as a record of their basis for determining eligibility of an employee to work in the United States. The form will be kept by the employer and made available for inspection by officials of the U.S. Immigration and Customs Enforcement, Department of Labor and Office of Special Counsel for Immigration Related Unfair Employment Practices.

Submission of the information required in this form is voluntary. However, an individual may not begin employment unless this form is completed, since employers are subject to civil or criminal penalties if they do not comply with the Immigration Reform and Control Act of 1986.

Reporting Burden. We try to create forms and instructions that are accurate, can be easily understood and which impose the least possible burden on you to provide us with information. Often this is difficult because some immigration laws are very complex. Accordingly, the reporting burden for this collection of information is computed as follows: **1)** learning about this form, 5 minutes; **2)** completing the form, 5 minutes; and **3)** assembling and filing (recordkeeping) the form, 5 minutes, for an average of 15 minutes per response. If you have comments regarding the accuracy of this burden estimate, or suggestions for making this form simpler, you can write to U.S. Citizenship and Immigration Services, Regulatory Management Division, 111 Massachuetts Avenue, N.W., Washington, DC 20529. OMB No. 1615-0047.

NOTE: This is the 1991 edition of the Form I-9 that has been rebranded with a current printing date to reflect the recent transition from the INS to DHS and its components.

EMPLOYERS MUST RETAIN COMPLETED FORM I-9
PLEASE DO NOT MAIL COMPLETED FORM I-9 TO ICE OR USCIS

Form I-9 (Rev. 05/31/05)Y

Department of Homeland Security
U.S. Citizenship and Immigration Services

OMB No. 1615-0047; Expires 03/31/07

Employment Eligibility Verification

Please read instructions carefully before completing this form. The instructions must be available during completion of this form. **ANTI-DISCRIMINATION NOTICE:** It is illegal to discriminate against work eligible individuals. Employers **CANNOT** specify which document(s) they will accept from an employee. The refusal to hire an individual because of a future expiration date may also constitute illegal discrimination.

Section 1. Employee Information and Verification. To be completed and signed by employee at the time employment begins.

Print Name: Last	First	Middle Initial	Maiden Name

Address (Street Name and Number)	Apt. #	Date of Birth (month/day/year)

City	State	Zip Code	Social Security #

I am aware that federal law provides for imprisonment and/or fines for false statements or use of false documents in connection with the completion of this form.

I attest, under penalty of perjury, that I am (check one of the following):

☐ A citizen or national of the United States
☐ A Lawful Permanent Resident (Alien #) A _____
☐ An alien authorized to work until _____

(Alien # or Admission #)

Employee's Signature	Date (month/day/year)

Preparer and/or Translator Certification. *(To be completed and signed if Section 1 is prepared by a person other than the employee.) I attest, under penalty of perjury, that I have assisted in the completion of this form and that to the best of my knowledge the information is true and correct.*

Preparer's/Translator's Signature	Print Name

Address (Street Name and Number, City, State, Zip Code)	Date (month/day/year)

Section 2. Employer Review and Verification. To be completed and signed by employer. Examine one document from List A OR examine one document from List B and one from List C, as listed on the reverse of this form, and record the title, number and expiration date, if any, of the document(s).

List A	OR	List B	AND	List C
Document title: _____		_____		_____
Issuing authority: _____		_____		_____
Document #: _____		_____		_____
Expiration Date (if any): _____		_____		_____
Document #: _____				
Expiration Date (if any): _____				

CERTIFICATION - I attest, under penalty of perjury, that I have examined the document(s) presented by the above-named employee, that the above-listed document(s) appear to be genuine and to relate to the employee named, that the employee began employment on *(month/day/year)* _____ and that to the best of my knowledge the employee is eligible to work in the United States. (State employment agencies may omit the date the employee began employment.)

Signature of Employer or Authorized Representative	Print Name	Title

Business or Organization Name	Address (Street Name and Number, City, State, Zip Code)	Date (month/day/year)

Section 3. Updating and Reverification. To be completed and signed by employer.

A. New Name (if applicable)	B. Date of rehire (month/day/year) (if applicable)

C. If employee's previous grant of work authorization has expired, provide the information below for the document that establishes current employment eligibility.

Document Title: _____ Document #: _____ Expiration Date (if any): _____

I attest, under penalty of perjury, that to the best of my knowledge, this employee is eligible to work in the United States, and if the employee presented document(s), the document(s) I have examined appear to be genuine and to relate to the individual.

Signature of Employer or Authorized Representative	Date (month/day/year)

NOTE: This is the 1991 edition of the Form I-9 that has been rebranded with a current printing date to reflect the recent transition from the INS to DHS and its components.

Form I-9 (Rev. 05/31/05)Y Page 2

LISTS OF ACCEPTABLE DOCUMENTS

LIST A		LIST B		LIST C
Documents that Establish Both Identity and Employment Eligibility	**OR**	**Documents that Establish Identity**	**AND**	**Documents that Establish Employment Eligibility**

LIST A

Documents that Establish Both Identity and Employment Eligibility

1. U.S. Passport (unexpired or expired)

2. Certificate of U.S. Citizenship *(Form N-560 or N-561)*

3. Certificate of Naturalization *(Form N-550 or N-570)*

4. Unexpired foreign passport, with *I-551 stamp or* attached *Form I-94* indicating unexpired employment authorization

5. Permanent Resident Card or Alien Registration Receipt Card with photograph *(Form I-151 or I-551)*

6. Unexpired Temporary Resident Card *(Form I-688)*

7. Unexpired Employment Authorization Card *(Form I-688A)*

8. Unexpired Reentry Permit *(Form I-327)*

9. Unexpired Refugee Travel Document *(Form I-571)*

10. Unexpired Employment Authorization Document issued by DHS that contains a photograph *(Form I-688B)*

OR

LIST B

Documents that Establish Identity

1. Driver's license or ID card issued by a state or outlying possession of the United States provided it contains a photograph or information such as name, date of birth, gender, height, eye color and address

2. ID card issued by federal, state or local government agencies or entities, provided it contains a photograph or information such as name, date of birth, gender, height, eye color and address

3. School ID card with a photograph

4. Voter's registration card

5. U.S. Military card or draft record

6. Military dependent's ID card

7. U.S. Coast Guard Merchant Mariner Card

8. Native American tribal document

9. Driver's license issued by a Canadian government authority

For persons under age 18 who are unable to present a document listed above:

10. School record or report card

11. Clinic, doctor or hospital record

12. Day-care or nursery school record

AND

LIST C

Documents that Establish Employment Eligibility

1. U.S. social security card issued by the Social Security Administration *(other than a card stating it is not valid for employment)*

2. Certification of Birth Abroad issued by the Department of State *(Form FS-545 or Form DS-1350)*

3. Original or certified copy of a birth certificate issued by a state, county, municipal authority or outlying possession of the United States bearing an official seal

4. Native American tribal document

5. U.S. Citizen ID Card *(Form I-197)*

6. ID Card for use of Resident Citizen in the United States *(Form I-179)*

7. Unexpired employment authorization document issued by DHS *(other than those listed under List A)*

Illustrations of many of these documents appear in Part 8 of the Handbook for Employers (M-274)

Tax-Related Forms

Attention:

This form is provided for informational purposes only. Copy A appears in red, similar to the official printed IRS form. But do not file Copy A downloaded from this website with the SSA. A penalty of $50 per information return may be imposed for filing such forms that cannot be scanned.

To order official IRS forms, call 1-800-TAX-FORMS (1-800-829-3676) or order online at Forms and Publications By U.S. Mail.

You may file Forms W-2 and W-3 electronically on the SSA's website at Employer Reporting Instructions & Information. You can create fill-in versions of Forms W-2 and W-3 for filing with the SSA. You may also print out copies for filing with state or local governments, distribution to your employees, and for your records.

a Control number	22222	Void ☐	For Official Use Only ▶ OMB No. 1545-0008		
b Employer identification number (EIN)			1 Wages, tips, other compensation	2 Federal income tax withheld	
c Employer's name, address, and ZIP code			3 Social security wages	4 Social security tax withheld	
			5 Medicare wages and tips	6 Medicare tax withheld	
			7 Social security tips	8 Allocated tips	
d Employee's social security number			9 Advance EIC payment	10 Dependent care benefits	
e Employee's first name and initial	Last name		11 Nonqualified plans	12a See instructions for box 12	
			13 Statutory employee / Retirement plan / Third-party sick pay	12b	
			14 Other	12c	
				12d	
f Employee's address and ZIP code					
15 State / Employer's state ID number	16 State wages, tips, etc.	17 State income tax	18 Local wages, tips, etc.	19 Local income tax	20 Locality name

Form **W-2** Wage and Tax Statement **2005**

Copy A For Social Security Administration — Send this entire page with Form W-3 to the Social Security Administration; photocopies are **not** acceptable.

Cat. No. 10134D

Department of the Treasury—Internal Revenue Service
For Privacy Act and Paperwork Reduction Act Notice, see back of Copy D.

Do Not Cut, Fold, or Staple Forms on This Page — Do Not Cut, Fold, or Staple Forms on This Page

a Control number	22222	OMB No. 1545-0008		
b Employer identification number (EIN)			**1** Wages, tips, other compensation	**2** Federal income tax withheld
c Employer's name, address, and ZIP code			**3** Social security wages	**4** Social security tax withheld
			5 Medicare wages and tips	**6** Medicare tax withheld
			7 Social security tips	**8** Allocated tips
d Employee's social security number			**9** Advance EIC payment	**10** Dependent care benefits
e Employee's first name and initial Last name			**11** Nonqualified plans	**12a** C o d e
			13 Statutory employee Retirement plan Third-party sick pay	**12b** C o d e
			14 Other	**12c** C o d e
				12d C o d e
f Employee's address and ZIP code				

15 State Employer's state ID number	**16** State wages, tips, etc.	**17** State income tax	**18** Local wages, tips, etc.	**19** Local income tax	**20** Locality name

Form **W-2** Wage and Tax Statement   **2005**   Department of the Treasury—Internal Revenue Service

Copy 1—For State, City, or Local Tax Department

---

a Control number		OMB No. 1545-0008	Safe, accurate, FAST! Use IRS e-file	Visit the IRS website at *www.irs.gov/efile*.
b Employer identification number (EIN)			**1** Wages, tips, other compensation	**2** Federal income tax withheld
c Employer's name, address, and ZIP code			**3** Social security wages	**4** Social security tax withheld
			5 Medicare wages and tips	**6** Medicare tax withheld
			7 Social security tips	**8** Allocated tips
d Employee's social security number			**9** Advance EIC payment	**10** Dependent care benefits
e Employee's first name and initial Last name			**11** Nonqualified plans	**12a** See instructions for box 12 C o d e
			13 Statutory employee Retirement plan Third-party sick pay	**12b** C o d e
			14 Other	**12c** C o d e
				12d C o d e
f Employee's address and ZIP code				

15 State Employer's state ID number	**16** State wages, tips, etc.	**17** State income tax	**18** Local wages, tips, etc.	**19** Local income tax	**20** Locality name

Form **W-2** Wage and Tax Statement   **2005**   Department of the Treasury—Internal Revenue Service

Copy B—To Be Filed With Employee's FEDERAL Tax Return.
This information is being furnished to the Internal Revenue Service.

Notice to Employee

Refund. Even if you do not have to file a tax return, you should file to get a refund if box 2 shows federal income tax withheld or if you can take the earned income credit.

Earned income credit (EIC). You must file a tax return if any amount is shown in box 9.

You may be able to take the EIC for 2005 if: **(a)** you do not have a qualifying child and you earned less than $11,750 ($13,750 if married filing jointly), **(b)** you have one qualifying child and you earned less than $31,030 ($33,030 if married filing jointly), or **(c)** you have more than one qualifying child and you earned less than $35,263 ($37,263 if married filing jointly). You and any qualifying children must have valid social security numbers (SSNs). You cannot take the EIC if your investment income is more than $2,700. **Any EIC that is more than your tax liability is refunded to you, but only if you file a tax return.** If you have at least one qualifying child, you may get as much as $1,597 of the EIC in advance by completing Form W-5, Earned Income Credit Advance Payment Certificate, and giving it to your employer.

Clergy and religious workers. If you are not subject to social security and Medicare taxes, see Publication 517, Social Security and Other Information for Members of the Clergy and Religious Workers.

Corrections. If your name, SSN, or address is incorrect, correct Copies B, C, and 2 and ask your employer to correct your employment record. Be sure to ask the employer to file Form W-2c, Corrected Wage and Tax Statement, with the Social Security Administration (SSA) to correct any name, SSN, or money amount error reported to the SSA on Form W-2. If your name and SSN are correct but are not the same as shown on your social security card, you should ask for a new card at any SSA office or call 1-800-772-1213.

Credit for excess taxes. If you had more than one employer in 2005 and more than $5,580.00 in social security and/or Tier I railroad retirement (RRTA) taxes were withheld, you may be able to claim a credit for the excess against your federal income tax. If you had more than one railroad employer and more than $2,943.60 in Tier II RRTA tax was withheld, you also may be able to claim a credit. See your Form 1040 or Form 1040A instructions and Publication 505, Tax Withholding and Estimated Tax.

(Also see *Instructions* on back of Copy C.)

a Control number		OMB No. 1545-0008	This information is being furnished to the Internal Revenue Service. If you are required to file a tax return, a negligence penalty or other sanction may be imposed on you if this income is taxable and you fail to report it.	
b Employer identification number (EIN)			1 Wages, tips, other compensation	2 Federal income tax withheld
c Employer's name, address, and ZIP code			3 Social security wages	4 Social security tax withheld
			5 Medicare wages and tips	6 Medicare tax withheld
			7 Social security tips	8 Allocated tips
d Employee's social security number			9 Advance EIC payment	10 Dependent care benefits
e Employee's first name and initial Last name			11 Nonqualified plans	12a See instructions for box 12
		13 Statutory employee / Retirement plan / Third-party sick pay		12b
		14 Other		12c
				12d
f Employee's address and ZIP code				

15 State Employer's state ID number	16 State wages, tips, etc.	17 State income tax	18 Local wages, tips, etc.	19 Local income tax	20 Locality name

Form **W-2**   **Wage and Tax Statement**   **2005**   Department of the Treasury—Internal Revenue Service

Copy C—For EMPLOYEE'S RECORDS. (See Notice to Employee on back of Copy B.)

Safe, accurate, FAST! Use

Instructions *(Also see Notice to Employee, on back of Copy B.)*

Box 1. Enter this amount on the wages line of your tax return.

Box 2. Enter this amount on the federal income tax withheld line of your tax return.

Box 8. This amount is **not** included in boxes 1, 3, 5, or 7. For information on how to report tips on your tax return, see your Form 1040 instructions.

Box 9. Enter this amount on the advance earned income credit payments line of your Form 1040 or Form 1040A.

Box 10. This amount is the total dependent care benefits that your employer paid to you or incurred on your behalf (including amounts from a section 125 (cafeteria) plan). Any amount over $5,000 also is included in box 1. You **must** complete Schedule 2 (Form 1040A) or Form 2441, Child and Dependent Care Expenses, to compute any taxable and nontaxable amounts.

Box 11. This amount is: **(a)** reported in box 1 if it is a distribution made to you from a nonqualified deferred compensation or nongovernmental section 457(b) plan or **(b)** included in box 3 and/or 5 if it is a prior year deferral under a nonqualified or section 457(b) plan that became taxable for social security and Medicare taxes this year because there is no longer a substantial risk of forfeiture of your right to the deferred amount.

Box 12. The following list explains the codes shown in box 12. You may need this information to complete your tax return. Elective deferrals (codes D, E, F, and S) under all plans are generally limited to a total of $14,000 ($17,000 for section 403(b) plans if you qualify for the 15-year rule explained in Pub. 571). Deferrals under code G are limited to $14,000. Deferrals under code H are limited to $7,000. However, if you were at least age 50 in 2005, your employer may have allowed an additional deferral of up to $4,000 ($2,000 for section 401(k)(11) and 408(p) SIMPLE plans). This additional deferral amount is not subject to the overall limit on elective deferrals. For code G, the limit on elective deferrals may be higher for the last three years before you reach retirement age. Contact your plan administrator for more information. Amounts in excess of the overall elective deferral limit must be included in income. See the "Wages, Salaries, Tips, etc." line instructions for Form 1040.

Note. *If a year follows code D, E, F, G, H, or S, you made a make-up pension contribution for a prior year(s) when you were in military service. To figure whether you made excess deferrals, consider these amounts for the year shown, not the current year. If no year is shown, the contributions are for the current year.*

A—Uncollected social security or RRTA tax on tips. Include this tax on Form 1040. See "Total Tax" in the Form 1040 instructions.

B—Uncollected Medicare tax on tips. Include this tax on Form 1040. See "Total Tax" in the Form 1040 instructions.

C—Taxable cost of group-term life insurance over $50,000 (included in boxes 1, 3 (up to social security wage base), and 5)

D—Elective deferrals to a section 401(k) cash or deferred arrangement. Also includes deferrals under a SIMPLE retirement account that is part of a section 401(k) arrangement.

E—Elective deferrals under a section 403(b) salary reduction agreement

F—Elective deferrals under a section 408(k)(6) salary reduction SEP

G—Elective deferrals and employer contributions (including nonelective deferrals) to a section 457(b) deferred compensation plan

H—Elective deferrals to a section 501(c)(18)(D) tax-exempt organization plan. See "Adjusted Gross Income" in the Form 1040 instructions for how to deduct.

J—Nontaxable sick pay (information only, not included in boxes 1, 3, or 5)

K—20% excise tax on excess golden parachute payments. See "Total Tax" in the Form 1040 instructions.

L—Substantiated employee business expense reimbursements (nontaxable)

M—Uncollected social security or RRTA tax on taxable cost of group-term life insurance over $50,000 (former employees only). See "Total Tax" in the Form 1040 instructions.

N—Uncollected Medicare tax on taxable cost of group-term life insurance over $50,000 (former employees only). See "Total Tax" in the Form 1040 instructions.

P—Excludable moving expense reimbursements paid directly to employee (not included in boxes 1, 3, or 5)

Q—Nontaxable combat pay. See the instructions for Form 1040 or Form 1040A for details on reporting this amount.

R—Employer contributions to your Archer MSA. Report on Form 8853, Archer MSAs and Long-Term Care Insurance Contracts.

S—Employee salary reduction contributions under a section 408(p) SIMPLE (not included in box 1)

T—Adoption benefits (not included in box 1). You **must** complete Form 8839, Qualified Adoption Expenses, to compute any taxable and nontaxable amounts.

V—Income from exercise of nonstatutory stock option(s) (included in boxes 1, 3 (up to social security wage base), and 5)

W—Employer contributions to your Health Savings Account. Report on Form 8889, Health Savings Accounts (HSAs).

Y—Deferrals under a section 409A nonqualified deferred compensation plan.

Z—Income under section 409A on a nonqualified deferred compensation plan. This amount is also included in box 1. It is subject to an additional 20% tax plus interest. See "Total Tax" in the Form 1040 instructions.

Box 13. If the "Retirement plan" box is checked, special limits may apply to the amount of traditional IRA contributions that you may deduct.

Note: *Keep Copy C of Form W-2 for at least 3 years after the due date for filing your income tax return. However, to help **protect your social security benefits,** keep Copy C until you begin receiving social security benefits, just in case there is a question about your work record and/or earnings in a particular year. Review the information shown on your annual (for workers over 25) Social Security Statement.*

---

a Control number		OMB No. 1545-0008		
b Employer identification number (EIN)			**1** Wages, tips, other compensation	**2** Federal income tax withheld
c Employer's name, address, and ZIP code			**3** Social security wages	**4** Social security tax withheld
			5 Medicare wages and tips	**6** Medicare tax withheld
			7 Social security tips	**8** Allocated tips
d Employee's social security number			**9** Advance EIC payment	**10** Dependent care benefits
e Employee's first name and initial Last name			**11** Nonqualified plans	**12a** Code
			13 Statutory employee Retirement plan Third-party sick pay	**12b** Code
			14 Other	**12c** Code
				12d Code
f Employee's address and ZIP code				

15 State Employer's state ID number	16 State wages, tips, etc.	17 State income tax	18 Local wages, tips, etc.	19 Local income tax	20 Locality name

Form **W-2** Wage and Tax Statement   **2005**   Department of the Treasury—Internal Revenue Service

Copy 2—To Be Filed With Employee's State, City, or Local Income Tax Return.

a Control number				
	Void ☐	OMB No. 1545-0008		

b Employer identification number (EIN)	**1** Wages, tips, other compensation	**2** Federal income tax withheld
c Employer's name, address, and ZIP code	**3** Social security wages	**4** Social security tax withheld
	5 Medicare wages and tips	**6** Medicare tax withheld
	7 Social security tips	**8** Allocated tips
d Employee's social security number	**9** Advance EIC payment	**10** Dependent care benefits
e Employee's first name and initial Last name	**11** Nonqualified plans	**12a** See instructions for box 12
	13 Statutory employee ☐ Retirement plan ☐ Third-party sick pay ☐	**12b**
	14 Other	**12c**
		12d
f Employee's address and ZIP code		

15 State Employer's state ID number	**16** State wages, tips, etc.	**17** State income tax	**18** Local wages, tips, etc.	**19** Local income tax	**20** Locality name

Form **W-2** Wage and Tax Statement   **2005**   Department of the Treasury—Internal Revenue Service

Copy D—For Employer.

For Privacy Act and Paperwork Reduction Act Notice, see back of Copy D.

Employers, Please Note—

Specific information needed to complete Form W-2 is given in a separate booklet titled 2005 Instructions for Forms W-2 and W-3. You can order those instructions and additional forms by calling 1-800-TAX-FORM (1-800-829-3676). You can also get forms and instructions from the IRS website at www.irs.gov.

Caution. *Because the SSA processes paper forms by machine, you cannot file with the SSA Forms W-2 and W-3 that you print from the IRS website. Instead, you can use the SSA website at www.socialsecurity.gov/employer to create and file electronically "fill-in" versions of Forms W-2 and W-3.*

Due dates. Furnish Copies B, C, and 2 to the employee generally by January 31, 2006.

File Copy A with the SSA generally by February 28, 2006. Send all Copies A with Form W-3, Transmittal of Wage and Tax Statements. However, if you file electronically (not by magnetic media), the due date is March 31, 2006.

Privacy Act and Paperwork Reduction Act Notice. We ask for the information on Forms W-2 and W-3 to carry out the Internal Revenue laws of the United States. We need it to figure and collect the right amount of tax. Section 6051 and its regulations require you to furnish wage and tax statements to employees and to the Social Security Administration. Section 6109 requires you to provide your employer identification number (EIN). If you fail to provide this information in a timely manner, you may be subject to penalties.

You are not required to provide the information requested on a form that is subject to the Paperwork Reduction Act unless the form displays a valid OMB control number. Books or records relating to a form or its instructions must be retained as long as their contents may become material in the administration of any Internal Revenue law.

Generally, tax returns and return information are confidential, as required by section 6103. However, section 6103 allows or requires the Internal Revenue Service to disclose or give the information shown on your return to others as described in the Code. For example, we may disclose your tax information to the Department of Justice for civil and/or criminal litigation, and to cities, states, and the District of Columbia for use in administering their tax laws. We may also disclose this information to other countries under a tax treaty, to federal and state agencies to enforce federal nontax criminal laws, or to federal law enforcement and intelligence agencies to combat terrorism.

The time needed to complete and file these forms will vary depending on individual circumstances. The estimated average times are: **Form W-2**—30 minutes, and **Form W-3**—28 minutes. If you have comments concerning the accuracy of these time estimates or suggestions for making these forms simpler, we would be happy to hear from you. You can write to the Internal Revenue Service, Tax Products Coordinating Committee, SE:W:CAR:MP:T:T:SP, 1111 Constitution Ave. NW, IR-6406, Washington, DC 20224. **Do not** send Forms W-2 and W-3 to this address. Instead, see *Where to file* in the Instructions for Forms W-2 and W-3.

Attention:

Do not download, print, and file Copy A with the IRS.

Copy A appears in red, similar to the official IRS form, but is for informational purposes only. A penalty of $50 per information return may be imposed for filing copies of forms that cannot be scanned.

You may order these forms online at *Forms and Publications By U.S. Mail* or by calling 1-800-TAX-FORM (1-800-829-3676).

See IRS Publications 1141, 1167, 1179, and other IRS resources for information about printing these tax forms.

9898 ☐ VOID ☐ CORRECTED

PAYER'S name, street address, city, state, and ZIP code	1 Gross distribution $	OMB No. 1545-0119 **2005** Form **1099-R**	**Distributions From Pensions, Annuities, Retirement or Profit-Sharing Plans, IRAs, Insurance Contracts, etc.**
	2a Taxable amount $		
	2b Taxable amount not determined ☐ Total distribution ☐		**Copy A** **For Internal Revenue Service Center**
PAYER'S Federal identification number	RECIPIENT'S identification number	3 Capital gain (included in box 2a) $	4 Federal income tax withheld $	File with Form 1096.
RECIPIENT'S name	5 Employee contributions or insurance premiums $	6 Net unrealized appreciation in employer's securities $	For Privacy Act and Paperwork Reduction Act Notice, see the **2005 General Instructions for Forms 1099, 1098, 5498, and W-2G.**
Street address (including apt. no.)	7 Distribution code(s) IRA/SEP/SIMPLE ☐	8 Other $ %	
City, state, and ZIP code	9a Your percentage of total distribution %	9b Total employee contributions $	
Account number (see instructions)	10 State tax withheld $ $	11 State/Payer's state no.	12 State distribution $ $
	13 Local tax withheld $ $	14 Name of locality	15 Local distribution $ $

Form **1099-R**   Cat. No. 14436Q   Department of the Treasury - Internal Revenue Service

Do Not Cut or Separate Forms on This Page — Do Not Cut or Separate Forms on This Page

☐ VOID   ☐ CORRECTED

PAYER'S name, street address, city, state, and ZIP code	**1** Gross distribution $	OMB No. 1545-0119 **2005** Form **1099-R**	**Distributions From Pensions, Annuities, Retirement or Profit-Sharing Plans, IRAs, Insurance Contracts, etc.**
	2a Taxable amount $		
	2b Taxable amount not determined ☐	Total distribution ☐	**Copy 1**
PAYER'S Federal identification number | RECIPIENT'S identification number	**3** Capital gain (included in box 2a) $	**4** Federal income tax withheld $	**For State, City, or Local Tax Department**
RECIPIENT'S name	**5** Employee contributions or insurance premiums $	**6** Net unrealized appreciation in employer's securities $	
Street address (including apt. no.)	**7** Distribution code(s) | IRA/SEP/SIMPLE ☐	**8** Other $ %	
City, state, and ZIP code	**9a** Your percentage of total distribution %	**9b** Total employee contributions $	
Account number (see instructions)	**10** State tax withheld $ .... $	**11** State/Payer's state no.	**12** State distribution $ .... $
	13 Local tax withheld $ .... $	**14** Name of locality	**15** Local distribution $ .... $

Form **1099-R**   Department of the Treasury - Internal Revenue Service

---

☐ CORRECTED (if checked)

PAYER'S name, street address, city, state, and ZIP code	**1** Gross distribution $	OMB No. 1545-0119 **2005** Form **1099-R**	**Distributions From Pensions, Annuities, Retirement or Profit-Sharing Plans, IRAs, Insurance Contracts, etc.**
	2a Taxable amount $		
	2b Taxable amount not determined ☐	Total distribution ☐	**Copy B**
PAYER'S Federal identification number | RECIPIENT'S identification number	**3** Capital gain (included in box 2a) $	**4 Federal income tax withheld** $	**Report this income on your federal tax return. If this form shows federal income tax withheld in box 4, attach this copy to your return.**
RECIPIENT'S name	**5** Employee contributions or insurance premiums $	**6** Net unrealized appreciation in employer's securities $	
Street address (including apt. no.)	**7** Distribution code(s) | IRA/SEP/SIMPLE ☐	**8** Other $ %	This information is being furnished to the Internal Revenue Service.
City, state, and ZIP code	**9a** Your percentage of total distribution %	**9b** Total employee contributions $	
Account number (see instructions)	**10** State tax withheld $ .... $	**11** State/Payer's state no.	**12** State distribution $ .... $
	13 Local tax withheld $ .... $	**14** Name of locality	**15** Local distribution $ .... $

Form **1099-R**   Department of the Treasury - Internal Revenue Service

Instructions for Recipient

Generally, distributions from pensions, annuities, profit-sharing and retirement plans (including section 457 state and local government plans), IRAs, insurance contracts, etc., are reported to recipients on Form 1099-R.

Qualified plans. If your annuity starting date is after 1997, you must use the simplified method to figure your taxable amount if your payer did not show the taxable amount in box 2a. See Pub. 575, Pension and Annuity Income.

IRAs. For distributions from a traditional individual retirement arrangement (IRA), simplified employee pension (SEP), or savings incentive match plan for employees (SIMPLE), generally the payer is not required to compute the taxable amount. Therefore, the amounts in boxes 1 and 2a will be the same most of the time. See the Form 1040 or 1040A instructions to determine the taxable amount. If you are at least age 70½, you must take minimum distributions from your IRA (other than a Roth IRA). If you do not, you may be subject to a 50% excise tax on the amount that should have been distributed. See Pub. 590, Individual Retirement Arrangements (IRAs), and Pub. 560, Retirement Plans for Small Business (SEP, SIMPLE, and Qualified Plans), for more information on IRAs.

Roth IRAs. For distributions from a Roth IRA, generally the payer is not required to compute the taxable amount. You must compute any taxable amount on Form 8606, Nondeductible IRAs. An amount shown in box 2a may be taxable earnings on an excess contribution.

Loans treated as distributions. If you borrow money from a qualified plan, tax-sheltered annuity, or government plan, you may have to treat the loan as a distribution and include all or part of the amount borrowed in your income. There are exceptions to this rule. If your loan is taxable, Code L will be shown in box 7. See Pub. 575.

Account number. May show an account or other unique number the payer assigned to distinguish your account.

Box 1. Shows the total amount you received this year. The amount may have been a direct rollover, a transfer or conversion to a Roth IRA, a recharacterized IRA contribution; or you may have received it as periodic payments, as nonperiodic payments, or as a total distribution. Report the amount on Form 1040 or 1040A on the line for "IRA distributions" or "Pensions and annuities" (or the line for "Taxable amount"), and on Form 8606, whichever applies. However,

if this is a lump-sum distribution, report it on Form 4972, Tax on Lump-Sum Distributions. If you have not reached minimum retirement age, report your disability payments on the line for "Wages, salaries, tips, etc." on your tax return. Also report on that line corrective distributions of excess deferrals, excess contributions, or excess aggregate contributions.

If a life insurance, annuity, or endowment contract was transferred tax free to another trustee or contract issuer, an amount will be shown in this box and Code 6 will be shown in box 7. You need not report this on your tax return.

Box 2a. This part of the distribution is generally taxable. If there is no entry in this box, the payer may not have all the facts needed to figure the taxable amount. In that case, the first box in box 2b should be checked. You may want to get one of the following publications from the IRS to help you figure the taxable amount: Pub. 560, Pub. 571, Tax-Sheltered Annuity Plans (403(b) Plans) for Employees of Public Schools and Certain Tax-Exempt Organizations, Pub. 575, Pub. 590, Pub. 721, Tax Guide to U.S. Civil Service Retirement Benefits, or Pub. 939, General Rule for Pensions and Annuities. For an IRA distribution, see *IRAs* and *Roth IRAs* above. For a direct rollover, zero should be shown, and you must enter zero (-0-) on the "Taxable amount" line of your tax return.

If this is a total distribution from a qualified plan (other than an IRA or tax-sheltered annuity) and you were born before January 2, 1936 (or you are the beneficiary of someone born before January 2, 1936), you may be eligible for the 10-year tax option. See the Instructions for Form 4972 for more information.

Box 2b. If the first box is checked, the payer was unable to determine the taxable amount, and box 2a should be blank. However, if this is a traditional IRA, SEP, or SIMPLE distribution, then see *IRAs* above. If the second box is checked, the distribution was a total distribution that closed out your account.

Box 3. If you received a lump-sum distribution from a qualified plan and were born before January 2, 1936 (or you are the beneficiary of someone born before January 2, 1936), you may be able to elect to treat this amount as a capital gain on Form 4972 (not on Schedule D (Form 1040)). See the Instructions for Form 4972. For a charitable gift annuity, report as a long-term capital gain on Schedule D.

(Continued on the back of Copy C.)

☐ CORRECTED (if checked)

PAYER'S name, street address, city, state, and ZIP code		**1** Gross distribution $	OMB No. 1545-0119 **2005** Form **1099-R**	**Distributions From Pensions, Annuities, Retirement or Profit-Sharing Plans, IRAs, Insurance Contracts, etc.**
		2a Taxable amount $		
		2b Taxable amount not determined ☐	Total distribution ☐	
PAYER'S Federal identification number	RECIPIENT'S identification number	**3** Capital gain (included in box 2a) $	**4** Federal income tax withheld $	**Copy C** **For Recipient's Records**
RECIPIENT'S name		**5** Employee contributions or insurance premiums $	**6** Net unrealized appreciation in employer's securities $	This information is being furnished to the Internal Revenue Service.
Street address (including apt. no.)		**7** Distribution code(s) ⎪ IRA/SEP/SIMPLE ☐	**8** Other $　　　%	
City, state, and ZIP code		**9a** Your percentage of total distribution　%	**9b** Total employee contributions $	
Account number (see instructions)		**10** State tax withheld $ $	**11** State/Payer's state no.	**12** State distribution $ $
		13 Local tax withheld $ $	**14** Name of locality	**15** Local distribution $ $

Form **1099-R**　　　　　　　　　　(keep for your records)　　　　　　Department of the Treasury - Internal Revenue Service

Instructions for Recipient *(Continued)*

Box 4. This is the amount of federal income tax withheld. **Include this on your income tax return as tax withheld, and if box 4 shows an amount (other than zero), attach Copy B to your return.** Generally, if you will receive payments next year that are not eligible rollover distributions, you can change your withholding or elect not to have income tax withheld by giving the payer Form W-4P, Withholding Certificate for Pension or Annuity Payments.

Box 5. Generally, this shows the employee's investment in the contract (after-tax contributions), if any, recovered tax free this year; the part of premiums paid on commercial annuities or insurance contracts recovered tax free; or the nontaxable part of a charitable gift annuity. This box does not show any IRA contributions.

Box 6. If you received a lump-sum distribution from a qualified plan that includes securities of the employer's company, the net unrealized appreciation (NUA) (any increase in value of such securities while in the trust) is taxed only when you sell the securities unless you choose to include it in your gross income this year. See Pub. 575 and the Instructions for Form 4972. If you did not receive a lump-sum distribution, the amount shown is the NUA attributable to employee contributions, which is not taxed until you sell the securities.

Box 7. The following codes identify the distribution you received. **1**—Early distribution, no known exception (in most cases, under age 59½). See the Form 1040/1040A instructions and Form 5329, Additional Taxes on Qualified Plans (Including IRAs) and Other Tax-Favored Accounts. For a rollover of the entire distribution, do not file Form 5329. See the Form 1040/1040A instructions for how to report the rollover. **2**—Early distribution, exception applies (under age 59½)*. **3**—Disability*. **4**—Death*. **5**—Prohibited transaction. **6**—Section 1035 exchange (a tax-free exchange of life insurance, annuity, or endowment contracts). **7**—Normal distribution. **8**—Excess contributions plus earnings/excess deferrals (and/or earnings) taxable in 2005. **9**—Cost of current life insurance protection (premiums paid by a trustee or custodian for current insurance protection, taxable to you currently). **A**—May be eligible for 10-year tax option. See Form 4972. **D**—Excess contributions plus earnings/excess deferrals taxable in 2003. **E**—Excess annual additions under section 415 and certain excess amounts under section 403(b) plans. Report on Form 1040/1040A on the line for taxable pension or annuity income*. **F**—Charitable gift annuity. **G**—Direct rollover to a qualified plan, a

tax-sheltered annuity, a governmental 457(b) plan, or an IRA. May also include a transfer from a conduit IRA to a qualified plan*. **J**—Early distribution from a Roth IRA, no known exception (in most cases, under age 59½). Report on Forms 1040 and 8606 and see Form 5329. **L**—Loans treated as distributions. **N**—Recharacterized IRA contribution made for 2005 and recharacterized in 2005. Report on 2005 Form 1040/1040A and Form 8606, if applicable. **P**—Excess contributions plus earnings/excess deferrals taxable in 2004. **Q**—Qualified distribution from a Roth IRA. You are age 59½ or over and meet the 5-year holding period for a Roth IRA. See the Form 1040/1040A instructions*. **R**—Recharacterized IRA contribution made for 2004 and recharacterized in 2005. Report on 2004 Form 1040/1040A and Form 8606, if applicable. **S**—Early distribution from a SIMPLE IRA in first 2 years, no known exception (under age 59½). May be subject to an additional 25% tax. See Form 5329. **T**—Roth IRA distribution, exception applies. You are age 59½ or over, disabled, or are the beneficiary of a participant who died. (You may not meet the 5-year holding period.) See the Form 1040/1040A instructions.

If the IRA/SEP/SIMPLE box is checked, you have received a traditional IRA, SEP, or SIMPLE distribution.

Box 8. If you received an annuity contract as part of a distribution, the value of the contract is shown. It is not taxable when you receive it and should not be included in boxes 1 and 2a. When you receive periodic payments from the annuity contract, they are taxable at that time. If the distribution is made to more than one person, the percentage of the annuity contract distributed to you is also shown. You will need this information if you use the 10-year tax option (Form 4972).

Box 9a. If a total distribution was made to more than one person, the percentage you received is shown.

Box 9b. For a life annuity from a qualified plan or from a tax-sheltered annuity (with after-tax contributions), an amount may be shown for the employee's total investment in the contract. It is used to compute the taxable part of the distribution. See Pub. 575.

Boxes 10–15. If state or local income tax was withheld from the distribution, these boxes may be completed. Boxes 12 and 15 may show the part of the distribution subject to state and/or local tax.

*You are not required to file Form 5329.

☐ CORRECTED (if checked)

PAYER'S name, street address, city, state, and ZIP code		**1** Gross distribution $ **2a** Taxable amount $	OMB No. 1545-0119 20**05** Form **1099-R**	**Distributions From Pensions, Annuities, Retirement or Profit-Sharing Plans, IRAs, Insurance Contracts, etc.**
		2b Taxable amount not determined ☐	Total distribution ☐	
PAYER'S Federal identification number	RECIPIENT'S identification number	**3** Capital gain (included in box 2a) $	**4** Federal income tax withheld $	**Copy 2** **File this copy with your state, city, or local income tax return, when required.**
RECIPIENT'S name		**5** Employee contributions or insurance premiums $	**6** Net unrealized appreciation in employer's securities $	
Street address (including apt. no.)		**7** Distribution code(s) IRA/ SEP/ SIMPLE ☐	**8** Other $ %	
City, state, and ZIP code		**9a** Your percentage of total distribution %	**9b** Total employee contributions $	
Account number (see instructions)		**10** State tax withheld $ $	**11** State/Payer's state no.	**12** State distribution $ $
		13 Local tax withheld $ $	**14** Name of locality	**15** Local distribution $ $

Form **1099-R**   Department of the Treasury - Internal Revenue Service

☐ VOID   ☐ CORRECTED

PAYER'S name, street address, city, state, and ZIP code	1 Gross distribution $	OMB No. 1545-0119	Distributions From Pensions, Annuities, Retirement or Profit-Sharing Plans, IRAs, Insurance Contracts, etc.
	2a Taxable amount $	2005 Form 1099-R	
	2b Taxable amount not determined ☐ Total distribution ☐		
PAYER'S Federal identification number	RECIPIENT'S identification number	3 Capital gain (included in box 2a) $	4 Federal income tax withheld $	Copy D For Payer
RECIPIENT'S name	5 Employee contributions or insurance premiums $	6 Net unrealized appreciation in employer's securities $	For Privacy Act and Paperwork Reduction Act Notice, see the 2005 General Instructions for Forms 1099, 1098, 5498, and W-2G.
Street address (including apt. no.)	7 Distribution code(s) IRA/SEP/SIMPLE ☐	8 Other $ %	
City, state, and ZIP code	9a Your percentage of total distribution %	9b Total employee contributions $	
Account number (see instructions)	10 State tax withheld $ $	11 State/Payer's state no.	12 State distribution $ $
	13 Local tax withheld $ $	14 Name of locality	15 Local distribution $ $

Form **1099-R**   Department of the Treasury - Internal Revenue Service

Instructions for Payers

We provide general and specific form instructions as separate products. The products you should use for 2005 are the General Instructions for Forms 1099, 1098, 5498, and W-2G and the 2005 Instructions for Forms 1099-R and 5498. A chart in the general instructions gives a quick guide to which form must be filed to report a particular payment. To order these instructions and additional forms, call 1-800-TAX-FORM (1-800-829-3676).

Caution: *Because paper forms are scanned during processing, you cannot file with the IRS Forms 1096, 1098, 1099, or 5498 that you print from the IRS website.*

Due dates. Furnish Copies B and C of this form to the recipient by January 31, 2006.

File Copy A of this form with the IRS by February 28, 2006. If you file electronically, the due date is March 31, 2006.

✸ Printed on recycled paper

Sample Résumés

00000 S. ABC St #000
Anytown, USA 00000

000-000-0000
0000@000.com

Marketing - #1 Before

Objective	Position in which I can demonstrate my industry and mathematical skills while utilizing my business degree and four years of marketing and client service experience

Experience

6/2000- Present   Cable Co   Englewood, CO

Field Service Analyst

- Coordinate operations and compile reports regarding field technician services and office management policies and procedures
- Process work orders via email and phone requests for HSP network
- Assist and market DirecTV services for dealer accounts
- Responsible for a high volume of retail calls and astute customer satisfaction

10/1999-2/2000   Advertising Co   Englewood, CO

Assistant Account Coordinator

- Assisted account coordinators with marketing and production of Ads for their clients
- Assisted with Internet advertising for employment opportunities
- Coordinated meetings and created proposals for prospective clients
- Office support and clerical duties

Education

1995-1999   University of Colorado   Boulder, CO

- Bachelor's of Science degree in Journalism
- Business Minor
- Graduated with distinction

Computer Skills   Proficient in Microsoft Office programs, ACT, STMS, CSG, and OMS

References available upon request

Resume provided courtesy of Coach Joan McMahon, SPHIR, of Career Solutions—Unleashing the Excellence Within (coachjoan@msn.com).

Susie Davis

44 S. Elmwood Lane, #1
Denver, CO 80237
Phone: (303) 555-4637 Email: candidate1@msn.com

SUMMARY: Experienced Marketing and Customer Service Professional with demonstrated abilities in internet research, data analysis and customer service. Strengths include training new employees, communication skills and report writing. Seeking an advertising or market research position in a dynamic environment where I can share my knowledge and experience for our mutual benefit.

PROFESSIONAL EXPERIENCE

DIRECT TV, Englewood, CO   2000–present
Field Service Analyst

♦ Effectively coordinate field technician services including implementing office management policies and procedures.
♦ Provide fast and efficient customer service to a high volume of retail calls resulting in problem resolution and customer satisfaction.
♦ Proactively correct work order errors to ensure smooth communication between DirectTV and the field sales force. Process work orders via email and phone requests for HSP network.
♦ Assist dealers with marketing DirectTV services by setting up showroom accounts and answering key commission questions. Persuaded hundreds of dealers to use retailer web site by discussing the features and benefits of site for their business.

NATIONWIDE ADVERTISING SERVICE, Englewood, CO   1999–2000
Assistant Account Coordinator

♦ Assisted account coordinators with marketing and production of ads for their clients including media placements and producing camera-ready art for publication. Provided administrative support including researching, copying and answering customer inquiries.
♦ Assisted with the internet advertising for employment opportunities by posting open positions.
♦ Provided administrative support to department including proposal creation, managing calendars and meetings for clients and prospects and assisting manager with new client files.

SPECIALTY SPORTS, INC., Denver, CO   Summer 98
Advertising Intern

♦ Selected and prepared artwork for current ads. Submitted the ads and artwork to local newspapers. Organized ad books for all 5 stores. Created original golf ad for Colorado Ski & Golf Store.

EDUCATION

UNIVERISTY OF COLORADO, Boulder, CO
♦ Bachelor of Science in Journalism with a Minor in Business, 1999
♦ Graduated with Distinction (3.75 / 4.00)

COMPUTER SKILLS

Proficient in MS Word, MS Excel, MS PowerPoint, MS Outlook, MS Access, ACT, STMS, CSG, and OMS (internal customer service and order processing programs).

Resume provided courtesy of Coach Joan McMahon, SPHIR, of Career Solutions—Unleashing the Excellence Within (coachjoan@msn.com).

Candidate #2 - Before
000 ABC Dr. • Anytown, USA 00000
0000@000.com • 000.940.2750

Freelance Web Design:

www.com - June 2000-present

- www.com - Conceptualized, designed, assembled and constructed website
- www.com - Conceptualized, designed, assembled and constructed website
- www.org - Conceptualized, designed, assembled and constructed website
- www.com - Conceptualized, designed, assembled and constructed website

Experience:

Internet Specialist / Project Manager - May 2000-April 2004
Mortgage Company, Huntingdon Valley PA • www.tollbrothers.com

- Project Manager of internal page, a website feature which allows users to save, sort and compare data from our website.
- Project leader/developer on *Selector* Flash application leading to more focused sales leads
- Web Designer responsible for design, development and updates of multi-page web sites delivering targeted marketing messages to consumers
- Responsible for over 20 web sites and their ongoing updates
- Production lead for all web related images: Maps, PDF's, Flash applications, Floor plans, Photos, Graphics
- Webmaster for *Investor Relations* section of web site including time sensitive press release postings
- Training / trouble-shooting for co-workers

Tennis Instructor - June 1995 – June 1999
Tennis Academy, Anytown, USA

- Supervised 4-6 Instructors managing 30+ children of varying ages
- One-on-one and group lessons

Tennis Instructor – June 1989 – June 1995
Racquet Club, Anytown, USA

- Supervised 6-8 Instructors managing 40+ children of varying ages
- One-on-one and group lessons

Skills:

- Flash, Dreamweaver, Fireworks, Freehand, Illustrator, Photoshop, Premiere, MS Office, HTML, DHTML, CSS, actionScript (Flash), Windows & Mac OS

Education:

- Associates of Communications – Film, Bucks County Community College, Bucks County, PA, May 1999.

Accolades:

- Web Marketing Association WebAward 2002 - Outstanding Website (www.com)
- 2002 Summit Award (www.com)

References: Will be provided upon request

Online Portfolio: www.com.html

Candidate #2-After

Email address: 00000@0000.com
Phone: (000) 000-0000

0000 ABE Drive
Anytown, USA 0000

SUMMARY: Professional Web Designer with demonstrated abilities in full-service graphical web design & construction. Strengths include client consulting, designing creative web concepts and constructing award winning, interactive web sites. Seeking a Web Designer position in a small to medium sized organization where I can use my creative, technical and project management skills for our mutual benefit.

PROFESSIONAL WEB DESIGN EXPERIENCE

THE ABC GROUP, Denver, CO   04—present
Contract Web Designer for ABC Co., Anytown, USA

- Provide graphic web design services for online learning company.

WWW.COM, Arvada, CO   00—present
Freelance Web Designer

- Conceptualized, designed, and constructed websites for small business owners including:
- www.1.com; www.2.com, www.3.org, www.4.com, www.5.com; and www.6.com.

MORTGAGE CO., Anytown, USA www.abc.com   00—04
Internet Specialist / Project Manager

- **Project Management**: Served as Project Manager for the creation of special home website feature which allowed users to save, sort and compare data. Led and developed *Selector* Flash application resulting in more focused sales leads for company. Served as Webmaster for *Investor Relations* section of web site including time sensitive press releases.
- **Web Design & Creation**: As Web Designer, provided design, development and updates to over 20 websites including multi-page websites delivering targeted marketing messages to consumers. Served as Production Lead for all web related images including maps, PDFs, Flash applications, floor plans, photos and graphics for site. Provided training and troubleshooting for team.

TENNIS INSTRUCTOR CAREER

ABC TENNIS ACADEMY, Anytown, USA   95—99
123 RACQUET CLUB, Anytown, USA   89—95

- Supervised 4-6 Tennis Instructors who managed the tennis programs for 30+ children of varying ages. Provided one on one and group tennis lessons to patrons.

EDUCATION

123 COMMUNITY COLLEGE, Bucks Co., PA
Associates of Communications in Film, May 1999

TECHNICAL SKILLS: Flash, Dreamweaver, Fireworks, Freehand, Illustrator, Photoshop, Premiere, MS Office Suite, HTML, DHTML, CSS, actionScript (Flash), Windows & Mac OS.

ACCOLADES

- Outstanding Website Award for www.1.com, Web Marketing Association, 2002
- 2002 Summit Award for www.1.com

Candidate #3 – Before
123 Main Street
Anytown, USA 00000
E-Mail: 00000000@000.com
Cell: (000) 000-0000

QUALIFICATIONS:

Highly adaptable individual with innovative thinking, excellent communication, and enthusiastic team-building skills. Combines high energy and motivation with strong organizational planning and leadership abilities. Meets deadlines in a high stress work environment.

EXPERIENCE:

Sales Account Representative   (1/04-10/04)
DELIVERY CO. - Anytown, USA
- Extensive sales training program
- Business to business cold calling
- Gathering daily leads to meet quota
- Setting daily appointments
- Meeting with CEO's,CFO's and Controllers
- Constantly closing business
- Set up and management of multiple accounts
- Build and maintain client relationships
- Create organized proposals to meet client needs
- Strong closing skills and problem solving required daily
- Self motivation and strong drive to succeed
- Meeting monthly sales quotas

Program Account Coordinator/ Field Staff   (7/03-12/03)
CABLE CO., Anytown, USA
- Client Communication
- Handled multiple tasks simultaneously
- Designed organized and creative proposals for our clients program.
- On-site management of transportation, hotel arrangements, tours and theme parties.
- Met with our clients before, during and after program to ensure satisfaction.
- Assisted with all aspects of sales and management of corporate special events
- Creative concepts, theme development and budgeting
- Logistics and vendor interface
- Selected décor for events, assisted with set up, and performed site inspections.

Promotions and Marketing Representative   (12/02-6/03)
Radio Station – Anytown,USA
- Collaborated with Account Executives to create and execute listener promotional campaigns.
- Planned and executed all aspects of on-site events
- Managed coordination of numerous events to achieve higher listener awareness and loyalty.
- Responsible for screening, interviewing and hiring individuals

for internship positions.
- Supervised and delegated responsibilities to interns
- Worked with on-air personalities to create exceptional special events
- Maintained relationships with local media buyers through special events and press releases.

Manager of Marketing and Promotions   *(1999-2004)*
Marketing Co., Anytown, USA
- Designed and implemented consumer product promotions at various special events
- Evaluated the progress and quality of staff's communication and marketing skills
- Used creative strategies and strong interpersonal skills to increase market awareness and sales.

COMPUTER SKILLS:

Superior computer skills using: Microsoft Windows operating systems, Microsoft Office (Word, Excel) Outlook, Microsoft Internet Explorer, Netscape Navigator and other communication databases.

EDUCATION:

BACHELOR OF ARTS DEGREE – COMMUNICATION
Minor in International Studies
The University of Arizona   *(Winter 2002)*

LA UNIVERSIDAD DE SEVILLA – SEVILLE, SPAIN
Study Abroad Program – Spanish and Language Culture   *(Spring 2001)*
Proficient in Spanish

ACTIVITIES:

- Community Involvement Includes: "Make a Wish Foundation" volunteer, Juvenile Diabetes Foundation, Boys and Girls Club, Poway Softball League

Candidate 3 – After
123 Main Street
Anytown, USA 00000
E-Mail: 0000@000.com
Phone: (000) 000-0000

SUMMARY: Experienced Sales & Marketing Professional with strong skills in on-site product promotions, event planning, and building customer relationships. Experience includes field marketing, working with branding strategies, and road show customer service. Strengths include adaptability, creativity, high energy and strong motivational skills. Seeking a marketing, sales or promotions position where I can use my education, customer service skills and sales and marketing skills for our mutual benefit.

EDUCATION & TRAINING

UNIVERSITY OF ARIZONA, Tucson, AZ
Bachelor of Arts in Communication with a minor in International Studies 2002

LA UNIVERSIDAD DE SEVILLA, Seville, Spain
Study Abroad – Spanish and Language Culture
Proficient in the Spanish language

XYZ SALES TRAINING, 2004

PROFESSIONAL EXPERIENCE

INDEPENDENT CONTRACTOR, Denver, CO
Sales & Marketing Representative   Jul 04 to present
Provide a variety of marketing services throughout the Denver metro area:
Onsite Product Promotions

◆ *Brand Ambassador*: Through XYZ Group, executed onsite promotional events. Created unique promotional material designed for target market. Worked with management to enhance enjoyment and awareness of new product. Train new agents and created follow-up reports to evaluate events. Through 123 Talent Agency, assisted at the Auto Show Registration booth for the duration of the event. Performed an onsite promotion for XYZ cable on many college campuses, weekend promotion for ABC's Animal Expo and a 2 week long field promotion for Flower Company.

◆ *Event & Roadshow Management*: Through ABC Marketing, created marketing and sales strategies in order to introduce a new gourmet soda pop beverage and nutritional bars into target market. Performed multiple product demonstrations daily to encourage sampling and selling of the product resulting in increased sales of approximately 100 cases / day. Managed and executed initial road show set up and breakdown including product placement and customer friendly design. Worked with a traveling road show to promote XYZ salsa and ABC Tea. Assisted with the sales and promotion of 123, a Vitamin B supplement. Through ABC Promo Company, worked the game booths and festivals at el cinco de mayo event in Anytown, USA.

◆ *Marketing Assistant*: Provide administrative assistance to marketing company including correspondence and office organization.

XYZ COMPANY, Anytown, USA   Jan 04 to Oct 04

Sales Account Representative

♦ **Sales:** After receiving extensive sales training, launched and managed sales cycle for this xxx company including business to business lead generation, cold calling, setting up appointments, and conducting successful sales calls to CEO's, CFO's and Controllers. Constantly closed business through building and maintaining client relationships.

ABC COMPANY, Anytown, USA   Jul 03 to Dec 03
Program Account Coordinator / Field Staff

♦ **Event Planning:** Assisted with all aspects of sales and management of corporate special events. Set up décor for events, assisted with setup, and performed extensive site inspections. Designed creative proposals for our client program. Generated creative concepts for events including theme development.

♦ **Customer Service:** Met with our clients before, during and after programs to ensure satisfaction. Provided on-site management of transportation, hotel arrangements, tours and theme parties for events.

Radio Station, Anytown, USA   Dec 02 to Jun 03
Promotions and Marketing Representative

♦ **Promotions:** Collaborated with Account Executives to create and execute listener promotional campaigns. Planned and executed all aspects of on-site events. Managed coordination of numerous events to achieve higher listener awareness and loyalty. Screened, interviewed and hired individuals for internship positions. Supervised and delegated work to interns. Worked with on-air personalities to create exceptional special events. Maintained relationships with local media buyers through special events and press releases.

MARKETING COMPANY, Anytown, USA   1999 to 2004
Manager of Marketing and Promotions

♦ **Marketing:** Designed and implemented consumer product promotions at various special events. Evaluated the progress and quality of staff's communication and marketing skills. Used creative strategies and strong interpersonal skills to increase market awareness and sales.

123 TOURS, Tucson, AZ   1998-2002
Promotions and Sales Representative

♦ Promoted, sold and coordinated 8 trips for college community for 200 people over a 4 year timespan.

OTHER

♦ Community involvement includes serving as a volunteer for: "Make a Wish Foundation" foundation, Juvenile Diabetes Foundation, Boys and Girls Club and Poway Softball League.

♦ Computer Skills: Superior computer skills including MS Office software (Word, Excel, Outlook), MS Internet Explorer, and Netscape Navigator.

Candidate #4 - Before

000 Main Street, Anytown, USA 00000
h. (000) 000-0000   f. (000) 000-0000
email: 000@000.com

Experience:

April 2001 to Present   **SUBSTITUTE TEACHER**
                                   XYZ School District; Anytown, USA

Substitute teaching assignments for grades K-12 in general education, special education, and tech lab settings. Collaborating with staff and volunteers to meet the needs of all children.

January 2001 to Present   **BUSINESS MANAGER (Part Time/Evenings)**
                                   ABC, Inc.; Anytown, USA

Manages website and online-shopping cart content. Receiving and filling of retail and wholesale orders. Maintains inventory. Researches new products and develops promotional material. Responsible for AR/AP. Responsible for IT administration. Maintains records on QuickBooks Pro 2003. Attends major trade shows and promotes company and products.

January 2003 to November 2004 **MEMBERSHIP ASSISTANT (Part Time)**
                                    Society for XYZ; Anytown, USA

Special projects within the membership department including special mailings, membership filing, and renewal processing.

1989 to 2002   **4-H VOLUNTEER ORGANIZATIONAL LEADER**
                                   CSU Cooperative Extension – Any County
                                   4-H Youth Development Program; Anytown, USA

Developing, implementing, and teaching 4-H project curriculum to school age children.   Managing county 4-H events. Being a team player in communicating, problem solving, and developing new ideas with County Extension staff, volunteers, and parents

Education:

2004 – Present   **UNIVERSITY OF PHOENIX**
                                   Seeking an MBA in Technology Management

1996 – 2000   **METROPOLITAN STATE COLLEGE OF DENVER**
                                   Degree: Bachelor of Arts in English – Elementary Education

COMPUTERS:

Very proficient installing, maintaining, teaching, and trouble-shooting:
- *Networks*: Windows NT, Macintosh OSX
- *Operating Systems*: Windows 2000, Windows XP, Macintosh OS
- *Software Applications*: Microsoft Office (Word, Excel, PowerPoint, Access, Outlook) Adobe Acrobat, Microsoft FrontPage, QuickBooks, FTP, Microsoft PhotoDraw, and more.
- *Membership Software*: iMIS

Candidate 4 - After

000 Main Street
Anytown, USA 00000
Home Phone: (000) 000-0000   Email: abc@123.com

SUMMARY: Experienced Manager with strong skills in project management, technology and teamwork. Strengths include problem solving, accuracy with numbers, and website design/maintenance. Experience working as a substitute teacher for grades K-12, as a volunteer in non-profit organizations and as a Business Manager in a small company. Seeking a business management position in a dynamic organization where I can use and develop my leadership and project management skills for our mutual benefit.

EDUCATION

UNIVERSITY OF PHOENIX, Denver, CO
Currently enrolled in MBA program with an emphasis in Technology Management

METROPOLITAN STATE COLLEGE OF DENVER, Denver, CO
Bachelor of Arts Degree in English and Elementary Education, 2000

PROFESSIONAL EXPERIENCE

ABC, INC., Anytown, USA (Part Time / Evenings)   Jan 01–present
Business Manager

- **Technology:** Manage website and online shopping cart content for animal protection business. Responsible for all aspects of IT administration for company.
- **Financial:** Perform Accounts Payable and Accounts Receivable including maintaining all accounting records on QuickBooks Pro 2003.
- **Marketing:** Attend major trade shows and promote company and products. Receive and fill retail and wholesale orders. Research new products and develop promotional materials.

XYZ SCHOOL DISTRICT, Anytown, USA   Apr 01–present
Substitute Teacher

- Provide substitute teaching for grades K-12 in general education, special education, and tech lab settings. Collaborate with staff and volunteers to meet the needs of all children.

SOCIETY FOR 123, Anytown, USA   Jan 03–Nov 04
Membership Assistant (Part – time)

- Performed special projects within the membership department including special mailings, membership filing, and renewal processing.

ABC Club, Anytown, USA   1989–2002
Volunteer Organizational Leader (CSU Cooperative Extension & Youth Development Program)

- Developed, implemented and taught 4-H project curriculum to school age children. Manage county 4-H events. In a team environment, communicated, problem solved and developed new ideas with the County Extension staff, volunteers and parents.

123 LEARNING CENTER, Anytown, USA   1996–2001
Infant Supervisor / Group Leader

- Served as liaison between parents and center management. Supervised 10 infants and directed the day to day operations of the staff and teaching assistants. Calmly solved complex problems with all parties on a regular basis.

TECHNICAL SKILLS: Install, maintain, train and troubleshoot the following:

Networks: Windows NT, Macintosh OSX
Operating Systems: Windows 2000, Windows XP, Macintosh OS
Software: Microsoft Office: (Word, Excel, PowerPoint, Access, Outlook), Adobe Acrobat, Microsoft FrontPage, QuickBooks, FTP, Microsoft PhotoDraw and more.
Membership Software: iMIS

Candidate #5 - Before
000 Main Street, #000
Anytown, USA 00000
000-000-0000
Email address

Objective:

Seeking a position in the health care field to further my education and experience.

Education:

University of Northern Colorado, Greeley, CO
B.A. English, December 1999

Experience:

October 2004 – Present. XYZ Hospital, Health Information Management, *Medical Records Processor*: Employed to the initial processing of outpatient medical records. Successfully established high levels of standards of accuracy and efficiency.

- Instigated additional steps that better helped my co-workers. Additionally, streamlined the processing task and saved 10-15 hours per week for other projects.

September 2001 – October 2004. XYZ Hospital, Health Information Management, *Analyst*: Responsible for interpreting data for all outpatient medical records to ensure compliance for hospital standards.

- Contributor to the implementation of a new computer program. Provided crucial information and insight for its design.
- Assisted in overhauling department criteria for the analysis of outpatient records.

January 2000 – September 2001. XYZ Hospital, Health Information Management, *File Clerk*: Hired to file outpatient charts, medical folders and loose papers. Provided information to hospital and other area hospitals with patient medical information.

- Contributed to the overhaul of the work flow in the file room.

June 1999 – December 1999. 123 Entertainment, *Guest Service Associate*: Provided assistance to customers in the purchasing of books, CDs, DVDs and computer software.

June 1999 – September 1999. XYZ Clothing Company, *Customer Service Sales Associate*: Assisted customers in the purchasing of clothing for men, women and kids.

Activities:

September 2004 – March 2005. Leader for "Games and Trivia" at XYZ Retirement Community.
September 2004 – November 2004. "Spanish for Health Care Professionals I" class.
February 2001 – March 2001. Arapahoe County Victims Advocate Training.
American Heart Association Basic CPR certification.

Skills:

Keyboarding; Windows 95, 98 and XP; Microsoft Word, Works and Outlook; Terminal Digit Order.

Candidate # 5 - After
123 Main Street, #000
Anytown, USA 00000
Phone: (000) 000-0000
Email address: 000@000.com

SUMMARY: **Experienced Medical Records Professional** with 5+ years experience managing all aspects of outpatient medical records processing at major metro hospital. Experienced with medical records assembly, analysis, organization and data integrity processes. Strengths include providing excellent customer service, working well in a complex, team environment, initiating effective process improvements, and using superior organizational skills. Possess special knowledge of HIM, hospital, and JCAHO rules and standards for records completion. Seeking an **xxx** position in an established company where I can use my education, customer service skills and process improvement skills for our mutual benefit.

EDUCATION & TRAINING

UNIVERSITY OF XYZ UNIVERSITY, Anytown, CO
Bachelor of Arts in English, 1999   GPA 3.22 / 4.0
Bachelor of Arts in Theater, 1999

St. Anthony Central Education Dept., Spanish for Health Care Professionals I, 2004
ABC County, Victim Advocate Training, 2001
American Heart Association, Basic CPR certification, 2004

PROFESSIONAL EXPERIENCE

XYZ HOSPITAL, Health Information Management Dept., Denver, CO   **2000 to present**
Medical Records Processor (Oct 04-present)

- **Records Processing:** Successfully perform initial processing of an average of 200 outpatient medical records daily from multiple departments for busy metro hospital. Serve as a resource within HIM department for overall knowledge of the entire outpatient process. Effectively interact with many hospital departments, doctors, managers and coders on a daily basis.
- **Process Improvements:** Streamlined the data entry process for coders which enabled a more effective work flow and resulted in a greater financial recovery for the department and the hospital. Successfully managed tasks resulting in a cut of 10-15 hours weekly to provide additional assistance to the department.

Analyst (Sep 01-Oct 04)

- **Records Processing:** Using Terminal Digit Order (TDO) process, interpreted a variety of outpatient medical records data, effectively ensuring compliance with HIM, hospital, and JCAHO rules and standards for record completion.
- **Process Improvements:** Contributed to the implementation of a new computer program for our department including providing crucial input and insight for its design. Assisted in overhauling department criteria for the analysis of outpatient records resulting in an effective, department-wide change in work flow process.

File Clerk (Jan 00-Sep 01)

- **Records Processing:** Responded to patient medical information requests via telephone and fax from hospitals, clinics, doctors and insurance companies following department's release of information procedure and HIM guidelines for releasing Protected Patient Information (PPI). Effectively interacted with all nursing units and hospital departments, former patients, HIM professionals, attorneys' offices, and County Coroner's Office. Efficiently filed folders, outpatient charts and loose papers using TDO.
- **Process Improvements:** Contributed to the overhaul of the work flow in the file room resulting in more efficient and equitable distribution of work, faster work processes and morale improvement.

123 ENTERTAINMENT, Anytown, USA   Jun - Dec 1999
Guest Service Associate

♦ Provided assistance to customers in the purchasing of books, CDs, DVDs and computer software.

ABC CLOTHING COMPANY, Anytown, USA   Jun - Sep 1999
Customer Service Sales Associate   May - Aug in 96, 97 and 98

♦ Assisted customers in the purchasing of clothing for men, women and kids.

OTHER

♦ Volunteer, Games & Trivia Leader, ABC Retirement Community, Sep 04-Mar 05
♦ Skills: Keyboarding; Windows 95, 98 and XP; Microsoft Word, Works and Outlook; Terminal Digit Order.

Answers to Practice Problems

Chapter 8—Answers (Interest)

1. Adjustable-rate mortgages, credit card interest rates, inflation, cost of doing business, earnings on CDs, earnings on savings accounts, earnings on bonds, earnings on money market accounts, etc.
2. Same, but the effects are opposite.
3. Is the interest rate (often advertised at 0% or 2% or something similar) only offered on balance transfers from another card?

   What is the interest rate on *new* purchases? It may be quite high.

   How long does this special interest rate last?

   Is there an annual fee with this new credit card?

   Is there a fee for balance transfers?

   How long is the grace period?

   What is your payment going to be?

   How long will you have to make the payments?
4. Martha is not going to be able to use her debit card. Anything she buys is going to be immediately deducted from her checking account and she doesn't have enough money. Her card will be declined.

Chapter 9—Answers (Inflation)

1. If you didn't get raises that kept pace with inflation, your standard of living would have to drop (fewer meals out, delaying the purchase of a home) or you would need a roommate, maybe a new job, or maybe you need to go back to school to become "promotable."
2. Subjective—no right or wrong answer.

Chapter 10—Answers (Time Value of Money)

1. Patrick is going to need over 14% per year as a total rate of return. It has been many years since this sort of return occurred with any regularity. The likelihood of this return being seen again is pretty slim, but it could happen. Patrick is a gambler, though, not an investor. Use the Rule of 72: 72 ÷ 5 years = 14.4%.
2. Briana may be too conservative for her own good. If you use the Rule of 72 she is going to double her money in a very long 18 years, but inflation and taxes will take their toll. Since she earns 4% and inflation is 3% she is only earning a "real" return of 1%. In addition, she is losing 0.8% of her interest earnings to taxes. That means in "real" terms her $10,000 is only gaining 0.2% in value every year—that's $20. There is a very high

price to pay if you are too conservative, yet people who wait to invest until they are in their 30s and 40s have no choice but to be conservative to avoid losing money.

3. If you earn 5% simple interest on $1,000 you earn $50 per year. To earn another $1,000 would take 20 years.

   If you earn 5% compound interest on $1,000 the Rule of 72 shows it will take about 14.4 years to double your money. Quite a big difference in time and money.

Chapter 13—Answers (Getting and Using Credit Cards)

1. Types of credit cards and uses

   Secured cards. Payment on these cards is assured since you have to set aside an amount equal to the "credit limit" on the card.

   A person might want this type of card when rebuilding credit after a bankruptcy. When monthly payments are made on time and in full, without dipping into the money securing the card, that is a good thing.

   Traditional cards. This is the type of credit card most people think of (and want). You get a credit limit—maximum you can owe the lender—based on your reputation (your credit report/score).

   People want this type of card so they don't have to carry so much cash or write checks. They are also able to buy things they might not be able to pay cash for, at least not right away.

   Bank debit cards. These are often the same as ATM cards, but they also work like cash or a credit card. Since your bank won't allow you to go into debt (you are limited by the amount of money in your accounts), these cards are much like prepaid or secured cards.

   If you need to get money from your checking account (or savings account in some situations) and also want to "charge" some expenses that you can't write a check for, these cards can be a good idea. If you habitually run out of money in your checking account, these cards are going to either not work or get you in even more trouble!

   Check guarantee cards. These cards are often ATM cards and don't work like a debit card otherwise. You can't normally use them for purchases.

   Most people would not want to be without either a debit card or a check guarantee card. Without one or the other, it would be very hard to get cash without a trip to the bank.

   Preloaded cards. These cards look like credit cards but aren't even close. They do nothing to help (or hurt) your credit rating. You can only use them until the amount loaded on them is gone.

   People who travel often and don't want to carry and change cash often find these useful. They often work as ATM cards, and also work much like a credit card (until the value has been used up). These cards can also be reloaded when you get back to the bank that issued them.

2. Explain the grace period.

   The grace period is the time between making a charge and having to pay for the charge. After the grace period ends, you are charged interest.

3. What can the CCCS do for you if you get into financial trouble and can't pay your bills?

   CCCS can help you arrange payment programs and manage your bills and debt. Using the services of CCCS can help you avoid bankruptcy and learn to manage debt.

4. What is "skimming"? What can you do to prevent this happening to you?

   Skimming is someone taking your credit card, often at a restaurant, and making an electronic copy (by "swiping" it) at the same time they process a legitimate charge. Later the person makes a printout of the card data (and may even make an actual card) and uses your credit card data to make purchases.

The best prevention is to never let your card out of your sight or possession. Always look at your monthly statements to make sure all the charges are yours. Notify your credit card company right away if you think your card was, or may have been, skimmed.

Never lend your credit card to anyone.

5. List three uses for a credit card that are "wants" rather than "needs."

This list could be huge, but here are a few things you could probably do without in the interests of debt reduction, debt management, or savings:

- Treating your friends to drinks and meals. Once in awhile on a rotating basis is great; routinely or frequently is not so good.
- Eating out more than once or twice a week when the only way you can pay is with a credit card.
- Charging a trip because you "need the break."
- Buying two pair of jeans when you only need one.
- Buying things you never use, or only use once or twice.
- Buying gifts that you can't really afford.
- And on and on . . .

Chapter 14—Answers (Manage Credit Cards and Avoid Being a Fraud Victim)

1. What is the biggest difference between a loan and a credit card?
   There are no real differences. Both depend on your ability to repay money and the issuer's (lender's) opinion of your reliability and willingness to pay them back. Both are due on set dates and usually have short grace periods. Both get you in lots of trouble if you pay late, don't pay enough, or miss payments.
2. List at least five things you should do to protect and manage your credit cards and credit rating. Here are some, but far from all, of the things you can do:
   - Always pay on time.
   - Make sure you keep the lenders informed of your current address.
   - Don't get another credit card because the one(s) you have is at the limit.
   - Never use a credit card for cash advances—the charges are horrendous.
   - Never use one credit card to make the payments on another credit card.
   - Never get a second credit card until you can manage the first one, and always earmark the second card for a specific purpose.
   - Always get credit for a specific purpose and use it for that purpose only.
   - Read the credit card agreement in full.

Chapter 16—Answers (Managing Credit)

1. What can hurt your credit rating and score?
   Paying late, missing payments, making less than the minimum payment, only making minimum payments, declaring bankruptcy, etc.
2. What can cause the interest rate you pay to go up?
   All the things in #1.

3. What can cause your credit cards to be canceled?
   All the things in #1.
4. Name at least three problems you may encounter in the future if you declare bankruptcy.
   • Getting a job that requires a security clearance (government, military, defense, etc.)
   • Getting future loans or credit cards
   • Getting the best rates on insurance
   • Renting an apartment
   • Leasing a car

Chapter 17—Answers (Identity Theft)

1. What do you consider the three most important things you can do to protect your credit?
   This is fairly subjective, but here are some ideas:
   • Guard your Social Security card and number.
   • Always report stolen personal information to the police and the credit bureaus.
   • Put a "fraud watch" on your account.
   • Never give out credit card or Social Security numbers on an unsecure website.
   • Read your credit card statements each month to look for signs of unusual activity/purchases.
   • Don't lend your personal documents to anyone.
   • Keep your passport, birth certificate, and Social Security card in a safe place.
   • Only give out personal information if you initiated the contact.
2. What steps you do you plan to take to avoid becoming a victim of identity theft?
   The steps in #1 will make you much less at risk.
3. What is "phishing"?
   Trying to get your personal information (passwords, credit card data, bank account/checking account numbers, Social Security number, and so on) by impersonating a place with which you do business. Some of the most commonly impersonated places include: banks, credit unions, ISPs, places with which you do online or electronic business, employers, insurance companies, and so on.
4. When can a place or person request your SSN?
   Generally only if there is a need to report financial information or obtain financial information.
5. What places/people should not request/need your SSN?
   Some prime examples are:
   • Health insurance companies
   • Medical services providers (doctors' offices, hospitals)
   • Schools (unless it is for your loan file)
   • Stores or other merchants

Chapter 18—Answers (Taxes, Deductions, and Your Income—The Basics)

1. When you are still living at home, what deduction or exemption do you normally *not* take?
   You normally don't take the personal exemption. Your parents take this exemption while you are dependent on them.

2. Why do you forgo this deduction?

   Your parents are almost certainly in a higher tax bracket so the exemption saves them far more in taxes than it would save you. Only one tax return can claim someone as a dependent—you can't be declared on two tax returns.

3. The employer's contribution to your pension or retirement plan savings is often referred to as "free money." Why is it called "free money"?

   Because as long as you meet certain requirements (time at the employer) you can contribute to the pension plan and get some kind of additional money from your employer—for free. Not all employers offer this plan. Never turn down free money!

4. What is the difference between tax-free, tax-deferred, and tax-deductible?

   Tax-free money is exempted from federal tax, and often state taxes. Examples: A Roth IRA is tax-free when you take the money at retirement, but the contributions are taxable. The growth on a Roth IRA is free from any taxes. Money from a tax-free investment is free of most income taxes.

   Tax-deferred money is deducted from current income, after Social Security and Medicare taxes are paid. Eventually taxes that have not yet been paid will be due.

   Tax-deductible money is things such as tax deductions when you itemize your tax return, or deductible IRA contributions.

Chapter 19—Answers (Taxes, Deductions, and Your Income—The Details)

1. Name at least eight kinds of taxes or other deductions you might find have come out of your paycheck.
   - State taxes
   - Local/city taxes
   - Head or use taxes
   - Retirement plan contributions
   - Voluntary short-term disability insurance contributions
   - Voluntary long-term disability insurance contributions
   - Voluntary life insurance
   - Health insurance premium—employee portion
   - Other voluntary deductions (specialty insurance, loan payments, savings bond purchases, United Way contributions, etc.)

2. What is the difference between total (gross) pay and take-home pay?

Your total pay is the amount your employer agreed to pay you when you were hired. You "gross" that amount. However, there are many things that conspire to reduce your pay, resulting in your take-home (net) pay. Some things you have no control over, such as paying income, Social Security, and Medicare taxes. Other things you do have control over, such as the number of exemptions you have, the benefits you choose to pay for, the amount you contribute for retirement, cafeteria, and Section 125 plans, and so on.

Bottom line? Your net (take-home) pay is what makes it into your checking account if you have your check deposited electronically.

Chapter 33—Answers (Paying for College)

1. What are some of the means to fund education? Which do you think might make sense for you and your siblings?
   - Roth IRA
   - Coverdell Education Savings Account (formerly the "Kiddie" or education IRA)
   - Section 529 Prepaid Tuition Plan
   - Section 529 College Savings Plan
   - Uniform Gift to Minors Account/Uniform Trust for Minors Account (UGMA/UTMA)
   - Traditional investment accounts
   - Government savings bonds
   - UGMA/UTMA
   - Employer-paid programs
   - Student loans
   - Grants
2. List some nontraditional funding options.
   - Work-study programs
   - Employer-paid programs
   - Military scholarships (ROTC, Academy)
   - Co-op programs

Chapter 39—Answers (Auto Insurance)

How might you make your auto insurance more affordable?

- Increase your deductible
- Keep good grades
- Don't get into an accident
- Keep a good credit score

Chapter 40—Answers (Personal Property Insurance)

1. What are the three ways to cover personal property inside your car?
   - Homeowner's insurance
   - Renter's insurance
   - Condo insurance
2. Why do you think it is smart to have replacement coverage on your renter's insurance policy?
   It costs a lot to replace stuff and insurance companies only pay the actual cash value (which may be next-to-nothing) for stolen or destroyed items.

About the Author

Janet Arrowood is the author of numerous financial and educational books and articles for both investors and professional advisors. She develops training materials for financial advisors and has also worked as a financial advisor.